Competing Responsibilities

Competing Responsibilities

The Politics and Ethics of Contemporary Life

SUSANNA TRNKA AND
CATHERINE TRUNDLE, EDS.

Duke University Press / Durham and London / 2017

Printed in the United States of America on acid-free paper ∞
Typeset in Minion Pro and Scala Sans by Graphic Composition, Inc., Bogart, GA

Library of Congress Cataloging-in-Publication Data
Names: Trnka, Susanna, editor. | Trundle, Catherine, editor.
Title: Competing responsibilities : the politics and ethics of contemporary life / Susanna
  Trnka and Catherine Trundle, eds. Description: Durham : Duke University Press, 2017. |
  Includes bibliographical references and index.
Identifiers: LCCN 2016042488 (print)
LCCN 2016043716 (ebook)
ISBN 9780822363606 (hardcover : alk. paper)
ISBN 9780822363750 (pbk. : alk. paper)
ISBN 9780822373056 (e-book)
Subjects: LCSH: Responsibility—Political aspects. | Citizenship. | Political rights. |
  Responsibility—Social aspects.
Classification: LCC JA79 .C647 2017 (print) | LCC JA79 (ebook) | DDC 172/.1—dc23
LC record available at https://lccn.loc.gov/2016042488

Contents

INTRODUCTION. Competing Responsibilities:
Reckoning Personal Responsibility, Care for the Other,
and the Social Contract in Contemporary Life

SUSANNA TRNKA AND CATHERINE TRUNDLE

Calls to be responsible pervade contemporary life.[1] In many Western countries, the drive for responsibility is often portrayed as being at the heart of public and political institutions. Governments around the world regularly list one of their main priorities as responsibly managing national finances; large multinational corporations increasingly promote their efforts to be socially and environmentally responsible and responsive; and in many workplaces, employees are increasingly being responsibilized through new modes of audit and assessment. Every day we hear myriad different appeals to responsibility, demanding that people must be held accountable for personal failings, social ills, and accomplishments. In the global arena, responsibility and its absence are often cast as the crux of conflict and its resolution. Responsibility is an ideal, it seems, we can never have too much of; calls for responsibility frequently index a lack, an aspiration, an achievement, or an obligation that is hard to refute.

The increasing pervasiveness of responsibility in contemporary discourse, and often the lack of reflexivity about its inherent social worth, are precisely what necessitates a closer examination of this concept. The task of unpacking and critiquing ubiquitous social concepts is particularly imperative when they begin to appear morally untouchable and it becomes increasingly difficult to locate the language to argue against them, as has been the case with words such as *freedom* in the United States in the wake of 9/11 or *human rights* on the global stage. We suggest that the time has come to similarly sharpen our scholarly and critical attention to understanding what exactly *responsibility* has come to convey. Turning our focus to claims about responsibility can reveal much about the visible and opaque workings of contemporary modes of power, as we can see in examples ranging from universities where students making demands for more protection from sexual violence on campus are told to wear sneakers and carry whistles and flashlights (Radio New Zealand 2014), to debates over the extent to which international corporations, from steel magnates and mines to the tobacco industry, are responsible for the health and well-being of local communities (Benson and Kirsch 2010; Trnka 2017; Welker 2009).

This book emerged out of a desire to apprehend the increasing discursive power of this term. Collectively, our contributors trace the efficacy and effects of a variety of claims to responsibility. As their chapters demonstrate, when responsibility is debated, such contests can reveal how individuals, governments, institutions, corporations, and communities envisage and constitute interrelationality. At other times, responsibility unassumingly and almost invisibly undergirds some of our most fundamental social practices wherein examining its role enables us to reveal the taken-for-granted assumptions, practices, and moral sensibilities that underpin our experiences of family, friendship, work, illness, love, and violence.

Much of recent scholarship on responsibility within the social sciences has focused on the link between calls to responsibility and modern forms of governmentality, suggesting that one of the key mechanisms of advanced liberal forms of governance, also widely referred to as *neoliberalism*, is *responsibilization*. The concept of *responsibilization* is most often used to refer to the increasing divestiture of obligations from the state onto individuals who are under growing pressure to formulate themselves as independent, self-managing, and self-empowered subjects (cf. Rose 2006). We can see this at play in the most dramatic of circumstances as well as in the most mundane, for example, through new self-motivating apps that enable novel forms of self-surveillance and care, the medicalized self who must take responsibility for her or his pathology or illness, or the production of self-reliant citizens who do not make too many demands on government services.

Despite, however, the pervasive and diverse deployments of neoliberal rhetorics of responsibilization, in everyday practice responsibility—including self-responsibility—entails a much broader range of meanings. The autonomous, responsibilized subject idealized by advanced liberal theory is in fact enmeshed in a variety of interdependencies within their families, to their schools or workplaces, to the environment, to the state, or to global communities (cf. Rose 2006). Allowing debates about responsibility to become a guise for promoting neoliberal values of individual self-sufficiency thus ignores the variety of modes of obligation, accountability, interdependence, and culpability that emerge out of and motivate social action.

We therefore argue for a new approach to understanding responsibility based on the concept of competing responsibilities. Our motive is twofold: we do so out of concern that the term *responsibility* is in danger of being colonized in public life and political rhetoric by neoliberal discourses of responsibilization. We also see the need to broaden scholarly debate and discussion so that the nuances of multiple responsibilities become central to academic analyses.[2]

With this in mind, we propose a new approach to responsibility that reclaims the diverse meanings and enactments of this concept by placing advanced liberal governments' emphases on responsibilization alongside other prevalent ways that responsibility is currently enacted: that is, other forms of personal responsibility; care for the Other; and social contract ideologies. Our argument has three facets. First, we wish to point out that neoliberal moves to inculcate self-responsibility constitute one particular kind of self-cultivation project, among many others. Second, one of the counterpoints to self-reliance, we argue, is care or the recognition of and response to the needs of the Other, often manifested through intimate, face-to-face relationships that predicate a fundamental, if often understated, mode of social obligation. Finally, while care for the Other foregrounds interrelational dependency, another mode of social obligation we wish to highlight is the interdependencies between larger collectivities, including the reciprocal responsibilities between individuals and the state that are enshrined in social contract ideologies. Calls upon the state, and increasingly upon other institutional forms such as corporations, may frequently align with neoliberal ideals but can also often be used to crosscut or overturn the values of individualism.

Inspired by current examinations of neoliberal projects of responsibilization, but also looking beyond them, the framework of competing responsibilities enables us to examine modes of responsibility that extend, challenge, or coexist with neoliberalism's emphasis on a particular kind of individual cultivation of the self.[3]

Responsible Subjects

To understand the emergence of modern notions of responsibility, an exegesis of contemporary assertions of responsibilization, interwoven with a brief examination of the roots of the word *responsibility* itself, is required. First used in English during the eighteenth century, according to the *Oxford English Dictionary*, *responsibility* is etymologically rooted in the twelfth and thirteenth centuries, in Christian church practices of singing or stating liturgical responses, taking on the additional meanings of being capable of responding to a question, accusation, or request. In contemporary usage, *responsibility* is often used to reference individual or collective accountability through judgments of one's rational capacities, assessments of legal liabilities, and notions of moral blame. Issues of responsiveness and answerability as well as agency and being capable of owning one's actions are thus at the heart of how responsibility has long been envisioned (cf. Hage and Eckersley 2012; Kelty 2008; Laidlaw 2014).

One of the theoretical domains in which responsibility has been highlighted is in relation to newly emerging neoliberal citizen-subjects. Engaging Foucauldian insights into techniques and technologies of the self, Peter Miller and Nikolas Rose (2008) have examined responsibility as a facet of advanced liberal forms of governance that are portrayed by their proponents as enabling individuals' "independence" and "empowerment." Advanced liberal governance, neoliberalism, or "neoliberalization" (Peck and Theodore 2012) refers to a set of ideals and practices that involve a shrinking state mandate, deregulation and privatization, a faith that markets can govern social life, and an increased emphasis on personal choice and freedom. Miller and Rose chart the rise of such advanced liberal forms of state-citizen relations and corresponding subjectivities since the 1970s, describing a sociopolitical transformation that "entailed a new conception of the subjects to be governed; that these would be autonomous and responsible individuals, freely choosing how to behave and act" (2008, 18).

The "responsible citizen" itself is, however, a much older concept (Kelty 2008). Originating during the French Revolution and related shifts toward democratic government, responsibility became a necessary—but also naturalized—capacity of individual personhood and rights as universal suffrage in Western Europe transformed ideas about where responsibility for governance was vested (McKeon 1957). As Richard McKeon argues, "the earlier formulation of this conviction tended to be restrictive: representative government or democracy will work only if the people is ready for it, that is, responsible. The reformulation inverts the relation: responsible government depends on a responsible people but a people acquires responsibility only by exercising it" (1957, 24, as quoted in Kelty 2008, 10). In a similar vein, T. H. Marshall's (1950) analysis of changing forms of citizenship through the eighteenth, nineteenth, and twentieth centuries reveals how a certain form of citizen-subject, imbued with specific civil rights and a newfound sense of collective loyalty and responsibility to contributing to society, coincided with the extension of formal political rights.

But while responsibility has been a key means of constituting the citizen-subject over the last two centuries, what *responsibility* signifies has significantly shifted during this period (Kelty 2008) and is frequently used today, in both scholarship and public life, to refer to a set of specific techniques of constituting a particular kind of self in relation to government and society at large. From President Obama's (2009) hailing of his presidency as the start of a "new era of responsibility" to calls for senior nurses in Scotland to take more "responsibility and accountability" for cleaning up their workplaces (*BBC News* 2012), "responsibility" and the "responsible citizen" have become buzzwords for the adoption and internalization of some of the core ideals of neoliberal or advanced liberal governance, in particular the devolution of what were formerly states' obligations and duties to other parties. In 2012, for example, the deputy mayor of Wellington, New Zealand, could refuse residents' requests to put up barriers at a crosswalk where numerous pedestrians had been hit by buses, on the grounds that it is not up to the city to provide such protection as "personal responsibility remains key" for pedestrian safety ("Personal Responsibility Key" 2012).

These instances highlight one of the central themes of advanced liberalism or neoliberalism, namely, that while the state appears to step back from its direct involvement in the lives of its citizens, personal choice and autonomy are in fact enacted as a mode of governance. As Rose has cogently put it with respect to the individual's responsibility for his or her health,

> the state tries to free itself of some of the responsibilities that it acquired across the 20th century for securing individuals against the consequences of illness and accident. Thus we have seen an intensification and generalization of the health-promotion strategies developed in the 20th century, coupled with the rise of private health insurance industry, enhancing the obligations that individuals and families have for monitoring and managing their own health. Every citizen must now become an active partner in the drive for health, accepting their responsibility

FIGURE I.1. Another example of the proliferation of responsibility discourse in government is Auckland Council's 2012 rebranding of "dog owner licenses" as "responsible dog owner licenses." Pictured is the council's 2015 brochure, which alerts residents of the many responsibilities of dog ownership. Used with permission from the Auckland Council.

FIGURE I.2. Personal responsibility also figures in a range of self-help discourses, including this shareable poster featured on a website devoted to encouraging living a happy life. Used with permission from the artist, Robert Tew, LiveLifeHappy website.

for securing their own well-being. . . . This new "will to health" is increasingly capitalized by enterprises ranging from the pharmaceutical companies to food retailers. . . . Within this complex network of forces and image, the health-related aspirations and conduct of individuals is governed "at a distance," by shaping the ways they understand and enact their own freedom. (Rose 2001, 6)

It is important to note, however, that there is significant debate over the increasing variety of social and political forms of what is referred to as neoliberal (Ganti 2014; Goldstein 2012; Hilgers 2012; Kingfisher and Maskovsky 2008) and over the accuracy of the term itself (chapter 1, this volume), as well as suggestions that many formerly neoliberal states may in fact be shifting into "post-neoliberalism" in the wake of the 2008 global financial crisis (Jessop 2013). Drawing from examples from around the globe, our contributors demonstrate the particularities and situatedness, tensions and instabilities inherent in the development and uptake of neoliberalizing reforms. Their accounts also reveal how the late twentieth- and early twenty-first-century emphasis on inculcating individual responsible subjects has traveled across a range of sites, constituting a potent ideal that both recasts politics and policy and is frequently hotly contested.

Personal Responsibility

Much of this scholarship is inspired by Foucault's insights into the intertwining of governmentality and subjectivity. In his analysis of the lineage of the concept of the care of the self, Foucault underscored the inherent politics of personal responsibility and showed how the agendas of government have become intertwined with projects of self-realization. While Foucault focused on self-care both as developed in ancient Greek society and its manifestations within modernity, other scholars have extended his analysis to consider the ways that audit culture in the late twentieth and early twenty-first centuries creates particular kinds of responsibilized subjects through the uptake of self-surveillance and self-assessment techniques (Strathern 2000b). As Cris Shore and Susan Wright (2011) have shown, techniques of modern management and financial accounting that at first might appear apolitical—that is, as just another routine measure of performance—are in fact aspects of modern forms of governmentality. Such techniques encompass accounting practices staged not only for the self but also with respect to a broader audience, through which personal and institutional responsibilities are surveilled from above and below.

While recent Foucauldian approaches have been fruitful for demonstrating the capillary modes of contemporary power and the links between the structures of politics and the most intimate domains of personal life, there are limits to what this form of analysis can offer. Rose and Lentzos's work on resilience, for example, warns against the scholarly and political dangers of reductionist equations of self-responsibility to a tool of right-wing political agendas. In chapter 1, Rose and Filippa Lentzos argue that the popular tide of interest in resilience should not be discredited by the left as yet "another twist in the obligations of responsibilization, in which the state and public authorities relinquish their obligations for the provision of security and well-being, turn a willfully blind eye to structural inequalities and disadvantage, devolving to individuals and communities the responsibility to manage their own insecurities, or even abandoning them to their fate." Rather, they suggest that resilience constitutes another, potentially fruitful way of both analyzing contemporary governance and providing an opening for progressive politics. As they put it, "resilience responds to a perception that our futures are not predictable and not calculable."

Correspondingly, many of the other chapters in this book demonstrate how calls for responsibility, including self-responsibility, cannot be analytically reduced to a facet of governing at a distance. Not only is there a variety of forms of responsibilities that govern social and political life, but there are also the myriad ways that people respond to calls to be responsible. Assuming personal responsibility can be either enabling or a burden, or frequently both. People may respond to demands to be personally responsible through resolute acts of "irresponsiblization" (Hunt 2003) or by recasting accountability and obligation onto others, including the state and other collective forms (chapters 3, 8, 10, this volume; Trnka 2017).

Indeed, as noted by Foucault, Rose, and others, despite responsibilization having become one of the trademarks of advanced liberalism, projects of inculcating self-responsibility in and of themselves are not necessarily linked to any particular form of governance. In his work on self-care and sexuality, Foucault distinguished two modes of self-cultivation that were popular during the Greco-Roman period: letter writing and the compilations of *hupomnēmata* or aide-mémoire. The hupomnēmata consisted of short texts or sayings that individuals recorded in order to guide themselves through meditation or in their daily behaviors (a sort of homemade, individualized version of the books of inspirational quotes for living that are popular today).

The second, correspondence or letter writing, which Foucault (1997) tellingly refers to as "self writing," consisted of the often daily review of one's most mundane practices, included detailed descriptions of activities undertaken, bodily sensations, and health afflictions. Foucault points out that unlike the later Christian examinations of conscience, such forms of opening up and accounting of oneself were submitted to the gaze of another (i.e., the correspondent who received the letters and often wrote back with commentary or even judgment) not as a means for rooting out evil, but rather as an aid to self-cultivation. Letter writing was thus "a question of both constituting oneself as an 'inspector of oneself,' and hence of gauging the common faults, and of activating the rules of behavior that one must always bear in mind" (Foucault 1997, 220). Many centuries prior to the auditing techniques promoted by advanced liberalism, letter writing resulted in "a whole set of meticulous notations on the body, health, physical sensations, regimen and feelings [that] shows the extreme vigilance of an attention that is intensely focused on oneself" (Foucault 1997, 220; see also Foucault 1988).

While not all cultures engage in such intensive projects of self-care, we can find similar emphases on self-cultivation across a range of different sociocultural and historical contexts. As Michael Carrithers (1985, 248) argues, the figure of the individual engaged in self-reflection and self-cultivation is central to a range of philosophical vantage points, each of which begins with "images of human beings alone: communing with Nature for the German Romantics, acting according to his own intrinsic human nature for the Stoics, meditating in the forest for Theravāda Buddhists, struggling in one's room in prayer for Protestant Christians" (a point also made in Laidlaw 2014; and in Reiser 1985). Another example comes from chapter 3 in this volume, which considers how calls for greater personal responsibility in the Czech Republic focus on rallying citizens to combat civic apathy. As Susanna Trnka notes, "in this context . . . responsibility and self-empowerment are understood not with respect to self-reliance as in Western neoliberal discourses of responsibilization but in terms of the need to stand up for oneself in order to make (collective) political demands on the state. Self-responsibility becomes political responsibility." Similarly, chapter 9 suggests that in Poland the values of self-care and cultivation of the self have long preceded their manifestations as part of contemporary neoliberal discourse. Simply put, advanced liberal responsibilization projects have a particular political agenda attached to ideas of self-care and should not be misrecognized as subsuming the entire category of self-responsibility and self-cultivation.

As this and other examples furthermore demonstrate, there are often close links between care for the self and responsibility for the Other. Foucault has made this point in a less noted aspect of his examination of self-care, suggesting how in ancient Greece care of the self was in fact deeply and ethically relational: "In the case of the free man . . . a person who took proper care of himself would, by the same token, be able to conduct himself properly in relation to others and for others" (1997, 287). As we examine below, this interrelational dimension of responsibility, inherent even in personal responsibility, not only underscores the need to turn our attention to how intimate relations with the Other and between larger collectives are essential to understanding the constitution of obligations and duties in social and political life, but also further complicates the image of the autonomous self that is propounded by neoliberal discourses of responsibilization.

Competing Responsibilities, Care for the Other, and Social Contract Ideologies

One promising line of critique of advanced liberalism's emphases on responsibilization that we seek to further encourage has been the destabilization of the purported ideal of the self-actualized and self-managing individual that stands in the center of neoliberal rhetoric. Autonomy and choice may not always be realized, or even desired, despite being fundamental to neoliberal representations of the self (Rose 2001). Even the most impassioned images of contemporary self-managing individuals often reveal a subject entangled within widespread ties, dependencies, and duties to others, be they kin, neighborhoods, schools, workplaces, or other institutions. Indeed, what has been called "the death of the social" simultaneously created new notions of community and spaces for collective action and responsibility (Rose 1996b), whether through biosocial communities in which citizens come together around a specific health issue or the rise of corporate social responsibility (CSR) programs.

There is clearly no singular response to how neoliberal visions of the responsibilized citizen-subject are enacted. Nor are neoliberal rhetorics promoting the autonomous individual watertight. Rather, many modes of collective association exist under the frameworks of advanced liberal governance. Moreover—and for our purposes here, more importantly—advanced liberalism's emphasis on responsibilization, no matter how varied, cannot encompass the breadth of subjectivities and interrelations that constitute contemporary enactments of responsibility. Crosscutting forms of identities and collective and interpersonal ties can sometimes intersect, and at other times contest, neoliberal frames. Social actors also move between different moral, ethical, and affective valences of what it means to be responsible subjects without necessarily feeling conflicted, in need of resolution, or necessitating "moral breakdown" (Zigon 2011; see also Kleinman 2006; Robbins 2009). Like shifting linguistic registers, such differences are not necessarily perceived as contradictory but can be encompassed within a single individual. Sometimes they constitute overlapping ethical domains. In outlining other modes of responsibility that are at play in social and political life through the tripartite framework of personal responsibility, care for the Other, and the social contract, we hope to further encourage critique of neoliberal conceptions of responsibilization as well as draw scholarly attention to the myriad of ways that responsibility is currently lived out.

Care for the Other

Obligations and ties enacted through relations of care constitute a fundamental, if currently often understated, form of responsibility in contemporary social life. Care is enacted across various levels of relationality, manifest through intimate, face-to-face relationships (such as between parent and child) or in relationships between collectivities (e.g., teachers and students; citizens and the nation). Crucial to these examples is the distinction between care and responsibilization, the latter of which, as we have highlighted, foregrounds the autonomous individual as making his or her own choices about how to act. In contrast, the care for the Other that we discuss here is constituted through the dual aspects of recognition and action motivated by one's commitment to the welfare of the Other.

In her influential comparison of the meanings of choice and care in practices of modern health care, Annemarie Mol (2008) argues that, inspired by neoliberal models of personhood that center on the value of choice, individual patient choice is increasingly cast as an unquestioned social good, associated with rights, autonomy, and empowerment, and often contrasted with paternalistic control and constraint, and patient passivity. Mol suggests, however, that we step outside neoliberal frameworks to consider how health care is practiced when predicated upon the logic of care. Unlike models of patient choice, relationships of care, she asserts, cannot be reduced to a transaction, with clear beginning and end points of responsibility, but involve an open-ended relationship in which power is negotiated between parties. Importantly, such relationships of care do not require affective qualities such as love, affection, and intimacy, but rather are constituted by a certain kind of interpersonal relationship that can be uncomfortable, conflicting, or pro forma and emotionally uninvolved.

In many circumstances, care can thus be best understood in relation to responsibility rather than love. Rather than enabling choice and independence, this type of care necessarily involves taking responsibility for recognizing what needs to be done for another (Gilligan 1982; Held 2006). Sometimes this involves negotiation, and at other times it involves taking over the capacity to make decisions (Mol 2008); what it does not necessarily involve is handing the responsibility for decision making over to the Other. In contrast to neoliberal rhetorics of partnership that emphasize the equality and agency of both sides (however superficial such rhetorics may be), relations of care are not inherently equal but may allow for different degrees of dependence and need. They may furthermore sometimes allow for shifting roles and obligations and are not necessarily contingent upon each partner upholding his or her side of the exchange.

The open-endedness that care for the Other necessitates is demonstrated in chapter 2, on drug treatment programs in Canada. Arguing against the programmatic modes of traditional harm reduction treatments, Jarrett Zigon reveals the conscious and unconscious ways that responsibilized subjectivities associated with advanced liberalism are inculcated through such seemingly apolitical programs. In contrast to what he describes as their "closed normalization of responsibility," experimental forms of drug treatment as exemplified by the Vancouver model represent what Zigon refers to as the concept of attunement or world building, an open-ended interrelationality that generates multiple possibilities for action. In such a world, social institutions operate on many levels, actively repurposed by those who engage with them, enabling, for example, a bank to become a site of social support, detox referrals, and employment advice.

As in Zigon's depiction of attunement, many popular descriptions of care assume an enduring commitment between parties. But care can also be a process that is fleeting and circumscribed, as, for example, in charity relief centers, hospitals, educational facilities, or courts of law. Care is often thus defined as a commitment to the welfare of the Other—a duty of care—no matter how brief it might be. It is, moreover, a duty that does not necessarily supersede other kinds of ties; care might lie in conflict with the values of responsibilization, but can also be incorporated alongside practices that employ the logic of choice.

One realm in which care for the Other is often distinct from but also intertwined with neoliberal modes of responsibility is that of kinship. Parenthood and childhood in present-day Western society are being reshaped by neoliberal forces that demand different kinds of behaviors and capacities (Tap 2007). The categories of mother, father, and child, the forms of relationality they require, and the sorts of (maternal, paternal, and filial) responsibilities they entail, are re-formed but never fully encompassed by the values of advanced liberal governance. A telling example is Aihwa Ong's (1999) account of "flexible citizenship." Ong describes how transnational Chinese subjects are shaped by the citizenship and residency regimes of specific nation-states and the logic of the marketplace, as well as by Confucian ideals of filial piety (*xiao*) and *guanxi* networks that govern relations between culturally defined superiors and inferiors, such as fathers and sons, husbands and wives, older brothers and younger brothers, and so on. Confucian ideals are neither reshaped by neoliberal logics nor seen as antithetical to the laws of the marketplace and citizenship requirements, but it is precisely the intersections of flexibility, Confucian piety, and market logics that "provide the institutional contexts and the webs of power within which Chinese subjects (re)locate and (re)align themselves as they traverse global space" (Ong 1999, 113).

In other contexts, the drive to realize the reforms and values of advanced liberalism generates new kinds of collective ties. In chapter 3, Jessica Robbins-Ruszkowski describes how the call for an engaged civil society in eastern Europe incites forms of mutual responsibility and sociality, resulting in the yearning among older Poles to seek out new forms of relationality. Here then, the neoliberal focus on self-responsibility that drives the establishment of programs to instill self-care and better living skills activates older values of *aktywność* (activity, activeness). Intersecting with the practices of Catholicism, nationalism, class, and traditional gender roles, these emergent practices of aktywność are constituting new kinds of intimate ties between age mates, replacing forms of intimacy that were once realized through work and kin.

In other cases, competing modes of responsibility necessitate a radical breaking away from neoliberal conceptualizations of individual responsibility, revealing how contestations between contrasting modes of care and accountability can occur even within a single individual. In chapter 8, Barry D. Adam outlines the different ways that accountability for HIV infection and treatment have been cast in Anglo-Saxon nations, describing the layers of discourse that have accumulated during the epidemic: in the late 1980s, debates over HIV were dominated by moral castigations and cultural contestations over the meanings of family and gender; in the 1990s, responses to HIV were coordinated by legal and biomedical services shifting to a marketplace model; and today HIV prevention and treatment have become incorporated within a neoliberal ethic of individual responsibility. Such an ethic, however, Adam reminds us, is never all encompassing. Rather, "everyday life often presents competing and inconsistent emotions and rationalities that make the execution of a singular ethic hard to realize even with the best of intentions." Focusing on the level of the individual, Adam has elsewhere shown that even those who wholeheartedly embrace the "every man for himself" ethic can run into trouble in seeing this through when faced with the prospect of having harmed a partner. In his examination of the revived phenomenon of barebacking, or unprotected casual sex between men, Adam finds that many of the same men for whom "[unprotected] sex is justifiable through a rhetoric of individualism, personal responsibility, consenting adults, and contractual interaction" will in fact blame themselves if they inadvertently expose their partners to HIV (Adam 2005, 339). One man interviewed by Adam, for example, described being so upset to have potentially infected a casual partner that he insisted on finding immediate postexposure treatment for him. Such "instances of disruption," Adam concludes, "expose the limits and failings of the rhetoric of [neoliberal] responsibility" in which these men otherwise wholeheartedly engage (2005, 343). What is significant for our argument here is Adam's careful depiction of intimate relations as entailing multiple framings of responsibility and at times necessitating a switch between neoliberal logics of self-responsibility and care of the self, and other forms of interpersonal responsibility and obligation.

While not requiring long-term commitment, such moves demand attentiveness and a willingness to respond. Even more fundamentally, they require the act of recognition, as prior to attempting to further the needs or interests of the Other, one must first recognize the existence not only of the Other, but of an "Other in need." Indeed, as Elise McCarthy argues, "Responsibility [as] a guide to ascertaining appropriate conduct . . . would seem to presuppose a field of recognition—literally recognizing one's self, one's place and one's time vis-à-vis others" (2007, 4). It is this act of recognition that then allows one to take up the duty of care and shoulder the responsibilities not only of oneself but of another.

Equally important to understanding care's links to responsibility is the notion of response. To explore this, many scholars have taken their cue from the philosophical work of Emmanuel Levinas, who argues that human interrelationality is premised upon an encounter with the face of the Other—that is, another person who has not been totally subsumed within the ego's preconceived cognitive categories of order (such as gender, race, class, and religion). Such encounters lead the ego to recognize that the Other is neither an extension of the self nor truly knowable to the self: "The relationship with the other is a relationship with a Mystery" (Levinas 1990, 63). As such it acts as a means by which the boundaries, powers, and limits of the ego and its comfortable sense of the world are revealed and challenged. Encounters with the vulnerable otherness of another thus involuntarily call forth "real choices between responsibility and obligation to the Other, or hatred and violent repudiation" (Davis 1996, 49). It is in this asymmetrical response to the Other, which challenges the ego's making and remaking of the world for itself, that different types of responsibility and care are borne. Levinas's approach locates care as a type of obligation at the core of universal, ontological being. As anthropologists and other scholars have shown, however, practices of recognition and response within care are in practice culturally calibrated and expressed; it is thus important to attend to the fact that to whom and how we respond and recognize are always shaped by cultural, political, and historical ideals and practices (e.g., Shaw 2005; Trundle 2014).

The empirical and philosophical framings of care vis-à-vis responsibility detailed above take care as primarily a form of benevolent engagement. Caring for the Other here assumes an alliance, or at least an alignment, of interests between the carer and the cared-for. Responsible care may, however, be configured otherwise. When actors disagree about what constitutes care for the Other, one person's interpretation of care may be deemed by another as harmful, just as caring for one entity may also involve harming another. Thus spanking a child can be seen as an act of responsible care or irresponsible cruelty depending on one's values or vantage point; partners in abusive relationships often explain perpetuating and accepting domestic violence in terms of caring love; and acts of war may involve the destruction of enemies in order to care for the nation (cf. Stevenson 2014). Defining what constitutes responsible care is thus not a straightforward matter.

Chapter 7 demonstrates this deftly. Writing about the aftermaths of violence in Sierra Leone, Rosalind Shaw describes how despite intending to heal and care for a society, certain forms of restitution, including international justice courts and truth and reconciliation commissions, in fact create or reveal social enmity. Actors for the international justice courts viewed the process of caring for a wounded society through a different lens than local community members who were trying to remake social life in the aftermath of violence.

Locals—both perpetrators and victims—perceived the court's and tribunal's processes as threatening the delicate social fabric they were trying to weave back together.

Not only do claims regarding the presence of care illuminate the workings of responsibility, but equally so do claims about the absence of care. Perceptions of a lack of care or the wrong type of care often become the basis for the assignment of particular types of responsibility, namely blame and culpability (e.g., Laidlaw 2014). These issues are raised in four chapters of this volume, each of which looks at debates and contestations around the assignation of blame. Chapters 6 and 7 both examine the aftermath of state violence in which the assignment of blame, or the inability to do so, are used for strategic social and political ends. Writing about reconciliation processes and the search for the missing dead in Cyprus, chapter 6 describes how the desire of the kin of victims of political violence to attribute culpability for their relatives' deaths is frequently counterposed by the activities of the forensic scientists employed by the state who are determined to leave unresolved both the specificities of violent events and their attribution to particular parties. Elizabeth Davis shows that the acts of harm continue when appropriate forms of care are not offered to the dead and the living. Care here comes to be enacted through painstaking efforts intended to redress the balance that often does not feel complete to victims' families.

Moving out of the realm of political violence and into more structural considerations of violence, chapters 3 and 10 consider claims against the state focused on the environment and health. Catherine Trundle, in chapter 10, examines understandings of the gene and genetics among aging British veterans who believe their health and lives have been adversely affected by radiation exposure at Pacific nuclear tests in the 1950s. Test veterans utilize emergent theories in radiobiology, which allows them to environmentally trace radiation harm through their own bodies to their wives' ill health, in order to deal with a sense of guilt and blame, and to render the state ultimately culpable for misfortune at a familial level. This biologized explanation has the effect of "de-emphasizing individual effort and empowerment, and recasting the biopolitical categories of victimhood and blame and the stakes of financial accountability" faced by the state (Trundle, chapter 10). Her chapter shows how refusing to be held individually responsible often involves attempts to relocate responsibility onto others, inciting new obligations of care and citizenship in the process.

Trnka, in turn, looks at how in the Czech Republic respiratory illness is cast as a citizenship issue, inspiring national debate over whether the state or multinational corporations are the ultimate guarantor of citizens' rights. Chapter 3 depicts how the Moravian city of Ostrava, once known as a heartland of industrial progress, has become famous in the Czech Republic—and increasingly throughout Europe—for its residents' acute respiratory problems, with some scientists contending that Ostrava's children suffer from the world's highest rates of asthma. Activists point the finger at Ostrava's steelworks, presently owned by the multinational ArcelorMittal, which in turn suggests that local residents should do more to improve their own living conditions and their own health. As Trnka shows, despite ArcelorMittal's robust community outreach and CSR program, legal claims and other activist efforts focus on the state as the site of blame, potential recompense, and hoped-for alleviation of suffering.

Such broad-scale debates over citizens' rights and the roles of states and companies in how obligation and culpability are—and should be—distributed lead us to a third dimension of responsibility: the social contract.

Social Contract Ideologies

As demonstrated, ideals of care focus on ties of dependency between the self and the Other that need not be reciprocal and symmetrical in nature and which occur at different scales, from relations between a parent and a child to those between a state and its citizens. By contrast, social contract ideologies focus on the founding principles of government and reveal myriad relationships within larger collectivities built on reciprocal bargains, pacts, or promises that demand something specific of each party. The underlying premise of social contract ideologies is that members of a group relinquish a portion of their individual autonomy and responsibility in order to gain protection and security and ensure that the wider collective assumes some measures of responsibility for and over them. Conceptualizations of such exchanges of responsibility have a long legacy within Western philosophical thought. Plato's *Crito* dialogues, for instance, demonstrate the notion of a necessary exchange between citizens and society. *Crito* details how instead of decrying Athenian society and its laws that have imprisoned and sentenced him to death, Socrates argues that his very existence and life have been enabled by the law and that he is thus obliged to obey it; it has responsibility over him, and he has responsibility toward it (Plato 1907).

Numerous influential theories of social contracts have followed, suggesting various accounts of the evolution of political life. While Hobbes ([1651] 1963) argued that through the social contract people invest a strong sovereign with absolute authority and responsibility, relinquishing a portion of their freedom in order to escape a "brutish" state of nature and gain the protection offered by society and politics, for Locke ([1699] 1967) life prior to the social contract was governed by laws of nature and if those collectively entrusted to rule become tyrannical and irresponsible, then the social contract could be overthrown. Rousseau (1762) in turn maintained that the first form of social contract protected the interests of the elites and argued for the need for the "general will" to drive direct democracy. Multiple imagined contracts can thus be invoked, with models by Plato, Hobbes, Locke, and Rousseau each investing responsibility in distinct actors and processes.

A recent iteration of the notion of social contracts is Ghassan Hage's (2003) concept of "mutual obligation." Writing against neoliberal conceptions of society and paranoid forms of nationalism, Hage articulates an alternative vision of society, one that distributes hope and recognizes and honors its members: "It is when we have a society which, through the bodies that govern it, feels 'obliged' to offer spaces that 'honor' its members as 'important' human beings, and when these members, in turn, experience an ethical obligation towards it—which means nothing other than becoming practically and affectively committed to it, caring about it—that we have a structure of 'mutual obligation'" (2003, 148). Crucial to Hage is the fact that social contracts are not reducible to the calculated exchange of rights between "homo economicus" and the state, but intersect with ideas of care and commitment, fundamentally driven by reciprocity rather than self-interest.

However, as many scholars have demonstrated, the ideal of social contracts contrasts with the political arrangements putatively enacted in its name, as what we take to be the rational rule of law often entails considerable levels of violence against those who are governed (Asad 2003). Furthermore, both the idealized image and the practice of social contracts for most of its history have sidelined women and children, slaves, and others as incomplete subjects unworthy of membership (Young 1989). Social contracts are thus best understood as ideologies that mask other forms of relations, including exploitative ones (Rawls 1971).

These forms of "mutual obligation" are, moreover, usually not consciously adopted or entered into; no one chooses to enter into a social contract as a "free," "rational" actor (Held 1993). Rather we are socialized within its ideology and rhetoric to envisage a certain kind of responsible individual and collective social responsibility (Rawls 1971, 13). The motivations for enacting such responsibilities at any given time are as likely to include affect or sensation as they are moral or ethical decision making (Trnka, Dureau, and Park 2013b; see also Fassin 2014). As James Laidlaw points out in a reading of responsibility that centers on the importance of affects and intersubjective ethics, our affective responses to events (particularly negative ones) frequently determine the attributions of meaning and ascriptions of intentionality that we make. As he puts it, "assessing and assigning responsibility" stems from "considerations that excite or inhibit . . . reactive attitudes such as gratitude and resentment, indignation, approbation, guilt, shame, pride, hurt feelings, forgiveness or love" (Laidlaw 2014, 185; see also Laidlaw 2010). Although Laidlaw focuses his discussion on interpersonal relations, the affective dimensions of responsibility and attributions of agency are, as many of our contributors demonstrate, also central to relations between citizens and states.

Most often, social contract ideologies are explicitly raised for reflection and debate through calls upon long-standing principles of citizens' rights or new forms of claims making. One novel type of group to actively articulate social contract ideals that has emerged since the 1980s has been biosocial communities or collectivities centered on shared bodily suffering, affliction, disease, or stigma, who demand more resources to improve members' health and well-being. Such communities do not merely attempt to fill in the gaps of services vacated by the state, but rather make claims for new forms of social inclusion. Engaging in discourses of responsibility and accountability, these groups direct demands toward the state, (private or public) scientific entities, and corporate business, seeking not only care, research, and investment, but also the extension of decision making beyond both the state and the realms of scientific enterprise through public-private "partnerships" envisioned to enable greater degrees of "patient choice" (Epstein 1996). This process is evident among the nuclear test veterans described in chapter 10 who, in the wake of state denials of responsibility, form groups in order to demand more access to health care and health monitoring and increased entitlement to disability pensions. In doing so they forge relationships with scientists and become actively engaged with understanding, promoting, and critiquing scientific processes of truth and evidence (see also Trundle and Scott 2013).

Social contract ideologies, furthermore, increasingly involve not only citizen-state relations but citizen-corporation relations as corporations are held to account not only for their viability in terms of generating profit but also on the basis of publicly perceived moral values. Since the late 1960s and early 1970s, CSR programs, which attempt to build public trust and moral standing through the language of accountability and responsibility, have been instituted by a range of national and transnational corporate organizations. These programs entail two levels—both the undertaking of projects that focus on social and environmental improvement and the publicly visible recording of these projects through various practices of reporting and accounting that legitimize and frame action as morally virtuous and responsible (Hage and Eckersley 2012; Welker 2009).

This aspect of being held to account deals less with meeting targets and legal requirements and verifying productivity, and focuses more on public forms of moral reckoning as the means by which individuals and entities build trust and collective ties through displays of responsible behavior, showcasing how they are ostensibly acting for the benefit of the wider public good. The very existence of CSR programs thus recognizes standards and moral values outside of profitability as important alongside those of the production of capital, as well as the failure of previous models of free-market capitalism to deliver significant and widespread social benefits. Moreover, as Marina Welker (2014) has shown, these programs and the values they promote can be hotly disputed within a single corporation. Indeed, neoliberal perspectives can constitute one of multiple orientation points for the actors who "enact" the corporation (Welker 2014). What is key, however, is the way that the corporation can come to be positioned as rightfully taking on social responsibilities divested from the state. In effect, the corporation is being positioned as another participant in the reciprocities that are taken as fundamental to the (state-citizen) social contract.

Corporate social responsibility is, however, often circumscribed, with certain responsibilities performed in order to foreclose others. These new forms of responsibility can, moreover, usually be explained in relation to the logic of markets and their drive for expansion; while CSR demonstrates the emergence of new rhetorics of moral responsibility, as many scholars point out, ultimately CSR often works to deradicalize alternative intentions, motivations, or effects that may lie within or emerge from its dynamic structures (e.g., Frynas 2012; Smith and Helfgott 2010).

Chapter 4 takes up this point to examine how audit culture has become a key instrument for producing responsibilized subjects on the one hand, but irresponsible and increasingly unaccountable financial institutions on the other. Cris Shore suggests that corporate responsibility raises important questions about the relationship between responsibility, power, and the limits of corporate obligation, arguing that in fact the law of limited liability works to protect companies from being responsibilized and held to account for their actions.

In her detailed account of CSR within the mining industry, Jessica Smith in chapter 5 makes a related point, underscoring the voluntary nature of CSR programs and the ways in which CSR programs and publications circumvent discourses of rights and obligations characteristic of government policy. But rather than critiquing CSR programs as "mere greenwash," she argues that much can be gained by focusing attention on the specificities of how responsibility is being redefined in corporate contexts. The shift toward relinquishing the term *responsibility* and replacing CSR with creating shared value (CSV) is, Smith suggests, indicative of the emergence of new corporate perspectives on relations between corporations, states, and citizenry that are in fact more closely aligned with the values of advanced liberal projects of responsiblization.

The question of what exactly CSR (or CSV) should entail, and where the lines should be drawn between state, corporate, individual, and community responsibilities, can turn into a high-stakes battleground, as Trnka's analysis of the political and scientific struggles to definitively locate the source of high rates of respiratory illness in Ostrava demonstrates (chapter 3). Showing how a consortium of interest groups made up of environmental activists, politicians, scientists, and the media draws upon deeply held convictions about the state's obligations to both recognize and adequately recompense masculine, working-class labor and protect vulnerable children, Trnka suggests how engaging in a "politics of last resort" results in collective claims on the state eschewing the new socialities offered by corporate social responsibility in order to reinvoke the fundamental principles of the citizen-state social contract.

As these chapters illustrate, ideologies of social contracts rest upon long-standing notions of relations between self and state, or self and collective, that can both invoke neoliberal ideals and crosscut neoliberal values and perspectives of the individual and his or her place in society. The notions of responsibility inherent in social contracts are much broader than those espoused by contemporary neoliberal rhetorics; they are not necessarily incompatible with neoliberalism, but they exceed it. They thus demand a different kind of analytical attention than scholarly critiques of neoliberal responsibilization can often afford and, in turn, can open up alternate ways of conceptualizing how ideas about responsibility, obligation, and duty shape contemporary life.

Conclusion

Our aim in this introduction has been to expand the conceptual framework through which responsibility is considered in order to shed light upon these sometimes competing and sometimes complementary modes of engagement. While we see advanced liberal modes of responsibilization as increasingly pervasive and powerful technologies of governance, we also see the need for analyses of competing responsibilities that reveal how the responsible subjects promoted by neoliberal ideologies exist within a matrix of dependencies, reciprocities, and obligations.

We have foregrounded some older and enduring views of responsibility not in order to subvert scholarly examinations of neoliberal responsibilization, much less of other newly emergent forms of responsibility, but to enable us to examine how a multiplicity of responsibilities can work with and against each other, sometimes reinforcing neoliberal responsibilization, and at other times existing alongside or undercutting it. We are aware that the phrase "competing responsibilities" necessarily highlights conflicting responsibilities, rather than those that smoothly align or intersect with practices of responsibilization. There is a political motivation for this choice; spotlighting alternatives is an important means of challenging the dominance of discourses of neoliberal responsibilization. Nevertheless, as the chapters in this volume illustrate, the concept of competing responsibilities encompasses responsibilities that relate in diverse ways to responsibilization projects.

Our goal has been to broaden scholarly discussions of what we see as a key concept in both scholarly discourse and contemporary social life. Personal responsibility far surpasses modes of self-accounting and governing at a distance that dominate late twentieth- and early twenty-first-century political life. Care for the Other and social contract ideologies, which foreground forms of dependency, interdependency, and recognition that are often downplayed in neoliberal rhetorics, offer further conceptual and empirical challenges to neoliberal perspectives on responsibility and broaden the definition of responsibility in academic and public debate.

This book is intended as a step toward a new direction in scholarly and public understandings of responsibility. The pages that follow propose novel perspectives on how responsibility is cast within the domains of governance and the interpersonal politics of community life, as well as within the ethical and moral entanglements inherent in everyday living.[4] By ethnographically analyzing enactments and understandings of responsibility across a range of geographic and cultural settings, this book's authors challenge universal and globalizing visions of responsibility as a singular mode of ethical and social engagement. They reveal both the different ways that the implementation of neoliberal projects of responsibilization has been taken up, transformed, and elided and the possibilities of other modes of ethical and social life.

Our contributors reconceptualize responsibility on three levels. The first is empirical, offering up ethnographically rich accounts of the multiplicity of ways that individuals, ethnic groups, professional communities, states, and corporations enact, debate, and contest obligations and duties. The second is theoretical, advancing new analytical perspectives and approaches in a range of areas, from the formation of intimate ties through friendships, families, and sexual relations (chapters 8, 9, 10) to recasting understandings of CSR (chapters 4, 5) or the unspoken politics inherent in forensic investigations (chapter 6), truth and reconciliation commissions (chapter 7), and struggles over the fundamental rights to health and well-being (chapters 2, 3, 8, 10). The third and final is political, calling for the need to carefully attend to how responsibilities are deployed, and can be deployed, across a range of state, activist, educational, corporate, and philosophical rhetorics. Countering an emerging scholarly tendency to reduce responsibility to neoliberal responsibilization, our authors delineate a complex conceptual terrain that is variegated and wide ranging. We hope our readers will take up the call made by these chapters to engage with the major trends and subtexts, crosscutting currents, alliances, and resistances in the politics and ethics of contemporary responsibility that emerge from these accounts. This challenge requires us both to undertake a sharper critique of moral claims of responsibility and, conversely, but equally important, to uncover the diverse ways that conceptualizations of responsibility enable us to reimagine social and political life.

NOTES

1. Some of the ideas presented here were first explored in Trnka and Trundle (2014); at the "Rethinking Responsibilities" workshop hosted at the Radcliffe Institute for Advanced Study, Harvard University, April 9, 2014; and at the Competing Responsibilities Conference in Wellington, New Zealand, August 15–17, 2014. We would like to thank our interlocutors at these and other forums for helping us articulate our thinking on these themes, in particular Nikolas Rose, Cris Shore, Thomas Strong, and Sarah Pinto.

2. The material for such an undertaking can be found across a range of social science disciplines, even though it may not be conceptualized under the category of responsibility. In anthropology, for example, if we consider Barry Barnes's statement that "all societies are systems of responsibilities" (2000, 8), then an examination of responsibilities, in terms of both how they are envisioned and how they are allocated, has long been at the root of anthropological enterprise. Indeed, as suggested by Max Gluckman (1972), many classic anthropological texts easily lend themselves to being reread as accounts of responsibility and obligation (see also Douglas 1980). Through analyses of religion, morality, politics, community, gender, kinship, or health care, anthropology has frequently taken note of responsibilities, albeit often under the rubric

of other themes. Our suggestion is that much of this material may be of particular use in rethinking how responsibility is formulated.

3. Given the broad range of meanings of responsibility, we have necessarily had to restrict our examination to particular types of social relationships, leaving aside important areas such as debates over the responsibilities humans have to the environment (e.g., Ingold 2000), linguistic treatments of responsibility (e.g., Hill and Irvine 1993), and ethical issues inherent in social science research (e.g., Shore and Trnka 2013).

4. The definition of *politics* we adopt here is essentially a Foucauldian view of how governmentality shapes not only large-scale political decision making but also the very intimate domains of social life. Our perspective on social ethics is akin to Michael Lambek's (2010a) delineation of "ordinary ethics" or the ways in which the moral and ethical are enacted through language and action as part of quotidian experience. Similar perspectives are promoted by Cheryl Mattingly (2014) and Paul Brodwin (2013).

Part I. Theoretical Departures

ONE. Making Us Resilient:
Responsible Citizens for Uncertain Times

NIKOLAS ROSE AND FILIPPA LENTZOS

To breed an animal that can take responsibility for its actions—perhaps even for its desires[1]—has not this, to misquote Friedrich Nietzsche, been the aspiration of all those who would govern human conduct—to rear a person who can not only *take* responsibility but *be held* responsible? Nursemaids and governesses, mothers and fathers, priests and politicians: this has been the ambition of all those for whom incessant coercion or mere obedience to external authority was either undesirable or unachievable. Responsibility in this sense is both ethical and technical. It is both a value and a set of values for living by. It is also a technical achievement, a work of the self upon itself under the tutelage of others: the condition of what we have come to term "liberty."

Responsibility and liberty have long been twinned. For people to live at liberty, they must be able to exercise responsibility over themselves and be willing to be held responsible for their actions. Hence, as Mariana Valverde (1996) has pointed out, there is a certain "despotism" at the heart of technologies for enabling liberty by inculcating the obligations of responsibility—"responsibilization" as the rather ugly term has it. She quotes J. S. Mill's *On Liberty* to demonstrate that this despotism was a key part of such liberal thought: despotism, Mill (1975, 15–16) argued, was necessary in order to turn children into subjects capable of living in liberty, and also to "improve barbarians" even if they would rarely, if ever, achieve that condition. Responsibility entails the capacity to subjugate the lower passions to the well-trained will, to subdue them by virtuous habits; the responsible adult has to exercise a continuous scrutiny of the self and, on occasion, a renewed despotism of self on self is required to ward off the temptations of vice.

For Norbert Elias (1978), the ability to take responsibility for oneself is the ultimate achievement of the "civilizing process": to incorporate conscience and hence the capacity for guilt, self-judgment, and self-control into the human soul itself as restraints on fundamental human drives. But our focus is different. It is on the variety of ways of thinking that invoke self-responsibility as a solution to certain problems, and on the diverse strategies, techniques, and tactics by which various authorities seek to inculcate it. Not the civilizing process, but "citizenship projects" and their associated "technologies of citizenship"—the practices for civilizing human subjects by turning them into responsible citizens. Such projects for inculcating responsibility divide subjects into actual citizens, potential citizens, failed citizens, or anticitizens on the basis of their presumed or demonstrated capacity—or lack of capacity—to exercise responsibility; or their willful refusal of the demands to become responsible.

To govern through responsibility is not just to install a certain form of self-reflection, but to create an ethic—a set of techniques of self-government. Such strategies for governing conduct form part of what one of us once termed "ethopolitics"—though this awkward term never really caught on.[2] Ethopolitics emphasized the ways in which values, sentiments, moral beliefs, and so forth are deployed by authorities as a kind of "medium" through which the self-mastery of the individual can be linked with the imperatives of good government. While discipline shapes conduct in terms of adherence to an externally imposed norm, "'ethopolitics' concerns itself with the self-techniques by which human beings should judge and act upon themselves to make themselves better than they are" (Rose 1999b, 27). Ethopolitical strategies are thus concerned with the value—and the values—of different ways of living: they problematize in terms of ethics and seek to act by means of ethics.

In this chapter we first explore some of the configurations for "the conduct of conduct" that work through the ethic of responsibility. Our aim is to dispel the contemporary tendency to associate responsibilization with something termed "neoliberalism." Following that, we suggest that this ethic of responsibility is being reworked in the context of a pervasive concern with managing individual and collective conduct in the face of unpredictability, adversity, insecurity, and uncertainty. It is here, we suggest, that we can understand the current popularity of the term *resilience*. We conclude by suggesting that while some see the rise of resilience strategies as the apotheosis of reactionary individualism, these new strategies focused on resilience might provide opportunities for a more progressive politics.

Making Us Responsible

When it comes to a genealogy of responsibility, we could begin with the Greeks, or with the early Christians. Or we could consider the arguments of those groups and organizations at the start of the nineteenth century, such as the Society for the Suppression of Vice in the United Kingdom, for whom human depravity and corruption of the public morals was to be combated by religious authority, and the submission to government, laws, and moral principles. Or we might start with the prison and asylum, those archetypal machines of morality that emerged in the nineteenth century, which aimed to inculcate responsibility into failed citizens or anticitizens. As we know, a whole array of apparatuses for the management of conduct—hospitals, workhouses, museums, and, of course, schools—were invented in England, Europe, North America, and elsewhere during the nineteenth century. These were both disciplinary and ethical technologies, seeking to instill responsibility through the organization of architecture, time, space, gazes, and much more (Jones and Williamson 1979). Schools, both for the elite and for the poor, were crucial. The elite, those who would govern, had to acquire the forms of character and learn the ethical technologies appropriate for those who would wield authority over others. For the poor, as one of us argued many years ago,

> Schools for infants and for older children were to be the site of a variety of different programs for the shaping of character en masse. . . . The corporeal and moral habits of industriousness and obedience would be inculcated into the members of the laboring classes, to fit them to become good servants—good tradesmen—good fathers—good mothers, and respectable citizens. . . . New regimes of the body—its purity, its hygiene, its sexual continence—were to address problems posed in terms of sexuality, disease and virtue. New regimes of the intellect—numeracy, literacy, calculation—were to install foresight, prudence and a planful relation to the future. (Rose 1999b, 104)

The intellectual and the ethical were linked; these schools utilized both class-room and playground for the observation of character and for moral training, and inculcated habits of thoughtfulness, order, cleanliness, diligence. This was achieved by rewarding good conduct on the one hand, and by classifying and sanctioning misdemeanors on the other (Hunter 1994). While the "good Christians" of earlier interventions were to be obedient to a fixed set of moral codes, in the schoolroom, an ethic of self-scrutiny, self-mastery, and responsibility was becoming central, capable of a more flexible application to life's exigencies.

This may give the impression that responsibility is always inculcated by authorities "from above" in the service of "social control." But strategies "from below" also gave pride of place to the ethic of responsibility. Consider, for example, the role of the friendly societies set up by religious groups and trade unions in the second half of the nineteenth century, and the ethic of prudentialism that lay at the heart of their mutual schemes for insurance. As Pat O'Malley has argued, in these developments, the subject was enjoined to take a prudent and calculative relation to the future—each individual was bound into a collective endeavor that would encourage and enable them to take responsibility for their future and that of their family. These practices of prudentialism, whereby an individual joined a scheme set up by their co-believers or counionists and set aside a certain monetary contribution each week or month, required the exercise of foresight in relation to one's own future, guided and supported by others in the same position, securing each through the combination of the contributions of all: this was to be the way that the responsible worker was to ward off the specter of future dependency on charity or the workhouse.

It is tempting to believe that this emphasis on governing conduct by inculcating individualized responsibility and prudence was to give way, over the course of the twentieth century, to practices that thought in "social" terms, that construed problems in terms of a wider social connectedness of individuals, and believed that solutions were to be found through collective measures to ensure security. But the technologies of the "welfare state" did not abandon the imperative to govern individual self-conduct and to support prudence and self-responsibility. Indeed, an

> ethic of personal responsibility was integral to the language of democratic citizenship that took shape over the course of the twentieth century. From Beveridge's schemes of social insurance, through Reith's [vision of] a national broadcasting system, to a range of interventions

into the domestic space of the family and the productive space of the factory, responsibility for oneself, for one's family, for one's co-workers and fellow citizens was . . . to be achieved through the technical forms of regulation, folded into the person in habits of radio listening as well as in the content of broadcasts, in the little rituals of the stamping of national insurance cards, in participation in morale raising activities in the workplace, in the mother's newly educated ways of thinking and acting upon her children. (Rose 1996a, 318)

The security of welfare was never intended as one of total protection, in which all aspects of the lives of citizens would come under the benign guardianship of an all-seeing and omnipotent state. Even in its most emblematic form, as in William Beveridge's plan for social security to defeat the five giant evils of Want, Disease, Ignorance, Squalor, and Idleness, the challenge was to devise a system that did not eradicate the obligations of citizens to take prudential steps to secure their own future. In his report of 1942, Beveridge directly addressed the fear that the security he offered would undermine "initiative, adventure, personal responsibility." He argued that, given the British character, "security can be combined with freedom and enterprise and responsibility of the individual for his own life" (Beveridge 1942, para. 456). "There are some to whom pursuit of security appears to be a wrong aim," he writes. "They think of security as something inconsistent with initiative, adventure, personal responsibility. That is not a just view of social security as planned in this Report. The plan is not one for giving to everybody something for nothing and without trouble, or something that will free the recipients forever thereafter from personal responsibilities" (para. 455).

The criticisms of the welfare state in the last decades of the twentieth century were partly underpinned by the belief that, despite such hopes, Beveridge's plan had indeed weakened those crucial virtues of self-reliance and prudence (Rose 1996a). Once more, responsibility was the solution. The state was no longer to be the sole provider of security, although it might still remain its ultimate guarantor (Rose 1999a). A new market for security was created, in which individuals were to be "incentivized" to take personal responsibility to ensure their own security when it came to health, education, entry into the workforce, provision for old age, and protection against crime. In this new ethopolitics, freedom required not just autonomy and enterprise but also responsible individuals, not just taking risks, but assessing and managing risks, calculating about their potential implications for one's form of life in the future, and taking active steps to secure—and ensure—against them.

Pat O'Malley—in the context of his work on crime and risk—has termed this "the new prudentialism"—a partial transformation of the "actuarialism" that characterized social insurance schemes into what he terms "privatized actuarialism" or prudentialism—a range of interventions "that facilitate, underline and enforce moves towards government through individual responsibility" (1996, 199). As in crime, and in health, an image takes shape of a responsible, moral individual who must engage in rational calculations to assess and manage future risks, guided, of course, by a range of authorities who provide information, advice, and guidance. As Monica Greco (1993) has put it, the individual, in such a configuration, acquires a "duty to be well"—and indeed a duty to take prudent steps to secure security for his- or herself and dependents in all manner of arenas of personal life—for health, for old age, for employability, and so on—under the tutelage of experts.

We have preferred the term *advanced liberalism* rather than *neoliberalism* to refer to such hybrid rationalities and technologies of government. The attack on the rationalities of welfare came not just from the right but from all sides of the political spectrum: from the left, who argued that the welfare state, despite its apparent egalitarianism, actually enshrined inequality and generated a powerful and unregulated welfare bureaucracy whose primary function was social control; and from classical liberals with their concern for individual rights, who argued that the powers of professional expertise within the welfare apparatus violated rights and substituted professional discretion for due process. Almost all seemed to agree that state-organized welfare services, as they actually existed, destroyed informal practices of solidarity and social support, enshrined professional power, and produced clientism rather than socially responsible citizens.

If these criticisms are associated with right-wing politics, this is because it was the right, rather than the left, that turned these criticisms of technical and invented strategies to reshape the state of welfare around a new distribution of responsibilities. As we know, they sought to break up the welfare apparatus, to introduce markets and quasi-markets, to invent new uses for technologies of audits, standards, and budgets to govern these quasi-autonomous agencies "at a distance," to challenge the discretionary power of experts by turning their clients into customers, and so forth (Rose 1996b). Political government was to be relieved of its obligations to know, plan, calculate, and steer the whole of society and economy from the center.[3] The state was no longer to be required to answer all societies' needs for order, security, health, and productivity. But it was not to be passive; its role was to create the conditions under which individuals, firms, organizations, localities, schools, parents, hospitals, and housing estates could take on the responsibility for resolving these issues—whether by permanent retraining for the worker or neighborhood watch for the community. Organizations, institutions, and individuals that were once enmeshed in the complex and bureaucratic tentacles of the social state were to be set free to find their own destiny within a new set of sociopolitical arrangements. At the same time, they were to be made responsible for their destiny, and for that of society as a whole, in new ways.

But politics was to be returned to citizens not just in the form of individual morality but also in terms of community responsibility: governing through community. Human beings were imagined as enmeshed within webs of obligation, identification, and allegiance, developing within micromoral domains—family, workplace, neighborhoods, associations—communities that were "natural" as opposed to the artificial and invented solidarities of the social state. Most clearly in the politics of "the third way," strategies were developed for acting upon these associations, networks, and cultures of belongingness and identity, by building networks, enhancing trust relations, and developing mutuality and cooperation. The hope was for a new relation between ethical citizenship and responsible community, fostered by, but not administered by, the state. New ways were invented for governing the behavior of individuals through ethics and in the name of ethics—through the values that steer individuals in their day-to-day conduct and choices. As Prime Minister Tony Blair (1996) put it in a newspaper article titled "Battle for Britain," "the search is on to reinvent community for a modern age, true to core values of fairness, co-operation and responsibility."

This sketch has had only one purpose. While many associate responsibilization with something called neoliberalism, as Susanna Trnka and Catherine Trundle point out, responsible subjects are always "nested within multiple . . . dependencies, reciprocal ties and obligations" (2014, 136). The strategies for governing conduct that have responsibility at their heart are not inescapably individualistic. They embody a range of different conceptions of the subjects of responsibility, of their internal topography—and indeed they do not always have a human subject as their focus—for example, where responsibilities apply to a collective, or to a role, such as that of a public official, rather than to the person who is its incumbent. Further, strategies of responsibilization have no single political allegiance, and they are capable of being deployed in many different ways. Even in the forms criticized as neoliberal, responsibility can be demanded of collective entities such as organizations and communities, and that responsibility is inherently relational—it entails a set of obligations toward others, the obligation to care about the consequences of one's actions for others, and, reciprocally, an array of potential culpabilities for those who renege on these obligations. And as we know, critical thought itself often valorizes responsibility and demands it where it is thought lacking. We should want to be responsible toward those for whom we care, or should care, even though such responsibility imposes costs upon us—which raises a host of questions about the limits of such care. We want others—polluters, pharmaceutical companies, financial institutions, tax avoiders—to be responsible to those whom they claim to serve. At the same time we know that, all too often, responsibility is imposed in the service of contested norms, by those who wish to deny or escape their own responsibilities, upon those who are not responsible for their condition and do not have causal powers that responsibility attributes to them—as in the attribution of obesity in the poor to their unhealthy lifestyles rather than their obesogenic environment.

To criticize responsibilization per se is to take a political and ethical shortcut—the difficult questions concern the analysis and evaluation of who is being held responsible by whom for what, in relation to what, in what ways, and with what consequences. Before we rush to judgment, a critical work of description is required. Having worked hard to "cut off the king's head" in our political thought, we need to be careful that, in our compulsion to critique, the sovereign does not rise again, this time in the phantasm of an omnipotent neoliberalism.

Responsible and Resilient?

The theme of resilience reworks responsibility in the face of a particular perception of our problematic present: that we live in uncertain times, that things are changing fast, that the future will not resemble the present, that the dynamics of our interconnected world escape our rational and linear models of calculation and intervention, that we are vulnerable not only to known but to unpredictable threats such as jihadist terrorism and climate change, those "known unknowns," but also to "unknown unknowns" that we are unable to predict but for which, somehow, we must be prepared. This is not just a new way of speaking about risk or the risk society. Strategies of risk management imagine the future as somehow similar to the present; they believe that it is possible to bring the future into the present and make it calculable. But the theme of resilience responds to a perception that our futures are not predictable and not calculable in this way.

The *Oxford English Dictionary* gives us a number of definitions of resilience dating back to 1626. To put it at its most simple, resilience is the capacity to cope with adversity or to bounce back after a blow. In the industrializing societies of the mid-nineteenth century, the term was applied to the mechanical properties of materials that had these qualities. But it always had multiple metaphorical senses—individuals, families, and communities could be resilient as much as bridges and buildings. In a present that our authorities find difficult to decipher, and a future that seems to escape rational calculations of risks, where unknowable and catastrophic events seem both inescapable and unpredictable, the language of resilience has found many niches in which to flourish. It has become prominent in strategies ranging from biosecurity to community empowerment, from training in the U.S. military to the raising of children able to meet the demands of the future. This language is eminently translatable; it connects up distant places and occurrences, links the macro and micro, associates the institutional and the subjective, for instance making connections between the preparedness of a city's energy system to cope with flooding and the capacities of its citizens to manage such a disaster. As a personal capacity, resilience is both exceptional—some remarkable people have come through terrible ordeals only to bounce back stronger—and ordinary: all living systems and living individuals have the capacity to adapt to the challenges of turbulent environments. It is both natural—human beings are by nature resilient—and it can be taught, by consultants for governments and organizations, by psychologists and social workers for their clients, by parents for their children, by trainers for military personnel. We can be resilient as individuals to the small reversals of fortune that impact on our own lives, and we can be resilient as communities, nations, and populations to the major geopolitical and environmental challenges that will confront us. Hence resilience seems perfectly suited to our present, or rather to prepare for an uncertain future. The language of risk, of rational calculation and preparation for the future, is permeated with anxiety about what is to come. But the language of resilience, even though it posits a future that is in many respects incalculable, and not amenable to rational management by experts, is nonetheless saturated with a certain kind of optimism: if we are resilient, whatever is thrown at us, we can survive and thrive.

The rise of resilience strategies has been extensively critiqued by social and political theorists on the grounds that they are neoliberal. Critics suggest that resilience—whether it concerns children, citizens, or communities—is another twist in the obligations of responsibilization, in which the state and public authorities relinquish their obligations for the provision of security and well-being, and turn a willfully blind eye to structural inequalities and disadvantage, devolving to individuals and communities the responsibility to manage their own insecurities, or even abandoning them to their fate.

It is true that, in one sense, the ethic of resilience is linked to the belief—maybe the recognition—that the state and the political apparatus cannot guarantee total security. On the one hand, political authorities cannot, on their own, take the responsibility to redress social wrongs let alone provide all the conditions for a fulfilled life. On the other, the state cannot secure its citizens against all possible threats, whether they be pandemics, floods, or terrorism. However, these themes are not exclusive to neoliberalism: most contemporary political programs take the view that an all-seeing, all-knowing, all-powerful, and protective state is neither economically feasible nor politically desirable. As with responsibility, so with resilience: many different strategies valorize and seek to produce, support, or encourage resilience in individuals or communities. And resilience deserves some more nuanced analysis before we subject it to critique.

The Logic of Resilience

The logic of resilience in contemporary governmental rationalities is something like this: absolute security is impossible.[4] We will experience adversity, although we cannot accurately predict when, how, and in what form. Preparedness, planning, precaution, preemption, preclusion, and prevention—all these are necessary endeavors, but they can never be completely successful: the anticipation work of experts and authorities fails to predict many of the dangerous events that actually occur; plans that seem rigorous on paper often miscarry in practice; painstakingly organized systems of communication and direction break down in the face of disasters and crises. Hence such anticipatory activities are insufficient. So when dreadful events happen, how shall we respond—as individuals, as communities, as economies, as nations? Shall our defenses crumble, shall our systems collapse, shall our populations panic, shall each of us be paralyzed with dread or disabled by trauma? Shall our children, if they experience misfortune and suffering in their early lives, be condemned to a life of failure or criminality? Or can we resist the damaging blows, bounce back from disaster, recover from our tribulations, adapt to our new situation, perhaps even emerge stronger, fitter, more resourceful—in other words, be resilient? And if we can identify what it is that makes some resilient—some buildings, some systems, some economies, some communities, some individuals—can we not teach resilience, learn resilience, enhance resilience at all these levels? Can we not have experts of resilience, who are able to advise us how to become resilient? If no authorities can deliver total security, if total security is a costly fantasy, then perhaps resilience is a more economical alternative, indeed perhaps a more liberal alternative, drawing, as it does, not on an image of an overwhelming and powerful authority that will protect us, but on the resources of each of us and all of us as vital creatures, that is to say, creatures with the will to survive and the capacity to adapt to our milieu.

This is not the place for a genealogy of resilience.[5] But we can learn something from the history of the term in social and political science. Some suggest the term *resilience* first appears in its modern form in ecology, with the publication of Holling's "Resilience and Stability of Ecological Systems" in 1973, work that became the basis of the Resilience Alliance founded in 1999, which examines resilience in systems ranging from marine environments to urban ones.[6] For Holling, to put it briefly, resilience could refer to either the capacity of a system to return to its previous state, or its capacity to absorb disturbances, reorganize, and restabilize to retain its original functions and utility. Others find a key early use in Wildavsky's (1988) distinction between anticipation, where some central intelligence seeks to predict and prevent dangers before they emerge, and resilience, as having the capacity to cope with dangers that have not been anticipated. Still others see the first uses in studies of children who had suffered great adversity and yet went on to lead successful lives, for example Werner's work on the longitudinal study of the children of the Hawaiian island of Kauai, which commenced in 1955 (Werner, Bierman, and French 1971; Werner 1993; Werner and Smith 2001). However, before 1992, very few articles in social and political science have the word *resilience* in the title. In the 1970s, a few essays appear that speak of the resilience of regions or nations. In the 1980s, we see two additional uses of the term: on the one hand, there is increasing discussion of the resilience of economies; on the other, there are articles on the resilience of individuals, in particular of children, in the face of various kinds of adversity (Crittenden 1985; Garmezy and Masten 1986; Mrazek and Mrazek 1987; Rutter 1985) perhaps culminating in Michael Rutter's highly cited article of 1987 on "psychosocial resilience and protective mechanisms."

From this point onward, the use of the term burgeons. It begins to be applied to resilient families, and to resilience in survivors of abuse and maltreatment—women who have been sexually assaulted, prisoners of war, and so on, alongside reference to the resilience of soil and agriculture, and to states in crisis. But children remain the main focus of the social science literature on resilience across the 1990s with a growing interest in the character-istics of children who survive and flourish against the odds, especially black children in urban ghettos in the United States (Floyd 1996; Howard 1996; Rak and Patterson 1996) and the development of interventions that might foster or increase resilience (Fine 1991; Hoekelman 1991; Luthar 1991). We return to these resilient children later.

But resilience is for adults too. Consider the rise in the problematics of resilience in the U.S. military. The word *resilience* does not appear in Allan Young's classical study of post-traumatic stress disorder in the U.S. military, which was published in 1995. Yet in the years that followed, at least in the United States, resilience became central to understanding and managing the fitness of military personnel and their liability to breakdowns on returning from combat (O'Malley 2010).[7] Resilience was the latest mutation in a concern that arose first in the wake of World War I—how can one assess the liability of military personnel to break down during or after combat? How can one select, allocate, distribute human resources, organize, and train one's personnel to maximize their effectiveness and minimize the costs of warfare (Rose 1989, part I)?

In the first decade of the twenty-first century, the U.S. military began a program of research on the factors affecting resilience to stress. It identified factors ranging from neurobiological to hormonal, but placed great emphasis on the potential protective role of psychosocial factors such as "optimism, humor, cognitive flexibility, cognitive explanatory style and reappraisal, acceptance, religion/spirituality, altruism, social support, role models, coping style, exercise, capacity to recover from negative events, and stress inoculation" (Southwick, Vythilingam, and Charney 2005). Military training and selection began to focus on psychosocial factors in resilience, which became central to the Comprehensive Soldier and Family Fitness program launched in 2002. Although there was little evidence of efficacy, by 2013, the U.S. Army had put in place its comprehensive Ready and Resilient program, based on the belief that "individual resilience can be built, maintained, and strengthened . . . and acquired through regular training."[8] There were resilience inventories, designed to assess resilience in military personnel entering combat, linked to the perception that susceptibility to PTSD was a matter of low resilience. There were programs for enhancing resilience prior to combat, and rebuilding resilience in those who returned traumatized from combat. Most controversy focused on programs that sought to enhance resilience through "spiritual fitness"—"strengthening a set of beliefs, principles or values that sustain a person beyond family, institutional, and societal sources of strength"—which entailed prayer sessions and appeared to many to be promoting religion (Cornum, Matthews, and Seligman 2011; Pargament and Sweeney 2011; Peterson, Park, and Castro 2011; Sherbourne and Gaillot 2011).

Over the first decade of this century, resilience also becomes central to debates over disaster management—Hurricane Katrina, the 9/11 attacks on the United States and the 7/7 (July 7, 2005) Tube bombings in London (Bosher et al. 2007; Bruneau 2006; Comfort 2010; Manyena 2006; van Opstal 2006). There was much concern with infrastructural resilience (Coaffee 2010; Croope and McNeil 2011; D'Antonio et al. 2009; Doherty, Dora, and New-some 2012; Hynes and Purcell 2012). But the subjective capacities necessary to deal with such disasters were also central. We can also see this focus on the subjective in arguments about "human security" in the field of development. As Chandler has argued, in this new way of thinking, the subjects of development are viewed as not passive victims but active agents who participate in their own development, while vulnerable subjects are those that lack the capacities for resilience: intervention is increasingly rationalized as "facilitating, empowering or capacity-building the vulnerable subjects on the ground" (Chandler 2012, 217, 225). Resilience, that is to say, became an antidote to vulnerability.

We have come to think of ourselves and our societies as vulnerable in so many ways: vulnerable ecosystems, vulnerable infrastructure, vulnerable food supplies, vulnerability to climate change, vulnerability to economic shocks and turbulence, vulnerability to terrorism, or just vulnerability to the challenges of the rapidly changing world in which our children have to live. And, it seems, resilience is the best response. *America the Vulnerable* was the title of a book published in 2004 by Stephen Flynn, president of the U.S. Center for National Policy, reflecting on U.S. security policy post-9/11.[9] Three years later, resilience became his central theme:

> The United States needs the kind of resilience that the British displayed during World War II when v-1 bombs were raining down on London. . . . More than a half century later, the United Kingdom showed its resilience once more after suicide bombers attacked the London Underground. . . . That objective was foiled when resolute commuters showed up to board the trains the next morning. . . . Whereas increasing security measures is an inevitable answer to a society's fears, resilience rests on a foundation of confidence and optimism. It . . . [allows] Americans to remain true to their ideals no matter what tempest the future may bring. (Flynn 2008)

If we can only recover our resilience, learn to value and strengthen it, we can overcome our fears and face an uncertain and unpredictable future with optimism. The message is a powerful one, and its power lies in part in the very ambiguity of the term, its capacity to "translate" between the ethical, the subjective, the organizational, the institutional, and the political, to move from place to place, program to program, problem space to problem space, from program to technology to ethics (Rose and Miller 1992).

The Resilient Individual and the Resilient Community

Critics suggest that resilience thinking and resilience strategies are fundamentally neoliberal in that they displace responsibilities away from the state onto individuals who now acquire new obligations.[10] Resilient subjects should not hanker after the misleading illusion of a security provided by others, but must adapt to dangers and will thrive under pressure by becoming more resilient (Joseph 2013).[11] But this interpretation is rather misleading, for discussions of resilience seldom, if ever, frame it as a capacity to be instilled into an autonomous individual who must cope with adversity on his or her own. From the early work on children, resilience has been seen as not merely an individual capacity, but dependent on a whole range of transindividual protective factors. In their classic study of the children of Kauai, *Vulnerable but Invincible*, Werner and Smith (1982) argued that the resilience developed by children who were vulnerable because of adversity was grounded in their close relations with others, within the family and outside it, including emotional support from others—not only were these social factors protective, but the resilient children themselves engaged in socially responsible activities, playing their own part in these networks of support. And in his much-cited work on this theme in the 1980s, Michael Rutter pointed to the need for "compensating experiences outside the home, the development of self-esteem, the scope and range of available opportunities, an appropriate degree of structure and control, the availability of personal bonds and intimate relationships, and the acquisition of coping skills" (1985, 608).[12]

Similar themes are stressed in almost all subsequent work on resilience: subjective resilience grows out of protective sociality and generates such sociality in its turn. Thus all the contributors to Michael Ungar's "handbook of theory and practice," *The Social Ecology of Resilience*, stress, to quote his introduction, that "the resilience of individuals growing up in challenging contexts or facing significant personal adversity is dependent on the quality of the social and physical ecologies that surround them as much, and likely far more, than personality traits, cognitions or talents. . . . Social ecological factors such as family, school, neighborhood, community services and cultural practices are as influential as psychological aspects of positive development when individuals are under stress" (2011, 1).

Perhaps this emphasis is not surprising given that this volume focuses on the question of what it calls the social ecology of resilience. But consider this study of survivor reactions to the 2005 London bombings, "characterized by adaptive features, such as order, solidarity and mutual aid rather than the dysfunctional individualism and panic that characterizes psychosocial vulnerability. Importantly, it was the crowd itself that was the basis of the resilience displayed by survivors . . . a sense of psychological unity with others during emergencies is the basis of being able to give and accept support, act together with a shared understanding of what is practically and morally necessary, and see others' plight as linked to our own rather than counter posed" (Drury, Cocking, and Reicher 2009, 85). Far from individualism returning in the face of disaster, the researchers claimed to find just the reverse—collective self-help, cooperation, the development of informal social networks—what they termed "collective resilience."

Resilience both emerges naturally in individuals and groups, yet it is also something that can be enhanced. We need to move, says Bonnie Benard of Resiliency Associates, from a deficit perspective that focuses on youth and families at risk to one that recognizes what resilience research has shown, that most youths make it, that all individuals have the power to transform and change, that even for "children born into extremely high-risk environments, such as poverty-stricken or war-torn communities as well as families with alcoholism, drug abuse, physical and sexual abuse, and mental illness," researchers worldwide have documented the amazing finding that at least 50 percent and usually closer to 70 percent of these "high-risk" children grow up to be not only successful by societal indicators but "confident, competent, and caring" (Benard 2002). And Benard's study of "fostering resilience in kids" argues that "what began as a quest to understand the extraordinary has revealed the power of the ordinary. Resilience does not come from rare and special qualities, but from the everyday magic of ordinary, normative human resources in the minds, brains, and bodies of children, in their families and relationships, and in their communities" (2004, 10). Resilience is fundamentally socially embedded: it grows out of caring relationships, high expectations from others, and opportunities for individuals to participate, to take and be given responsibility for others, and to contribute to their communities (Benard 1991). Resilience is natural, but can be enhanced by education and training, by parents and teachers who know how to foster it, by learning "to model the caring, positive expectations, and invite the contributions that engage the innate resilience in our students" (Benard 2002, 27).

These resilience strategies are, it is true, postsocial strategies for governing—the imagined territory on which they act is not that of society but of community; the individual is imagined as a moral subject enmeshed in bonds of affinity with others in localized ties to a specific moral collectivity (Rose 1996c). And community, here, is a means of government—for the soldier in the U.S. military as much as for the child in adversity. Resilient subjectivity is to be shaped and supported by strategies to strengthen bonds of community allegiance and affinity (Bacon and Mguni 2010). Thus, a case study, "Urban Resilience in Situations of Chronic Violence" by Diane Davis, argues that in the insecure communities of Medellín, Colombia, plagued by violence, the state is largely absent but a range of strategies to enhance community resilience can enable communities to wrest control back from armed actors in their territory. Community resilience is not, here, portrayed as an alternative to a role for the state: "Resilience appears at the interface of citizen and state action, and is strengthened through cooperation within and between communities and governing authorities. . . . When citizens, the private sector, and governing authorities establish institutional networks of accountability that tie them to each other at the level of the community, a dynamic capacity is created to subvert the perpetrators of violence and establish everyday normalcy" (Davis 2012, 9).

On the one hand, securing individuals against adversity, whether poverty, urban violence, or even catastrophic external events such as floods or terrorist attacks, is beyond the power of the state alone; on the other, innovative actions—whether by loving parents, inspiring teachers, resourceful communities—can ensure not merely survival but flourishing in novel and more effective, perhaps more democratic ways, by maximizing resilience.

Beyond Critique?

Neoliberalism has become an all-purpose term of critique in much contemporary critical social science. It is often a means of avoiding the complexities of careful analysis and evaluation—what is happening: neoliberalism; why is it happening: neoliberalism; what's wrong with it: neoliberalism. We are not fans of such totalizing analyses.[13] Is neoliberalism an ideology, a doctrine, a political project, a strategy, an epoch? When the term is used, does it refer to actually existing neoliberalism, which takes complex and hybrid forms in different contexts, or is it an interpretive notion—even when the proponents deny it, behind their protestations really lies neoliberalism. Or is it merely a term of critique applied to policies that seem to turn their backs on the major structural reforms necessary to overcome poverty and disadvantage, leaving them to the mercy of markets, competition, and the search for private profit, while urging each individual to become an entrepreneur of himself or be consigned to a twilight world of exclusion?

In relation to resilience, it is this latter, pejorative rather than analytical use of the term that is dominant. Thus Dorothy Bottrell, writing in the context of Australian social policy, argues that the contemporary deployment of the language of resilience, even when it speaks of community resilience, ignores structural deficiencies, poverty, inequalities, and racisms to focus on the resilient individual rather than the collective, intersubjective, and infrastructural conditions for resilience:

> The emphasis on individuals, their skills and attitudes is an outmoded notion of resilience that decontextualizes it from cultural contexts, social structures and political processes. . . . The required subjecthood is concerned with conformity, acquiescence and limited choice . . . [constituting] further adversities of the least advantaged, intensifying their need for resilience . . . shifting responsibility from the state. . . . State rhetorical enthusiasm for resilient individuals and communities provides a smokescreen over its removal of barriers to market based accumulation . . . and policy failures in areas such as poverty reduction, educational equity and redress of damaging adverse conditions in marginalized communities. (Bottrell 2013, 2–4)

A damning verdict, and one that leaves little space for ambiguity or for optimism—even if one might feel that national productivity, global competitiveness, and stronger futures were not such dreadful things to hope for, or that a frank admission of the limitations of political action might be no bad thing, or that nostalgia for the welfare state conveniently forgets the many vigorous criticisms that progressives mounted against such policies in their heyday. Others, too, seek the comfort of critique. Thus Sandra Walklate and colleagues claim the language of resilience in counterterrorism strategies sidelines "the capacity of individuals to 'keep calm and carry on' in the face of adversities and catastrophes" and that resilience narratives promote a deficit model in which individuals lack resilience in order to develop strategies to implant it: a "quest to develop a resilient State that attempts to compel individuals, communities and voluntary agencies to perform security on its behalf" (Walklate, Mythen, and McGarry 2012, 185). "Authorities" deliberately underestimate the natural resilience of their citizens and populations to justify interventions that themselves require individuals to take responsibility for managing their own security, hence increasing the resilience of the state itself.

Framed in this way, there seems little virtue or promise in the current linking of resilience and responsibilization in policies and strategies, merely a monotonous narrative of authorities denying *their* responsibilities while imposing those responsibilities on the very individuals they are paid to serve. Of course resilience—like empowerment, recovery, and mindfulness—can rapidly switch from a radical alternative to a tool in the toolkit of professionals to be used coercively and as norms that can be used to judge: you *will* become resilient, and it is your responsibility if you fail. But we suggest that as with responsibility, so with resilience: perhaps we might do better to abstain from the rush to judgment, refrain from seeking some grand overarching logic such as neoliberalism as the basis for our assessment of resilience, and explore the polyvalence of resilience strategies, and ask whether, how, and in what ways we might find some handholds here for a more optimistic intellectual and political engagement. As someone once almost said, no doubt everything is dangerous, or carries the possibility of danger, but that does not mean that everything is bad, let alone to be denounced in favor of a better yesterday which has already failed, or a better tomorrow that is seldom specified (Dreyfus and Rabinow 1983).

Conclusion

As one of us argued nearly two decades ago, "We should not assume that all is for the worst in this 'post-social' age" but rather "identify the points of weakness that might be exploited if we are to maximize the capacity of individuals and collectivities to shape the knowledges, contest the authorities and configure the practices that will govern them in the name of their freedoms and commitments" (Rose 1996b, 353).

As we have seen, notions of resilience are providing a versatile framework for strategies for the management of individual and collective conduct at a time when the future seems not simply risky, but constitutively unpredictable, suffused with unknown unknowns, interconnected in ways that confound linear models of cause and effect, and where events respect no barriers of geography or culture in their implications.[14] In such a context, where fears of ungovernability might be overwhelming, the logic of resilience is a hopeful one. We may be vulnerable, but we can develop the capacities to bounce back from disaster, to recover from calamities, and to adapt to these dangers, and in the process we may even become stronger. Resilience is both natural and can be produced; it is both an everyday quality of normal human development and one that can confer extraordinary advantages on those individuals and communities that possess it. It can be fostered by experts, defined, categorized, measured, normed, and built into training manuals, but it also arises spontaneously out of the collective bonds of caring and allegiance of individuals in situations of threat or emergency. To foster resilience is not to create disciplined subjects whose conduct is fixed by norms and judged in terms of good and bad. It does not require some all-seeing governing agency that seeks to know and regulate everything within a territory. But nor does it seek to devolve all responsibilities to isolated, autonomous, responsibilized subjects seeking to live their lives as self-promoting enterprises, seeking only to maximize their utilities and responding to market incentives to do so. In their imagination, strategies of resilience seek to make use of the natural capacities of living human beings to cope with adversity, when they are part of supportive networks of community affiliation. Resilience does not entail the fantasy of the antiliberal and vastly expensive dystopias of total protection, prevention, precaution, and preclusion, based on the belief that threats and dangers can be identified and planned for in advance. It underpins a whole range of light, mobile, and highly translatable strategies for dealing with uncertainty and contingency, strategies that seem to reconcile the twin obligations of freedom and security.

Of course, there is much analytic work to be done if we abandon the blanket critique of neoliberalism. We need to identify the problematizations around which resilience appears as a solution; the kinds of explanations of problems that resilience provides, notably the centrality of the idea of vulnerability; the specific technologies being developed to enhance resilience; the forms of expertise that are taking shape to define and manage it; and the conceptions of personhood and techniques of the resilient self that are being put into place. There is certainly much to criticize here in the new obligations of parents, teachers, therapists, community workers—and ourselves—that are being deployed to "make us resilient"; demands for resilience without the collective and infrastructural powers and resources to realize resilience are disingenuous at best, toxic at worst. And indeed the very idea of resilience may be conservative in its implications—aiming to retain or re-create what is threatened, rather than to transform it. But perhaps there are some positive elements in resilience strategies that might provide handholds for a more progressive politics, once one recognizes that what must be entailed in such a politics is not the hope of not being governed, but of being governed differently. For resilience can offer individuals and collectivities a space of action and creativity; it creates possibilities for legitimate contestation in the name of resilience, and authorizes arguments concerning the distributed capacities and solidarities required to make resilience a reality. Perhaps, then, one should argue not *against* responsibility and resilience but *on the territory* of responsibilities and resiliencies, about who should be responsible for what and how they should be held accountable, about the power and resources required to make resilience a reality, about the collective conditions for responsibility and resilience. Perhaps, that is to say, in both resilience and responsibility, there is something worth affirming.

ACKNOWLEDGMENTS

This is a revised version of a paper Nikolas Rose presented at the Fourth Latin American Colloquium on Biopolitics: Common goods, governmental technologies and counterconducts at the National University of Colombia, September 2013. Thanks to all those who kindly gave comments and criticiswm, especially Pat O'Malley. It arises out of our joint work on rationalities and strategies of resilience, and previous versions of the argument have been presented at the Keele University and the London School of Economics in 2007 and 2008 and at the University of Sydney in 2011 (Lentzos 2006; Lentzos and Rose 2009).

NOTES

1. The reference is, of course, to the opening sentence of the Second Essay of Nietzsche's (1969) *Genealogy of Morals*.

2. Although there have been some interesting attempts to use and develop it.

3. The following paragraph reproduces some text from Rose 1999b.

4. Of course, the emergence of resilience and its multiple meanings has been much discussed in the literature (Holling 1973; Manyena 2006). Some authors focus on debates on resilience in critical infrastructure, often locating the rise of the term in a shift from anticipation, planning, prevention, and preparedness in the face of increasing uncertainty and unpredictability (Boin and McConnell 2007; Comfort 2010). Others have focused on resilience in debates on security (Walker and Cooper 2011). In keeping with the general overuse of the term *neoliberal*, some suggest that governmental strategies that frame themselves in terms of resilience are, in fact, forms of neoliberalism because they emphasize individual responsibility—this appears to satisfy the authors' will to critique without adding any analytical clarity to the issues involved (Joseph 2013). Pat O'Malley (2010), in the course of an argument about risk

and uncertainty, has helpfully examined the self-technologies of resilience in the U.S. military, and we draw on some of his arguments in what follows.

5. In an otherwise helpful account of the rise of resilience language in a number of practices, Walker and Cooper (2011) present a genealogy of resilience as part of their critique. Ignoring the strictures of genealogists on the fallacies of reading through the origin, they argue that the origins of resilience lie in Holling's ecological writings and the development of complex systems theories that reject notions of homeostasis; they then satisfy their critical ambitions by showing that complex systems theory is compatible with the work of the arch neoliberal devil Friedrich von Hayek—despite the fact that he never cited complex systems theory and the key authors in ecological systems theory never cited him, his hidden hand is found in the fact that planners in leading financial institutions are now using the language of complex systems. However, most other authors agree that psychological and psychiatric work from the 1940s on children brought up in deprived or otherwise damaging environments played a key role in shaping the use of the term to describe the capacity of individuals to resist stress and also in shaping the distinction and relation between resilience and "vulnerability" (Manyena 2006). The brief analysis of publications presented here shows something of the multiple pathways that have intertwined to give the notion of resilience such versatility and such a capacity to connect the subjective, the organizational, and the political.

6. Resilience Alliance, "About," http://www.resalliance.org/about.

7. The UK did not follow that path, not least because of the skeptical voices of some psychiatric researchers.

8. Army.mil, "Ready and Resilient," http://www.army.mil/readyandresilient.

9. See www.centerfornationalpolicy.org.

10. In his insightful comments on resilience self-help manuals, mostly emerging in the United States (Brooks and Goldstein 2004; Reivich and Shatté 2002; Siebert 2005), Pat O'Malley (2010, 506) suggests that the subject they seek to create, to cope with a radically uncertain future, is consistent with neoliberalism—flexible, adaptable, enterprising, innovative. Unlike many others, however, his analysis is modest in its scope and empirically grounded.

11. Julian Reid suggests that the idea that individuals no longer seek absolute security but are inherently flexible, dynamic, thriving on living dangerously, has become key to contemporary forms of neoliberalism: "The neoliberal subject [must not] conceive the possibility of securing itself from its dangers, but . . . [must believe] in the necessity of life as a permanently [sic] struggle of adaptation to dangers. . . . Building neoliberal subjects involves the deliberate disabling of the aspirations to security that peoples otherwise nurture and replacing them with a belief in the need to become resilient" (2012, 149).

12. This book had been cited over 3,000 times by July 2013.

13. Will Davies (2014) helpfully identifies some common themes of neoliberalism. He argues that neoliberal thinkers seek a new social and political model, which does not simply celebrate market forces, but seeks to create such forces, and targets institu-

tions and activities that lie outside of the market, such as universities, households, public administrations, and trade unions either to neutralize them or to make them work rather more like markets. To do this, the state must be an active agent, aiming to implant the rules of institutions and individual conduct, in ways that accord with a certain ethical and political vision. Central to this ethical and political vision is the idea of competitive activity rather than the creation of equality: competition is seen as a nonsocialist principle for society in general, through which value and scientific knowledge can best be pursued.

14. As we were preparing this chapter for publication, we became aware of the work of David Chandler, who argues that governmental strategies framed in terms of resilience go beyond neoliberalism and arise in particular in the face of perceptions of complexity, and the challenge of "governing complexity." While neoliberal strategies still hanker after predictability and knowability—to govern a realm was to be based on a knowledge of its laws and properties—the rise of resilience derives from the attempt "to rethink governance on the basis of unknowability . . . without assumptions of Cartesian certainty of Newtonian necessity" (Chandler 2014, 63). As will be evident, our argument has some similarities, but we suggest that the genealogy of resilience thinking is more complex and that resilience rationalities have gained their power because of their capacities to link diverse "problem-solution" complexes.

TWO. Attunement: *Rethinking Responsibility*

JARRETT ZIGON

"Meeting them where they are at" is one of the pillars of harm reduction, which can be defined as the "policies, programmes and practices that aim to reduce the harms associated with the use of psychoactive drugs in people unable or unwilling to stop. The defining features are the focus on the prevention of harm, rather than on the prevention of drug use itself, and the focus on people who continue to use drugs" (Harm Reduction International 2014, 1). Harm reductionists consider this "focus on people" and the "meeting them where they are at" approach to be quite progressive. It is not uncommon for harm reductionists to contrast their approach, which they see as tolerant and nonjudgmental toward drug users and use, with what they call behavior change approaches such as abstinence-based therapy, which are considered judgmental, conservative, and ultimately unrealistic. This contrast may work at the surface level, as it were, of the use of drugs or not. But it does not take account of the ways in which certain kinds of moral values and virtues, for a lack of a better term, are worked upon, altered, and embodied by means of the tolerant and nonjudgmental harm reduction practices. In this essay I consider this phenomenon by addressing the responsibilization that is at the very core of the harm reduction approach.

Of course pointing out that responsibilization is at the core of harm reduction is nothing new as several critical studies have already done so. Indeed in previous work I have pointed to some similarities in responsibilization practices between abstinence-based therapeutics and harm reduction (Zigon 2011). What I hope to do in this essay is not so much to argue that such responsibilization occurs in harm reduction practices as to suggest that it occurs because of the deep ontological assumptions enacted by the harm reduction approach, and that these are assumptions it shares with various hegemonic social and political projects of modernity, including but not limited to liberalism, socialism, and anarchism.

In the rest of this essay, then, I consider this relation between ontological starting points, harm reduction, and responsibilization. I begin with a brief discussion of the dominant modern form of ontology and its relation to familiar notions of morality and biopolitics. I then consider what I call the typical model of harm reduction as an illustration of the enactment of this ontology and how this results in what we call responsibilization. I then briefly and critically engage an influential alternative ontology offered by a prominent social theorist, and consider its shortcomings in taking up a Levinasian conception of responsibility. Finally, and in response to this critique, I turn to the unique case of Vancouver, Canada, and the enactment of what I call a politics of world-building (Zigon 2014b). In this final section I show that the approach taken in Vancouver differs significantly from the typical harm reduction model in that, in contrast to the linear and individualized approach taken by the latter, Vancouver agonists are in the process of creating a new world that is primarily characterized as being attuned with itself.[1]

Such attunement, in contrast to the closed normalization of responsibility, ultimately allows a world to remain open such that new possibilities regularly emerge and allow those who dwell in this world the possibility of becoming otherwise. The result, I argue, is that the politics of world-building currently under way in Vancouver reveals an alternative to the closed normalization of responsibility because it begins from and enacts another ontology. This politics may in fact allow us to leave behind the concept of responsibility altogether as a remnant of an ontology that no longer holds much social, political, or intellectual validity despite its continuing hegemony. Ultimately, I hope to show that the politics of world-building in Vancouver reveal that such alternative ontological starting points, and the other worlds that can be built from them, open new possible futures in ways that the temporalities of metaphysical humanism and its concepts such as responsibility cannot, and thus provide new paths for the rethinking of political action (see Zigon 2015).

The Modern Form of Ontology

What is the modern form of ontology? To begin with, there is what Karen Barad calls the metaphysics of individualism, which is the ontological foundation that grounds science, politics, and ethics, as well as the prevalent ways of being-in-the-world today. This is a metaphysics that posits "that the world is composed of individual entities with individually determinate boundaries and properties" (Barad 2007, 107). While the roots of the metaphysics of individualism go further back than the seventeenth century, there is much agreement that this ontology found firm ground in the new philosophy of Descartes and the new physics of Newton (Barad 2007, 97; Villa 1996, 176). Just as Newtonian physics started from the assumption of an observer looking onto, discovering, and representing a reality independent from the observation process (Barad 2007, 97), so too Descartes grounded the possibility of all knowledge on the self-certainty of one's own clear and distinct existence as consciousness, a consciousness that above all represents.

Within this ontology it is this capacity to represent that provides the foundation from which the objectivity of all other things could emerge. Or as Heidegger put it, "The Being of the one who represents and secures himself in representing is the measure of the Being of what is represented as such" (in Villa 1996, 176). Thus, it is by means of the emergence of representationalism out of the metaphysics of individualism that "man becomes the relational center of that which is as such" (176). This centrality was ultimately assured with Kant's Copernican revolution since it was his transcendental philosophy that "grounded the objectivity of the object in the subjectivity of the subject," thus cementing what Heidegger called the "modern form of ontology" (177).

This "modern form of ontology," which subjectivizes all that exists, and thus places humans in the godlike position of "the representative of that which is" (Villa 1996, 180), can be called metaphysical humanism. Metaphysical humanism is the contemporary form of the metaphysics of individualism. It is the ontology that places the human as an individualized entity with "determinate boundaries and properties" at the center of all existence, from which it projects these properties onto it and its constituent parts in the attempt to understand and know them by means of representation, as well as to control them. But even more importantly, metaphysical humanism enacts this project not merely for the sake of knowledge and control, but primarily as a means to secure and fix those "determinate boundaries and properties" that supposedly constitute humanness as such.

This ontological circle of metaphysical humanism, then, in the words of

Dana Villa (1996, 183), closes and "reifies the 'open possibility' of human existence into a 'what,' the better to provide an answer to the question 'Why is it necessary for man to exist at all?'" In other words, in the attempt to understand their own existence, humans have created an ontology—metaphysical humanism—that secures and fixes a particular conception of this existence by foreclosing all other possibilities for its own becoming. Thus, in carrying out this ontological project of metaphysical humanism, the subjectivization of all existence has been enacted such that the worldliness of all existents has been forgotten. In doing so, there has been a turning away from the open possibilities of being, and thus the closing off of worlds and their existents, humans being just one. As Dana Villa (192) puts it in describing Hannah Arendt's critique of modernity: "Science, philosophy, economic and political theory [and, I would add, much social theory as well]: all conspire to cover over both the phenomenon of world and the worldliness of phenomena."

Within the ontological conditions set by this metaphysics, worlds and their existents are closed and fixed. Worlds and the existents that populate them become quantized, as mathematics is projected onto them and understood as the language of nature. Meanwhile, humans and their activities, when not themselves quantized, are secured with properties such as responsibility, dignity, and rights, and thus grounded in a unique, distinct, and unworldly or transcendent set of moral values. As a result, Reason and Morality, the twin properties of humans posited and enacted through metaphysical humanism, have resulted in what Arendt calls world alienation. That is, this ontology has led to the alienation of humans from the worldliness from which the conditions of their very being emerge, as well as the open possibilities available to them (as well as all other existents) within those worlds. This ontology results in a leveling or the closing off of possibility and, as such, a closing off of the possibility of becoming otherwise that might be available if we lived within other ontological conditions. For as it currently stands, worlds conditioned by metaphysical humanism seem to foreclose possibilities of disclosive spontaneity while only supporting "normalized" behavior (Villa 1996, 173). It is for this reason that Arendt, in a sort of foreshadowing of Foucault, could so easily conclude that in the "modern age . . . life, and not the world, is the highest good" (Arendt 1998, 318).

It is important to point out that metaphysical humanism as the culmination of the metaphysics of individualism and representationalism is not simply a matter of philosophical writings and trends. Rather, metaphysical humanism emerged, gained hold, and became the dominant ontology today by means of diverse practices. In this sense, philosophy is itself merely just one of many practices that enact this ontology. Perhaps the most significant of these practices is scientific practice, which has come to stand for many as the sole basis of truth, and in its modern form emerged along with the metaphysics of individualism, as its methods were eventually secured through the binary and epistemological assumptions of metaphysical humanism. Similarly, capitalist and technological practices are based on the assumption that the earth (and increasingly that which is beyond it) exists simply as standing reserve—and this includes human labor as well as nonhuman life—for the purposes of human use, profit, and progress. But one of the most significant manifestations of metaphysical humanism today is the so-called biopolitical therapeutic regime by which "life, and not the world, is the highest good" and through which what Rancière (2010, 94) calls the police, or "the distribution of the sensible characterized by the imaginary adequacy of places, functions and ways of being," is enacted.

Just one example of such biopolitical therapeutic regimes is harm reduction. The enactment of metaphysical humanism and responsibilization is perhaps most obviously discerned in the very organization of most harm reduction services and the kinds of assumptions that go into this organization, as well as the way in which those who encounter these metaphysical assumptions in practice, in turn, come to embody such assumptions. In the following section I consider how this is the case.

Responsibilization and Harm Reduction

For what I call the typical model of harm reduction, "meeting them where they are at" indicates what is often called the reality that many people who use drugs are not ready or willing to stop their drug use. "Where they are at" indicates where an individual user is in terms of his or her own desires and capabilities. The *where* and the *at*, then, do not indicate a relationship to anything other than oneself and the contained attributes of that self. Beginning from this assumption of the isolated individual, the typical model of harm reduction offers services such as syringe exchange, condom distribution, and substitution therapy to these individuals with the primary aim of reducing harm that this individual can cause others or that others may cause the individual. Since harm reduction makes no formal attempt to help users stop using, the occasionally stated, but in most cases not stated, goal is to train users to become better managers of themselves and in so doing to take more responsibility for their own health and the effect they may have on others' health.

This potential effect on others is not the only way that harm reducers working within the typical model see drug users as in relations. I do not want to create the image that harm reducers do not recognize the various ways that drug users are intimately connected to their worlds, and the effects this has had on their drug use. Poverty, unstable family environments, lack of opportunities, and police oppression are all recognized as potential factors in why people begin and continue to use drugs. But these are viewed as just this, factors, things out there in the world that have happened to and thus shaped this individual. In this closed space of things, persons, and happenings—a space often referred to as society or community—individuals move about, and as they encounter other things and persons they are more or less affected by these encounters. The cause-and-effect imaginary is here something akin to the Humean billiard table. Harm reductionists hope to provide yet another knock-on effect through their encounter with users.

These encounters normally occur either at a fixed location, a mobile bus, or through peer outreach work. The latter two, in fact, are also usually located at one or a few fixed spots on a scheduled rotating basis. In this sense, harm reduction services fit into the predefined space of society or the community and in so doing offer just one more possible encounter in this closed space. The hope is that the effects of this other possible encounter will counteract the other potentially harmful encounters users will likely have. The fixed or semi-fixed location of the typical harm reduction model, then, provides a relatively safe place for users to go, and the opportunity to change themselves by being there. Again, this change is best described in terms of self-management and increased responsibility.

This model of harm reduction is far and away the dominant model and can be found nearly every place that harm reduction is practiced. It is not surprising, then, that in my research in Honolulu; New York City; St. Petersburg, Russia; and Denpasar, Indonesia, as well as other cities I've visited or read about, this is precisely the model that is enacted. Each one of these cities offers harm reduction services out of either fixed or semifixed locations. But the point to be made is not so much the fixity of the services as the fact that this fixity is regularly an isolated one. That is, these locations are typically found in areas of the city where either very little of anything else is actually taking place—for example, the back road by the docks in Honolulu where the mobile bus parks every day or the back road behind one of the main hospitals in St. Petersburg where a center is located—or in a part of town hectic with other activities completely distinct from, and in many cases, completely opposed to harm reduction practices, such as the middle of a busy street on the

Lower East Side of New York or in a residential neighborhood in Denpasar. Fixity in and of itself is not the problem. But isolated fixity is.

This is so because it spatially enacts the same metaphysics of individualism that supports the isolated individual model of the person, the very model that underpins the assumption that "where a user is at" is indicative of that person's ability or willingness to stop using drugs. Thus, whether we focus on the location of a service center or the conception of a person, both work together to make the assumption "that the world is composed of individual entities with individually determinate boundaries and properties" seem as though it is in fact the case. The way in which these different practices work together to support and bring into being a certain kind of reality becomes even clearer when we consider the activities that occur at these fixed locations of harm reduction. Furthermore, through these practices responsibility emerges as one of the primary value terms that signify, and thus further congeals, this reality.

The central activity of harm reduction is the syringe exchange program. This program provides the opportunity for drug users to bring used syringes to the exchange in order to receive clean and unused syringes in return, along with other necessary works such as cotton, sterile water, and bottle caps. In most cases the exchange is one for one, such that, for example, someone who brings in thirty used syringes can receive thirty new ones in return. In some locations, such as the exchange where I worked in New York, there is some leeway on this rule such that if a sufficient reason is given for why a person needs more syringes than he brought in, he is able to receive a certain number more. What counts as a sufficient reason is already predefined and listed on the form that needs to be filled out by the exchange worker during each exchange. Some possible reasons are (1) a planned upcoming trip during which there will be no access to clean needles; (2) the user lives far from the center and so the distance makes it inconvenient to come regularly; and (3) fear of carrying used syringes. Notice that each of these reasons is directly tied to the fact of the fixity of the center, which, as pointed out above, is normally in an area of town not particularly convenient to access for many users. And finally, in some locations, such as St. Petersburg, there are limitations on the number of syringes one person can receive on any given day. At the center in St. Petersburg this number is one hundred.

Thus, in addition to the access to clean syringes this exchange provides, and thus the potential harm it reduces by preventing the spread of infectious diseases, this exchange also provides an encounter through which individual users are disciplined to become better self-managers and more accountable for their actions. They must travel to a fixed location where they have been registered, oftentimes risking encounters with police who are aware that users are going to this location and will have pockets or a bag filled with a good number of used syringes, which still have heroin residue in them, and very possibly other illicit items and substances. They must make this risky trip during certain preset hours, which normally are those of a typical business or institutional temporality. Additionally, what they are able to receive from the center in terms of items and numbers is preestablished by the center and may not reflect the needs of the user. And finally, any attempt to deviate from these guidelines is met with a demand for an account of why this individual might be allowed to deviate—not to mention the fact that during these exchange encounters it is not uncommon that users will be asked whether or not they have recently been tested for HIV or hepatitis C, or would like some kind of counseling, or if they would like training in overdose prevention, or any number of other similar questions. Ultimately, then, users who come to a syringe exchange cannot help but get the message that they must become more accountable and responsible for their actions, and a good way to do this is to become better self-managers of their behavior, thoughts, emotions, and time.

A similar message is communicated through other activities that commonly occur in harm reduction centers. This was illustrated well in the center where I worked in New York City. In addition to the syringe exchange, this center also offers a number of therapeutic activities—ranging from group talk therapy to yoga—that take place in the so-called hangout space. A weekly schedule of these activities is posted near the front door, next to the house rules sign, by the reception desk. As one looks at the schedule to find the time of the activity one wants to attend, it is difficult not to notice the fact that no cursing, no arguments, and no dealing, among a number of other restrictions, are all prerequisites not only for joining an activity but also for being in the space at all. To be in the center, then, is to be a certain kind of person who can manage being that kind of person.

This, of course, does not go unnoticed by a number of users who frequent the center, and the restriction on cursing is the least of their concerns. Quite a few of these regulars have been around since the mid-1990s, when it was founded as a collective of user and AIDS activists who sought not only to reduce the harm of drug use but also to provide a space where "users could be users," as I was told by one of them. Back then, so the story goes, the center was a space where users could discuss, debate, and argue with one another over their needs, political, economic, social, health, or otherwise. It was a space where spontaneous concerts or poetry reading or art projects would occur. It was a space that was theirs, where they didn't have to become something they weren't—rather, the space became that which they made it.

Today, many of the same people and many of the more recent participants, as they are called, no longer make the space but are made by it. The center, as I was told several times, has been taken over by college-educated therapists and managers, and in so doing has become institutionalized. The so-called hangout space that was once open to become whatever the users there wanted to make of it, is now primarily where the therapeutic activities occur. And when the hangout space is free to be used for hanging out, it is dominated by a big-screen television that plays recent Hollywood hits at a volume that takes over the space. It has become, to a great extent, a waiting room for the next therapeutic session. It has become a place where most activities that occur are aimed at the learning of better self-management, accountability, and responsibility, or the place where one can wait until one is able—either according to the schedule or one's choice—to begin this self-work.

It is not uncommon for at least one of these therapeutic sessions to be aimed at participants gaining some skills—and this is usually in terms of emotional and self-management skills—for entering the labor market. Such a weekly session also takes place in the center in Honolulu. What is particularly noticeable in these sessions is that a good deal of emphasis is put on the distinction between good labor and bad labor. For example, sex work or working in bars is considered bad labor, the kind of work that denies one's dignity or self-respect. The message of these sessions is that participants must take responsibility for themselves and do the kind of training necessary to break away from the trappings of these bad jobs and make themselves into persons capable of getting good jobs. The unfortunate limitation of these sessions, however, is that the only kind of training provided is for peer work within the center itself or the HIV prevention organization with which it is affiliated. Such sessions, then, limit possibilities for labor to such an extent that in order to be considered as a responsible worker, one must—considering the frequent lack of education and training otherwise—become a worker within the very institutionalized and closed model of harm reduction that claims to offer possibilities to escape the world of drug use and the stigmas that go along with it. This not only closes possibilities to learn to labor in an acceptable way (e.g., not doing sex work), but further limits the skills one actually acquires to such a narrow set that one remains, as it were, trapped in the excluded zones rendered barely inhabitable by the drug war. Peer work may be considered a good job done by responsible workers, but it provides little or no possibility of transitioning to one entirely outside of harm reduction in particular or the biopolitical therapeutic industry in general.

In this section I have tried to show how what I am calling the typical model of harm reduction—and particularly its emphasis on responsibility—enacts and reproduces the contemporary form and values of metaphysical humanism. The forgetting of the world that further characterizes this practice results in precisely the kinds of labors and projects that Hannah Arendt predicted—that is, an unswerving focus on life and normalization. Recall that the primary focus of the typical model of harm reduction is preserving life by reducing the potential harm of drug use. The harm reduction project enacted is the maintenance of the health and life of individual humans through interventions on the being of those individuals, but not through any significant intervention in the world of these individuals. And as we saw, the most significant intervention into the life of individual drug users is not necessarily in terms of the provision of syringes, for example, but in the disciplining of self-management, accountancy, and responsibility. In the typical harm reduction model, then, we see a clear example of how the biopolitical focus on life, and the turning away from the world that accompanies this focus, results in the normalization and responsibilization of individuals in locations that have become institutionalized. It is a model that enacts a distribution of the sensible that Rancière calls the police. That is to say, the biopolitical focus of harm reduction is entirely on preserving life and in the process making individuals into a particular kind of being—a being that fits into a prior conception of what counts as human, that, as such, fits into a certain order of things; a being that is fit into a preconceived world rather than recognized as intertwined with and of a world.

What is the difference between being fit into a preconceived world and being intertwined with and of a world? And how might this ontological difference allow for ethics and politics that differ from that of metaphysical humanism? Some have argued that beginning from a different ontology can lead to different social and political ways of being and becoming. In the rest of this essay I would like to show how this in fact may be the case. But before turning to the example of what I call the Vancouver model of harm reduction, I first consider one of the more original, insightful, and influential contributions to the so-called ontological turn and its possible ramifications for social, ethical, and political theory.

Barad, Levinas, and Responsibility

It has become trendy in academia to eschew perspectives that focus on humans. Many of these studies rightly emphasize the shortcomings of humanism and attempt to provide an alternative to its human-centrism. These come in various guises ranging from new and vital materialisms to object-oriented ontology. What becomes clear when reading many of these alternatives, however, is that despite their claims of offering something new, they nevertheless continue the leveling of all beings that is characteristic of metaphysical humanism. If one of the most pernicious consequences of metaphysical humanism is the leveling of all existence by means of the projection of humanness onto all that is, then many of these so-called alternatives similarly level existence by means of projecting certain presumed qualities of objects or matter or what have you onto all that is. Thus whether we continue the old projections of metaphysical humanism or enact new ones with the variously new realisms, we continue the project of leveling with yet another flat ontology.

But perhaps an even more dangerous consequence of some of these alternatives—dangerous because unrecognized and adamantly denied—is that they tend to continue metaphysical humanism in another form. Whether it's forests thinking, carrots feeling, or chemical systems choosing a path of development, one thing that is not difficult to find in the writings of the so-called posthumanists is the language traditionally reserved for human capacities now assigned to nonhuman beings. I imagine that one possible response of posthumanists would be that such language is intentionally used in order to disrupt assumptions of human exceptionalism. That is, of course, a perfectly reasonable response. But as I have argued elsewhere (Zigon forthcoming), concepts tend to have a proclivity to resist the performative openness argued for by Butler and others, such that their accumulated historical use tends to make them stick to or slip back to or remain anchored to (or whatever metaphor you prefer) the range of possible meanings and practices they have acquired, as well as the institutions of power that have supported these meanings. Chemical systems may in fact spontaneously and inexplicably develop in certain ways under certain conditions of disequilibrium, but to refer to this as choosing—and to do so in a way that clearly draws on notions of human choice—at the very least resembles too closely the kind of metaphysical humanism that many posthumanists claim to be arguing against.

Perhaps the worst violator of slipping metaphysical humanism in through the back door of posthumanism is Karen Barad in her highly influential and deeply interesting *Meeting the Universe Halfway*. Here I am not referring to her reliance on quantum physics as providing the key to understanding the nature of reality. Unlike most posthumanists who have turned to science or mathematics as offering a nonhumanist approach to reality—despite the fact that these two practices are perhaps the most obvious culprits of metaphysical humanism—Barad, for the most part, tempers and alters her use of quantum physics just enough so as not to make this the most obvious contradiction of her own point. Rather, I am referring to her conclusion that the agential realism approach she offers results in "an ethical call . . . to take responsibility for the role that we play in the world's differential becoming" (Barad 2007, 396).

In the posthumanist world of agential realism, Barad claims, all existents must take responsibility for this becoming. Not only humans, but brittle stars, photons, and everything else is responsible for the world's becoming in Barad's view. As she puts it, "the becoming of the world is a deeply ethical matter" (Barad 2007, 185). It seems that it is not enough that politics and art have taken a deeply ethical turn (e.g., Rancière 2010)—and oftentimes with moralizing consequences (e.g., Brown 2001)—but now ontology and existence itself is ethical through and through. Indeed, as Barad (2007, 182) further explains, ethicality "is part of the fabric of the world; the call to respond and be responsible is part of what is. There is no spatial-temporal domain that is excluded from the ethicality of what matters." Not unlike some anthropologists who project metaphysical humanist notions of morality onto social life and argue that the social is ethical through and through (e.g., Lambek 2010a), Barad projects one of the twin pillars of this ontology, that is morality, onto all of existence. Indeed, this projection takes on a neoliberal tinge as we are told that questions "of responsibility and accountability present themselves with every possibility" (Barad 2007, 182). Just as the neoliberal free agent is personally responsible for every one of her actions, thoughts, and desires, so too the agent of agential realism is responsible and accountable to "each moment" of becoming (182). All of existence, so it would seem, must take on the heavy burden of a neoliberal-like responsibility and accountability.

Despite this metaphysical humanist leveling, Barad nevertheless maintains a privileged and exceptional place for humans in her supposedly posthuman world. For although all existents have responsibility and are accountable "for the becoming of the world," humans must take on more responsibility than any other. And here we return to human exceptionalism. Indeed this is not an uncommon result of posthumanist alternatives, and certainly not unexpected considering the prevalence of human-centric language projected onto other existents in these works. Thus, for example, the political theorist Jane Bennett concludes her *Vibrant Matter: A Political Ecology of Things* with a confession of sorts that she is unable to articulate any normative implications of her vital materialism and so falls back on what she calls a "Nicene Creed for would-be vital materialists" (2010, 122). The fundamental content of this creed, as it turns out, is that "a careful course of anthropomorphization" is the best way to combat the possible hubris of anthropomorphism. In the end, then, the best this vital materialist political theory can offer is a warning that we ought (and I intentionally use this term) to anthropomorphize a bit more carefully. This is certainly not a compelling alternative to metaphysical humanism.

And neither is Barad's adoption of Levinas and his central concept of responsibility for the Other. For Levinas, it may be the case that everyone is obliged with responsibility, but the key claim that Levinas makes is that one always bears full responsibility for the Other. Responsibility for Levinas, then, is always focused and centered; it is always "my" responsibility for the Other, and not, as we might hope, mutual responsibility for one another. Indeed, such mutuality is impossible for Levinas, as the Other is always infinitely separated from oneself along an infinite curvature of intersubjectivity; this is an infinite curvature that, like Descartes's infinite curvature between the human subject and God, forecloses any possibility for mutuality, reciprocity, or being-with. It is this human-centric, indeed metaphysically individualist, notion of responsibility that Barad adopts as the main ethical and political conclusion for her posthuman agential realism (cf. Washick and Wingrove 2015).

Barad, however, is seduced by Levinas's notion of proximity, which he characterizes as "difference which is non-indifference," and which he equates with responsibility (Levinas, in Barad 2007, 391). Barad reads proximity as similar enough to her notion of entanglement, which is the intimate intra-action of existents even if separated by large distances, such that she can make a case that entanglement, like proximity, is responsibility. But she does not account for the infinite curvature of intersubjectivity that Levinas places as the condition for his conception of responsibility for the Other. Intra-acting entanglement may, à la quantum physics, entail that all existents that are entangled respond to one another. But for Levinas there is no response of the Other to the one who is responsible; the infinite curvature between the two establishes an essential and insurmountable division that not even a quantum leap can overcome. In adopting a Levinasian notion of responsibility and trying to fit it with her quantum-inspired ontology, then, Barad only repeats in a differential form the very metaphysical humanist and individualist perspective she attempts to escape. Indeed, by adopting the central concept of perhaps one of the most individualist of all moralist thinkers, Barad risks espousing an ethical politics that isolates the human more than ever from the rest of existence.

If attempts to rethink ethics and politics through the rethinking of ontology have tended to do little more than repeat in a differential manner some of the most basic assumptions of metaphysical humanism, must we conclude that such a project is doomed to fail and is best set aside? In the rest of this essay I try to make the case that we need not give up yet. But in order to move forward it is imperative, as I hope to show, to move beyond the turn to mathematics, physics, and other natural sciences that has informed much of the ontological turn thus far, and as a result done little more than maintain a metaphysical humanist perspective in a manner similar to what Heidegger called technology. In the next section I hope to show that this moving beyond is possible not by turning to our best scientific explanations of reality, but instead by turning to the world itself.

Vancouver

While having a conversation with the director of one of the main organizations addressing the situation of the drug war in Vancouver, I mentioned how impressed I was that this organization, in alliance with several others, had been able to "build a parallel world" in the Downtown Eastside of the city. He immediately sat up in his seat and his facial expression changed, seeming to indicate a sense of recognition mixed with pride, as he replied, "Yes, that's exactly what we have done. No one's really put it that way before, but that's what we've done." This struck me as just a bit strange, and in fact I'm still not entirely sure he was being honest with me, since it seemed so obvious that this is exactly what has happened in this down-and-out zone of exclusion that was once the center of historic Vancouver.

Although a hundred years ago the Downtown Eastside was a center of business, commerce, and government in Vancouver, by the late twentieth century it had become the front line of the drug war in the city. Businesses and government offices had moved out to be replaced with single-room occupancy (sro) hotels and abandoned spaces. It was not uncommon that commuters who had no other option than to take a bus through this part of town could look out the window and see bodies dead from overdose lying on the sidewalks. The back alleyways that run throughout the neighborhood had become heroin shooting galleries, a place of business for sex workers, a place to sleep and congregate and buy and sell drugs, and yet another place to die from overdose. Hundreds of people a year, in fact, would die of overdose in this neighborhood alone. It was, as one eventual protest by drug users would call it, "the killing fields."

This neighborhood had become a world in which the people who lived there—a great number of whom were drug users—could no longer dwell. This world had become uninhabitable and unbearable. Those who lived there were reduced to objects that metaphorically and quite literally could become just another piece of trash on the sidewalk or in the alley. Where these users were at, then, was a world that no longer provided possibilities to become anything other than dead. Eventually many of these users and their neighbors and some of the organizations already working in the neighborhood—mostly SRO organizations—had enough and began to mobilize to address the fact of the unbearableness of this world. And while at first this meant the establishment of harm reduction services along the lines of the typical model I described above, soon the coalition of user and SRO organizations began to creatively experiment with a new model of harm reduction. Although several of the key players in this coalition were strongly influenced by various communal and radical leftist politics, ultimately their political experimentation is best understood as a postpolitical project that seeks to address the situated demands of the particular world where they happened to be (Zigon 2015). Thus, in contrast to attempts to implement a preknown and a priori political ideology—be this neoliberally infused biopolitics or anarchosocialism—the politics of world-building enacted by these Vancouver agonists simply attempt to remake their world by whatever means necessary so that they can once again dwell in it (Zigon 2014b). At the core of this experiment and this new model, then, was a shift of focus from individual drug users to the world with which drug users happen to be intertwined. With this shift—as I argue—there was an accompanying shift from a concern with self-management, accountability, and responsibility to something we might call worldly attunement.

Elsewhere I have argued that attunement in the ontological sense is that force of existence that allows relationships to assemble (Zigon 2014a). When speaking of the existent we call human, attunement is what allows it to be a being that is initially and always a being-in-relationships. Because of attunement humans are always and inseparably intertwined in the diverse relations that come to be a world. Similarly, attunement allows all nonhuman things to assemble and come to partially constitute worlds, and in so doing to be always and inseparably intertwined in diverse relations, just one of which is with what we call humans. Worlds come into being and maintain this being because existents become attuned and maintain this attunement in certain ways. I have called this maintenance of attunement ethics; we can call it an ethics of perseverance or fidelity. Worlds, however, become uninhabitable and unbearable when attunement can no longer be maintained. From the breakdown of a world, out of its unbearableness, a demand for another kind of ethics emerges; this is an ethics of dwelling, which we can also call politics—that is, politics as a process of world-building.

Such an ethics of dwelling as a politics of world-building is under way in Vancouver. It is not clear, however, to what extent this is recognized outside of the city. Certainly Vancouver has become a beacon of hope for harm reductionists and anti–drug war agonists around the globe, but this is primarily so because a coalition of users, harm reductionists, and SRO organizations was able to establish the first and only legally sanctioned safe injection site (Insite) in North America. The fact that this accomplishment—certainly a tremendous one—is what Vancouver is primarily known for says more about the assumptions and focus of those who remain within the limits of the typical harm reduction model than what Vancouver has actually become. For while the establishment of Insite is a central aspect of the new world that has emerged out of the breakdown of the Downtown Eastside, it is precisely just one aspect of this new world, within which it is now possible for drug users to dwell. This new world, created primarily by users and allied organizations who became motived by an ethics of dwelling to enact a politics of world-building, consists of among other things art galleries and studios, a bank, a grocery store, a dentist's office, a community center, and a network of social enterprises where users can be trained for employment and work and includes two cafés and various stores.

This is a new world attuned to itself and as such always open to becoming otherwise. For to be attuned to itself, a world must always be open to becoming something that it is currently not. Attunement entails a process of becoming. What does this mean and how is it different from the typical harm reduction model? Consider the following. One October morning I was standing outside of one of the social enterprise cafés talking with the manager of the café and the director of the First Nations program with one of the neighborhood organizations. The manager was telling me about how the social enterprises provide possibilities for persons to become connected to the neighborhood while also gaining skills that could provide opportunities outside of the neighborhood. Just then the director interjected and began telling me that unlike most service programs around the globe, Vancouver is unique in that they have built what he called a structure but I will call a world, in which any one of the programs within this world serves as an entry point for the others. The director went on to draw a distinction. As he put it, normally if one is seeking harm reduction services then one must and can find these services only at a particular location run by a particular organization that is generally disconnected from other kinds of programs and services. The director called this common way of providing and finding services linear because there is only one entry point—the harm reduction clinic—and it provides only one kind of service.[2] This linear track is characteristic of the typical harm reduction model I described above. Vancouver's Downtown Eastside, on the other hand, is a world of networked services and social enterprises into which one can enter at any point and be referred to, learn about, take advantage of any number of other available possibilities within this world.

The director continued and gave me the following example of how this emergence of possibilities happens. The bank, he said as he pointed to it across the street, can be an entry point for a range of possibilities. The bank is a space where tellers come to know local customers quite well as they all tend to be people from the neighborhood. Over time they hear their stories, see them in the streets and in the cafés, or in the community center, and thus a relationship is built. It is not uncommon, then, that someone might confide in a teller about some difficulties she might be experiencing, or the teller might simply be able to see that she is acting differently than usual, and thus the teller can suggest she go across the street to the detox center, for example, or to the dentist, or suggest she seek employment at one of the social enterprises within the neighborhood. The bank, then, becomes an entry point into a range of possibilities that emerges from a world that is attuned to the ways of being and becoming of itself. It is a space or clearing from which a world opens itself to one of its inhabitants and in so doing potentially opens itself to becoming a new world as the eventual feedback consequence of this original opening can never be known. This is attunement as a process of becoming.

The bank is not simply a place to keep one's money so that the bank can make profit; it also becomes an entry into a world specifically designed and attuned to those beings that dwell there. Thus, not only are the human tellers and customers attuned to these possibilities, but so too are the architectural space and technology of the bank. The lobby, for example, unlike in other banks, is not simply a place to fill out deposit slips or wait to meet a teller or service representative, it is also a space or a clearing for people in the neighborhood to hang out, drink the free coffee, and use computers and the Internet provided to anyone free of charge. The bank lobby is a clearing where it is possible to learn about what is happening elsewhere in the neighbor-hood—for example, political rallies, concerts, yoga sessions, or art exhibits—by talking with others or reading the announcements posted. It is also a clearing opening onto the globe as one can interact with others anywhere or learn about anything via the Internet. The bank lobby, then, is a clearing out of which possibilities of learning, acting, and becoming are opened. And just in case this is not enough, the lobby is also a space where anyone can go and get a safe crack pipe from a vending machine—this is likely the only bank in the world that offers a crack pipe vending machine. This bank, then, is a space of opening possibilities that go far beyond those of the linear or typical harm reduction model, and these possibilities become available because of the attunement that is built into the world of which it is a part.

The bank is not the only clearing in this world. Consider the life trajectory of Joan, a thirty-three-year-old woman who was born in the Downtown Eastside and has become who she is today because of the attunement of her world to itself, and the clearings available to her because of this attunement. Joan grew up living in the SROS and family housing units in the neighborhood with her heroin-using mother, and started using various drugs herself in her early teens. At one point she realized she wanted to find a job but didn't know how to do so since her background didn't exactly provide her with the kind of skills and education most employers look for. As is the case for most drug users around the globe, the larger world of Vancouver that Joan had been thrown into excluded her from most possibilities of becoming otherwise. Luckily, though, she had also been thrown into a parallel world created by a particular enactment of a politics of world-building, and this world had clearings that opened possibilities for Joan. Thus, she turned to the people working in the office of the housing unit where she was living at the time. They had known Joan since her childhood and could see that she was ready and willing to work and so helped her get her first job in their office. But soon everyone realized that such a job did not well suit Joan's creative interests, and so they helped connect her to an arts and crafts shop within the network where she could do her art and interact with people more regularly. Eventually, once Joan became pregnant and decided to stop using, she was easily able to access detox and other support services within the network and not have to worry about how the time spent on this might affect her job status. Today Joan lives with her husband and two-year-old son in new social housing that is a part of a new high-rise condominium of mixed social and private housing, a project that was initiated and fought for by the alliance of organizations engaged in this politics of world-building as they battle against encroaching gentrification. Joan continues to work in the arts and crafts shop, as well as in one of the neighborhood art galleries, and continues to do her art. The person Joan has become, then, is in a very real way a result of the possibilities for becoming available within this attuned world created through the politics of world-building under way in Vancouver.

This is not a world defined by the closed normalization of biopolitical metaphysical humanism, and neither is it a practice of harm reduction focused on responsibilization. Rather it is a world characterized by attunement, in which clearings become available that open possibilities for both the world and its inhabitants to become otherwise. With this simple shift by a few political agonists from the metaphysics of individualism to a world, we can witness a politics of world-building and the enactment of an entirely other form of ontology. This political event, I contend, provides us with something like hope.

Some Closing Words

Unlike the linear track offered by the typical harm reduction model, as well as most service organizations around the globe, the world built in the Downtown Eastside of Vancouver is rhizomatic in that a person can enter it at any point and find herself connected to any number of other possible points within this world. What is most interesting for our purposes about the Vancouver model is that where a person finds herself once having entered the rhizome may be someplace (both literally in terms of location and metaphorically in terms of existential possibilities) she had not expected or intended, or may not have known she was interested in or cared about, or perhaps even may not have known was possible. This new world gives an entirely other meaning to the harm reduction concern for "where they are at." For, as I hope I have made clear in this essay, this rhizomatic world opens possibilities for being and becoming that the typical harm reduction model normally does not provide. Whereas the typical model tends to limit being and possibilities to the normalized self-management and responsibility of a user who seeks to inject safely, the rhizomatic world is a world within which a user can do so safely, but also opens possibilities to become a person with a job and a savings account, have dentistry work done, build friendships and relations of trust, find good housing, and buy a cup of well-brewed coffee, among many other things. Thus, in their rejection of the linear model of harm reduction, as well as the metaphysical individualism and humanism that underpin it, the political actors in Vancouver's Downtown Eastside have enacted a politics of world-building through which they are creating a world attuned to itself. To some extent this attunement is similar to the care "enacted across various levels of relationality," about which Trnka and Trundle write in the introduction. But whereas their notion of care still seems to require an ontologically prior subject agent who can do such things as recognize, act, and commit to an Other, and thus in some sense still must choose to enter into a relationship, the attunement that I have written of here is an ontological infrastructure of relationality within which all beings—human and nonhuman alike—are already intertwined, the result of which is a modality of being we might call attuned care (see Zigon 2014a). This, then, is an attuned world that responds to the necessities of its constituent parts—human and nonhuman alike—and in so doing is in a continual process of becoming otherwise. The provocation Vancouver provides us, then, is to ask the question of how the politics of world-building they have undertaken can become motivation for other such political projects, through which being is never limited but is always open to possibilities, possibilities that become available through any entry point into an attuned world.

NOTES

1. I use the term *agonist* instead of *activist* in order to emphasize the agonistic nature of this political activity.

2. It should be noted that in many places such service centers do provide referrals to other services provided at other centers that are similarly linear. Thus, in contrast to a world of emerging possibilities, this referral system connects isolated points and involves a good deal of layered difficulties of bureaucracy and so forth.

Part II. States, Companies, and Communities

THREE. Reciprocal Responsibilities: *Struggles over (New and Old) Social Contracts, Environmental Pollution, and Childhood Asthma in the Czech Republic*

SUSANNA TRNKA

It was one of those miserable fall days, when you wake up in the morning with a throbbing headache. Out the window, it looks like a dark sack has been thrown over the whole town, just as it had all week. "Back into this shit," you mutter under your breath as you close the door. "God, what a stench! What the hell are they putting in the air? It's unbelievable: they're waging chemical warfare against their own people."

If you say you can't breathe, there are two meanings. The first is symbolic, that the mental environment is stifling, choked with lies and hypocrisy: there is no breathing room. The second meaning is more immediate, that the air itself is corrupted and you are literally choking to death. The first is a sigh of despair; the second a cry for help.
—ELECTRICAL ENGINEER EDUARD VACKA as quoted in a 1987
dissident publication (reproduced in Kilburn and Vaněk 2004)

Few visitors to Ostrava can escape the overwhelming sensation of being surrounded by a blanket of smog, particularly if they visit the Czech Republic's third largest city in the winter. Located in the industrial center of Moravia, near the borders of Poland and Slovakia, Ostrava's landscape has long been dominated by coal, iron, and smog, earning it the nicknames "black Ostrava" and "the steel heart of the republic." Today, Ostrava is famous throughout the Czech Republic for its residents' respiratory problems. Indeed, some Czech doctors and scientists have lobbied to have Ostrava recognized as having the highest rates of childhood asthma in the world.

It wasn't always so. Many of the air quality problems in Ostrava began after the establishment of the state-owned Nová huť Klementa Gottwalda (NHKG) steel plant in 1951. As one Ostrava resident remembers, when his parents moved to the region in the 1940s, they specifically chose to settle in the Ostrava district of Radvanice and Bartovice as his mother suffered from respiratory problems. They assumed the air there would be beneficial as the area had once been the home of a tuberculosis sanatorium. He recounts to me how on the day the NHKG steel plant first opened for production, "It was sunny and my father sat down to read the newspaper. Behind his back he could hear it start to rain. He kept on reading his paper until he realized it had been raining far too long. He turned around and looked out the window and saw it wasn't rain, but ash. And it never stopped falling."

The negative effects of such "rainfall" on local residents' health were largely hidden from wider public view until the 1989 Velvet Revolution. Following the overthrow of the government, not only did environmental conditions across the republic receive intensive media coverage, but nationwide economic restructuring resulted in the widespread closure of Ostrava's coal mines and the temporary cessation of production in many of the city's steelworks. While mining did not recover, much of the steelworks industry was bought and expanded by foreign companies. Luxemburg-based ArcelorMittal purchased the former NHKG, renamed it ArcelorMittal Ostrava, and refurbished it into what is today the largest steelworks in the Czech Republic, producing 3 million tons of crude steel per year. As a result, the air quality in Ostrava not only stopped improving but plummeted to the point that parts of the city (Radvanice and Bartovice) are widely considered to have the worst air quality in all of Europe, due to high levels of PM10, benzo[a]pyrene (BaP), benzene, and arsenic.[1] Data collected in Radvanice and Bartovice in 2013, for example, reveal that levels of PM10, which can lead to aggravated asthma, chronic bronchitis, and lung cancer, exceeded EU limits one hundred and twenty-nine days in the year, and levels of BaP, which causes cardiovascular diseases and damage to genetic material, exceeded EU directives by 900 percent (Czech Hydrometeorological Institute 2014). More recent reviews (e.g. Vossler, Cernikovsky, Novak, et al. 2015) paint a similarly grim picture.

The plight of Ostrava's 300,000 residents, and the half a million people living in the surrounding region, has elicited widespread media interest not only in the Czech Republic but across Europe. In part, this is due to high-profile protests during which local residents have repeatedly donned gas masks to highlight their concerns over air quality. Residents also wrote a petition, which garnered 19,000 signatures, demanding that steel companies and local and national government take action to stop the pollution. There has furthermore been a series of lawsuits against ArcelorMittal Ostrava as well as a lawsuit filed by the local Ostrava government against the Czech state.

The situation in Ostrava has inspired much public and legal debate over who is responsible for ensuring the health and well-being of Ostrava's residents. Many local residents, nongovernmental organizations (NGOs), physicians, and scientists look to the state—both local and national—as ultimately responsible for safeguarding Ostrava's inhabitants. At the same time, however, local and national politicians are struggling to resolve the crisis of rising unemployment. Compounded by the fact that there appears to be little scope for industry or commerce in the region other than through the steel industry, the unemployment rate ignites vociferous debate over how to best ensure residents' health and well-being. Meanwhile, the air quality has become so dire that the EU recently stepped in and attempted to force the Czech government to act. EU pressure has, however, proved ineffective thus far. In such a context, asthma and other respiratory illnesses emerge as a citizenship issue that provokes widespread and sustained interest, both within and beyond the city of Ostrava (see also Trnka 2017).

Some of this attention could be explained by the fact that air pollution knows no boundaries: everyone who lives in Ostrava suffers from the same overall environmental conditions. However, as Harper (2004) and Brown, Morello-Fosch, and Zavestoski (2011) have pointed out for the United States, the links between environmental conditions and respiratory illnesses are often most concerning for local, lower-income communities as concentrations of air toxicity can differ dramatically from neighborhood to neighborhood based on the location of industries, freeways, and bus depots, as well as wind direction. As Harper notes with respect to Houston, Texas, "All people living in the Houston area are breathing poisoned air, [but] the concentrations of ground-level ozone and air toxics are not equally shared by all" (2004, 308). This is also the case in Ostrava, where some parts of the city—most notably Radvanice and Bartovice—are getting more than their fair share of both air pollution and respiratory illnesses. That said, the environmental health movement in Ostrava has received national attention and become a rallying point for politicians, scientists, and physicians far outside the region. Here, then, environmental politics is not being ghettoized, but nationalized.

One reason why Ostrava's air pollution has come to occupy such prominence is the concerns it evokes over the appropriate roles of citizens, the state, and capitalist corporations in a fledgling democratic society. The stories that make the headlines are, furthermore, inflected with widely held traditional perspectives on masculine, working-class labor, women's domestic roles, and the need to protect vulnerable children. All that is missing from popular narratives—and conspicuously so—is the state's role in protecting its citizenry.

In depicting the Ostrava situation as a struggle between citizens who are suffering and a state that is not living up to its obligations, Czech activists draw upon deeply held convictions about the reciprocal relations and responsibilities envisioned to exist between states and citizens.[2] Moreover, as the epigraph at the beginning of this chapter demonstrates, the view that environmental health is inherently a citizenship issue harkens back to struggles against the state during the state-socialist regime.

As it is currently cast, the struggle in Ostrava evokes a generational politics of social contracts in which mothers and (male) workers contribute to the well-being of the nation-state through (female) reproduction and (masculine) labor, on the understanding that there will be a corresponding counter-contribution, namely the state's protection, if not of themselves, then, at the very least, of their children. As in all exchanges, temporality is crucial (Bourdieu 1972) in that state protection is particularly needed when citizens are young and vulnerable.

Didier Fassin (2013, 118) has pointed out the immense rhetorical power of children as iconic victims whose innocence and defenselessness cannot be questioned. When children's lives become the sites of political struggle, Fassin suggests, political debate shifts into a highly emotive register in which questions of responsibility take on a different kind of valence. One could argue that young children represent the outer limits of notions of individualized, personal responsibility, as they simply cannot take care of themselves and thus represent the inherent need for collective interdependence. For many adults, moreover, the image of the child in pain is a highly affective trigger, eliciting concern and a desire to alleviate suffering in a way that is qualitatively different from other political objects. The figure of the suffering child thus provides a powerful, emotive focal point for debates over the obligations of the state.

As with all social contracts, this is a nationalist story and the state's obligation to protect its people is heightened by the fact that the company in question is foreign owned. It is also an ethnic story, as citizenship is represented through the images of white families in pain. Not everyone can suffer, and Ostrava's Roma (gypsies) are left out of claims upon the state, literally erased from scientific and medical discourse. The social contract is thus drawn to encompass only those who are thought to have appropriate relations with the state—that is, those who give enough and do not take too much—and exclude those deemed to be outside of the reciprocal obligations of state and citizen.

It is also a story of how attachments to old social contracts can outweigh attempts to create new ones, as state-citizen relations are widely seen to trump ties between companies and local residents. ArcelorMittal has taken major steps, both in Ostrava and internationally, to portray itself as a moral actor, but much of this has fallen flat in terms of the company's local and national reputation. Despite the early postsocialist period during which conservative rhetoric promoted free markets and unfettered capitalism as being both the most natural and the most morally just economic and political system, most of Czech society appears unwilling to consider companies as acting within a moral framework. Cognizant of what Peter Benson and Stuart Kirsch (2010, 459) have referred to as the "token accommodation" of many corporate social responsibility (CSR) programs, activists, scientists, and local pressure groups continue to turn to the state as the only source of (potential) justice.

This then is a case in which the citizen-state social contract stands as a powerful ideal even when it is constantly being undermined. As Elizabeth Kirtsoglou (2010) has noted, modernization (locally glossed as Westernization) is often embraced for its promise to deliver the ever-deferred ideal of citizen-state relations, even though it is also the mechanism through which multiple exclusions and loopholes in social contract ideals are constantly being created. In continuing to hold the state to account, Czech activists demand that the state act as it should rather than as it does.

Significantly, what is at stake is more than the honoring of a contractual obligation per se (though that is important too). Indeed, the debates over air pollution in Ostrava demonstrate the often intense and enduring affective ties that exist between citizens and states (cf. Hage 2003; Trnka, Dureau, and Park 2013b), even when the capability of the state to act justly is held in question. For many Czechs, struggles such as the one over Ostrava's environmental destruction are not (just) a question of demanding one's rights but also of one's expectations of care. Citizens anticipate and hope for more than simply the return of services that is inherent in a state (or corporation) honoring a contractual obligation; they strive to receive care and recognition from the state as the representative of society writ large. Despite deep-seated skepticism and wariness over how the state has historically been the site of (Austro-Hungarian, German, and state-socialist) oppression, as well as contemporary concerns over political corruption, the state emerges as the only force considered strong enough to protect those who cannot protect themselves.

Such calls upon the state to protect the citizenry constitute a counterpoint to the "politics of resignation" that Benson and Kirsch have described as a component of global capitalism, "a symptom of the process through which corporate power normalizes and naturalizes risk and harm as inevitable conditions of modernity" (2010, 462). Instead, what emerges here is a politics of last resort in which protestors struggle to position the state as the ultimate moral agent that will protect its people in the face of rampant, capitalist industry.

Environmental Politics: Past and Present

While the activities in Ostrava outshine other environmental protests, throughout the Czech Republic demonstrations draw attention to the impact of air pollution on respiratory health. Public interest in this area can be traced back to an anticommunist environmental movement that cast environmental damage as one of the quintessential issues determining citizens' relationships to the state. Moreover, environmental damage has a visibility that many other political issues cannot garner (figure 3.1). As those who live in the regions most affected relate, you can often see the smog, feel it in your eyes, throat, and lungs, hear the coughs around you. The bodily discomfort, pain, and, in some cases, outright threat to life caused by air pollution has a lengthy history. So too has the collective outcry against it.

In 1987, two years before the dissolution of the socialist state, the first stirrings of a radical Czechoslovak environmental movement began to be felt. Initially, there was little government resistance to public interest in environmental issues as the Communist Party did not perceive environmental activism as a political threat (Vaněk 1996). In fact, some environmental activists initially received party authorization and set up their groups under the umbrella of the Communist Party's civic organizations. At the same time, however, a populist, underground environmentalist movement was also emerging. Located in northern industrial centers such as Teplice, populist movements initially focused on demanding environmental changes that would improve people's living conditions. Soon, however, activists' demands became more radical, culminating in calls for the government to step down. In the lead up to the November 1989 Velvet Revolution, thousands of residents of northern industrial cities took the streets, demanding clean air as a human right.

Historian Miroslav Vaněk, who grew up in Teplice, has no trouble ex-

FIGURE 3.1. Ostrava skyline, featuring ArcelorMittal's smokestacks. Photo by Susanna Trnka.

plaining how so many people were galvanized into action. "The pollution was so bad," he tells me, "so many children would get very sick every year. And everyone could see how sick they were. You would go to visit the doctor and the waiting room was full of sick children with stuffed noses, coughs, their eyes red and so swollen that they could not shut them. . . . This was *not* an ideological struggle like the dissidents' arguments about human rights, but it was something *everyone* in that area was living through."

A few months before the Teplice demonstration, another pivotal environmental group emerged. Based in Prague and thus closer to the cultural and political centers of power, the Prague Mothers stirred up antigovernment sentiment among members of the populace who weren't usually predisposed toward political activism. One of their founders, Jarmila Johnová, was the mother of three young children in 1989. No stranger to politics, she was a member of a dissident circle that included the future president, Václav Havel. Her husband was a prominent activist who later held a ministerial position in the first postsocialist government. During the 1980s, however, her husband spent long periods in prison. Johnová was also politically active, but acutely aware of her role in holding her family together. She remembers that when the secret police knocked on her door, one of her greatest fears was that if she too was arrested, no one would be left to look after their children.

Nonetheless, she and a group of Prague-based dissidents, all of whom were mothers of babies and young children, came together to raise public awareness about the effects of Prague's air pollution on children's health. Their primary complaint was the smog. "You could see it in the air," she explains, "and on the bad days, my son . . . went gray and had no energy. It was my own intuition that his listlessness was linked to the air quality, as we weren't doctors. But we knew there was dust in the air and we couldn't watch our children like this. If it was made public, we imagined the government would need to start caring about the environment." So in May 1989 Johnová organized a group of women who took their prams and parked them in the middle of the street, calling on the government to improve the air quality.

The inspiration to call their group Prague Mothers came from a male friend who convinced Johnová that a government that prided itself on protecting mothers and children wouldn't be able to brush them off. The name also proved to be an effective smokescreen, suggesting the protesters were not disgruntled dissidents but "just mothers with prams." As Michael Kilburn and Vaněk (2004) noted, "The parade of prams . . . left bystanders supportive and security forces completely disarmed."

By late 1989, the Prague Mothers' protests were having an effect on public consciousness about environmental destruction and its health impacts. Further buoyed by the activities of the Teplice protestors, these concerns were soon swept up into a much larger protest movement that culminated in the November 1989 Velvet Revolution and removed the state-socialist government from power (Fagan 2004; Holy 1996). The public prominence of environmental concerns meant that they received significant political traction with the new government. Across the nation, the air quality improved. That is, until, in the country's southeastern region of Moravia, it began to deteriorate again.

The Steel Heart of the Republic

Some 170 miles away from Prague, Ostrava is today the site of the republic's most intense air pollution and highest rates of respiratory problems. Since 2002, local residents have been mobilizing to raise awareness of the health situation and demand redress from local and national government and from the steelworks company ArcelorMittal Ostrava.

Science and medicine have been at the forefront of their political struggle. One of the locals who spearheaded the citizens' movement is pediatrician Dr. Eva Schallerová, who became a media figure and candidate for political office in her effort to draw attention to local children's respiratory problems. Dr. Schallerová and others also won the attention of a team of scientists at the Prague-based Academy of Sciences. Led by Professor Radim Šrám, this team has spent years studying the situation in Ostrava, aiming to conclusively demonstrate the health impact of air pollution on children.

Professor Šrám and his team have found that the rate of upper respiratory infections in infants in Radvanice and Bartovice is almost double that of infants in other Ostrava districts and that children in Radvanice and Bartovice also suffer much higher rates of pneumonia, tonsillitis, intestinal infections, and viral illnesses (Dostál, Pastorková, Rychlik, et al. 2013). Professor Šrám has also claimed that the air pollution in Ostrava causes inheritable DNA damage. But Professor Šrám's most striking and controversial finding has been that the rate of childhood asthma in Radvanice and Bartovice is 37 percent (Šrám, Blinková, Dostál, et al. 2013). This is not only three or four times higher than the rate in other parts of the Czech Republic (generally estimated at 8–10 percent), but would be the highest rate of childhood asthma in the world. (Most international rankings consider national rather than district-based statistics, according to which the world's highest rate of childhood asthma is in the United Kingdom and in New Zealand at around 25 percent.)

According to Professor Šrám, the extremely high rates of asthma in Radvanice and Bartovice are explained by the fact that it is situated downwind of ArcelorMittal Ostrava and thus directly in the path of airborne dust particles released by the steelworks. He has carefully plotted the asthma statistics for each district on a large map of Ostrava and shows me how the closer you get to the wind stream that distributes the steelworks' emissions, the more children's respiratory problems increase. Most of the health issues, he says, are due to the Ostrava operations, though some of the pollutants are propelled across the border from ArcelorMittal's Polish plant.

Like Dr. Schallerová, Professor Šrám is eager to pit medicine against unchecked industrialism. For him, though the science is complex, the political story behind it is simple: the emissions coming out of ArcelorMittal Ostrava are much higher than EU recommendations, but if ArcelorMittal was pressured to uphold EU norms, the Ostrava steelworks could easily be closed and production shifted to the Polish plant, less than sixty miles away. Given the economic situation in Moravia, it is hard for anyone in the region to complain. It is thus, Professor Šrám contends, the duty of the nation's political leaders to stand up and protect the citizenry. Otherwise, Professor Šrám warns, the effects on Ostrava's population will be dire, as the pollution is damaging not only the health of current residents, but even their DNA, impacting subsequent generations.

Some members of the government appear sympathetic to Professor Šrám's campaign, but others call his research pointless. Ostrava's deputy mayor, Dalibor Madej, called Professor Šrám's team's research "a waste of money because they probe into things we all know—that we have pollution here" (quoted in

Flemr 2011). The question for Madej and his supporters is not whether the pollution exists, but how to proceed given fears of further economic strife in the Ostrava region.

Since the massive closures of its coal mines, Ostrava has suffered severe economic hardship. Currently it has the nation's highest unemployment rate at 10 percent, as compared with the national average of 7.5 percent ("Czech Republic" 2013). The national government has announced numerous rescue packages for the region, none of which appears to be having much effect. Other than the steelworks, which are having economic difficulties of their own, there is little prospect for economic recovery.

Thus even among those who accept Professor Šrám's findings, many have trouble reaching the same political conclusions, instead suggesting that the actual lived impact of closing down the steelworks would be much worse than allowing them to break the emissions guidelines. As one ecologist pointed out to me, after the mining and steelworks closures in 1989, "The air certainly got better and people's health improved, but how could people be delighted to be able to breathe again when they had no jobs? Clean air means to people *both* improved health and lack of work."

In some respects, polluted air not only has been a part of the region's landscape for decades but was a signifier of prosperity from the very beginning. Ostrava first came to the fore with steel technology in the early 1800s. Following the discovery of black coal deposits, the first steelworks, Vitkovice Steel and Iron Works, was established in 1830 (figure 3.2). Its opening was a highly ceremonial event, presided over by representatives of industry and trade, local politicians, and religious leaders. As recounted in a local text: "Invited to the ceremony were the most prominent figures in local society. . . . A special mass was said and the new factory was blessed. The first puddle furnace in the entire Austro-Hungarian Empire was lit by the Ostrava priest Leopold Rada. The main orator at the ceremony . . . Kašpar Hauke (representing the town of Moravian Ostrava) . . . stated that 'the first blow of the hammer in this new works will awake the entire region from its sleep'" (Ostrava Město Kultury 2013).

The awakening announced by Hauke did indeed see the area shift from a primarily agricultural base to a center of European industry as mines and steelworks in the area proliferated. The state-socialist period, in particular, fostered the massive expansion of both industry and the city itself, through projects such as the building of the NHKG or New Ironworks of Klement Gottwald in the early 1950s, which was named in honor of the president, Klement Gottwald, who led the 1948 communist coup that overthrew the

FIGURE 3.2. Originally constructed in the nineteenth century, the lower section of Ostrava's Vitkovice Iron and Steelworks has been closed down and turned into a museum. Photo by Susanna Trnka.

elected, postwar government. Gottwald later increased his notoriety by overseeing political purges during which eleven politicians were found guilty of treason and executed.

Following the 1989 revolution, NHKG quickly dropped its association with Gottwald and was put up for sale as part of the state's privatization scheme. The plant was bought by the Indian-born, British-based steel magnate Lakshmi Mittal, who modernized and expanded its operations. In 2006, Mittal Steel acquired the world's second-largest steel-making business, Arcelor; the resulting merger created the world's largest steel company, ArcelorMittal. The merger also gained Mr. Mittal a few new monikers, including International Newsmaker of the Year 2006 from *Time* magazine.

Ostrava's steelworks have thus long been the focus of industrial growth, political symbolism, and, during certain periods, the expansion of personal wealth. But while mills such as Vitkovice and NHKG/ArcelorMittal Ostrava provided the backbone of the local economy for close to two hundred years and have been used to reflect the success and largess of their owners—be it the Austro-Hungarian Empire, the socialist state, or private, foreign ownership—they also raise profound questions about the social relations underpinning these enterprises.

Who Is Responsible?

The image of the steel mill's hammer swung by the united hands of religious authority, government, industry, and tradespeople to awaken a long-dormant region into industrial activity has today given way to intense struggles over how to ensure the health of the nation, in both economic and bodily terms.

Religious authorities have long exited the scene and are no longer viewed as central to industry, but three of the original participants at the founding of Ostrava's steel industry—government, industry, and trade—remain pivotal in contemporary debates over how to respond to air pollution. How should tradespeople and other residents of Ostrava engage with a steel plant that both provides them with much-needed employment and poisons their environment? What is the responsibility of government for ensuring economic prosperity (keeping the region awake) while protecting its citizenry against rampant profiteering? Can industry play a more active role in community protection, or has it taken over the role of the state in promoting industry over health and, in effect, engaging in what activists have referred to as "chemical warfare" (Vacka quoted in Kilburn and Vaněk 2004) against Ostrava's residents?

Since 2006, a series of public demonstrations, petitions, legal cases, and media announcements by NGOs, scientists, and company representatives has created a battleground over the question of culpability. One of the first points of contention was the origins of the air pollution. When activists initially called upon ArcelorMittal to improve Ostrava's air quality, the company denied being the source of the air pollution problems. Instead ArcelorMittal pointed a finger at other local steel plants and a large local heating plant as well as at individuals' automobile and home heating emissions. Scientists and NGOs stepped in to quantify the role each contributor plays in creating the city's air pollution. A study undertaken by the Technical University of Ostrava determined that emissions from the ArcelorMittal Ostrava steelworks contribute approximately 60 percent of airborne dust and almost 92 percent of arsenic and BaP found in the air around Radvanice and Bartovice (Peek et al. 2009). These findings, along with growing pressure from activist groups, led ArcelorMittal Ostrava's spokesman Sanjay Samaddar to admit, "We know that our company has a significant influence on the quality of the air in Radvanice and Bartovice. Of course we do not renounce our shared responsibility for the air quality and we will invest billions [of crowns] into its improvement" (quoted in Pleva 2008).

Samaddar's statement, made in October 2008, was considered a milestone by many involved in the environmental movement as the company had finally accepted responsibility for its role in damaging the air quality. But it was not the turning point that many had hoped for as the company continued its plan to build new and larger facilities. These facilities would be more environmentally friendly but, given their increased production levels, residents were concerned that the bigger facilities would result in the same levels of pollution. The question of taking responsibility therefore remained, and as the situation intensified, so did demands that the company, the local government, and the state take the necessary steps to rectify Ostrava's air quality.

With the support of the civic organization Vzduch (Air) and the environmental legal group Ekologický Právní Servis (EPS), local residents wrote a petition calling on the company to stop its polluting practices and on various branches of the government to stop capitulating to industry. This was accompanied by a series of court cases, the most high profile of which was filed by the city of Ostrava against the Czech state, the ramifications of which are discussed below.

In response to rising pressure, primarily from citizens' groups but also from local political bodies, ArcelorMittal promised to continue reforming its production processes in order to lower its emissions. In 2014 the company opened a new dedusting plant worth a billion crowns (approximately $50 million USD at the time). While these steps have been welcomed by activist groups, many see them as not going far enough and as a continued reflection of ArcelorMittal's primary commitment to ensuring profit over the health of local residents.

National government has also responded to the increasing pressure put upon it by announcing a series of programs to address the air pollution problems. These include a 220 million crown (approximately $11 million USD) boiler exchange, in which households with old, environmentally unfriendly boilers can replace them with new ones and a 90 million crown (approximately $4.5 million USD) scheme for building ecologically sound homes. The national government also promised to lend support to local government to create low-emission zones, akin to those in the United Kingdom and Germany, in order to cut down on vehicle emissions.

Even so, news reports suggest that Ostrava's future continues to look bleak. Despite various anti-pollution measures, the air quality ratings for Ostrava in 2013 were worse than in preceding years (Baroch 2014). As this decade unfolds, Ostrava's air pollution continues to cause serious health concerns and inspire both political activism and heated debate over how to rectify the ongoing environmental damage (Čisté Nebe 2016; Velinger 2015).

For many activists and scientists, the most viable solution is increased public pressure, which—they point out—requires citizens to take responsibility themselves.

Personal Responsibility: Combating Civic Apathy

In the midst of their many calls on government to rein in capital, activists are also occupied with exhorting the citizenry to stand up and pressure government to bend to their collective will. Indeed, some activist efforts focus as much, if not more, on educating and engaging the citizenry as they do on political lobbying. The NGO Vzduch, for example, has listed among its primary strategic priorities keeping citizens engaged and combating civic apathy (Skýbová 2009).

A politics of personal responsibility is thus inherent in these debates. In this context, however, responsibility and self-empowerment are understood not with respect to self-reliance as in Western neoliberal discourses of responsibilization (Rose 2006), but in terms of the need to stand up for oneself in order to make collective political demands on the state. Self-responsibility becomes political responsibility, drawing on decades of debate over the role of individuals in civil society, both during and after state socialism.

Those involved in the front lines of environmental health efforts frequently complain about high levels of public apathy. Professor Šrám, for example, while speaking very highly of what he referred to as the "ordinary mothers" who made up the 1989 Teplice environmental movement and the early activities of the Prague Mothers, complained that their sense of initiative has been lost. As he put it, "In the Ostrava region, people say that around election time, environmental degradation motivates their voting—it is their first or second priority [in choosing candidates]. But . . . at other times, no one cares."

Other activists express similar attitudes, with some of them specifically tailoring their data gathering to have the dual purpose of not only collecting data but also engaging citizens, especially children, in hands-on activities that will compel them to care. Many of the projects on environmental pollution organized by the Prague Mothers thus involve children recording air pollution and undertaking rudimentary analysis of this material. This way, Johnová explains, the children learn that it is every citizen's responsibility to ensure a healthy environment.

Dr. Jarmila Veselá, a public health specialist, holds a point of view similar to Professor Šrám's and is scathing about individual solutions to respiratory health.[3] "How should you solve the asthma crisis in this country?" she laughed sarcastically. "Don't live by a factory chimney!" More seriously, Dr. Veselá suggested, the problem is "that people prioritize their finances over their health, because they are not educated. They don't form groups and get active, but instead they go play football and don't worry about the environment."

Civic apathy is often described as a two-pronged problem: not only are people not educated or cultured (*vzdělané*) enough to be able to adequately understand what is happening and why, but they are also afraid to have an opinion and voice it. As one environmentalist colorfully put it, we call this "*přizdisráč*" (literally, "shitter by the wall"). She explained, "It means that you even shit by the wall, so if there is a big field and you can go shit in the middle of it, you shit by the wall, because you refuse to expose yourself." It is, I later realize, the Czech equivalent of the American term "chicken shit." What is different about these calls to stand up for oneself is the assumption that people's personal responsibility will lead to increased civic engagement and collective action.

Some activists worry, however, that the focus on personal responsibility can lead to blaming individuals and shifting attention away from industry. Explaining how their own research revealed that a significant proportion of the air pollution in Ostrava is caused by home heating, a spokesperson for the environmental NGO Arnika expressed concern that such findings do not result in a backlash against the city's residents. Many of Ostrava's residents have no choice over how to heat their homes, she said, and it is due to poverty, rather than apathy, that locals are infamous for heating their homes by assembling "Ostravian comets": empty plastic drink bottles filled with sawdust and oil that are burned in domestic coal heaters, resulting in a blast of heat and a variety of chemicals released into the air. Arnika and other groups thus embrace government programs like boiler exchanges and eco-friendly home grants as long as they constitute supplements to larger structural changes, rather than solutions in themselves.

The Company as a (Non)Moral Actor

In all of this talk of citizens and government, one aspect left out of many activists' sweeping visions is corporate responsibility. While they may call on industry to change its practices, many involved in these campaigns work on the assumption that there is little to be gained by appealing to corporate consciences as industry is beyond reason. Dr. Veselá was perhaps the bluntest in her assessment that "even when business thinks of the greater good," its focus is on making business opportunities and thus "the industrialists think to themselves, 'I employ 7,000 people, so one blue child [choking due to exposure to air pollution] doesn't matter.'"

Corporate social responsibility is new to the Czech Republic. While the CSR activities of some corporations, most notably Vodafone, are embraced by consumers (Trnka 2013), these tend to draw on a young and globally savvy consumer base. Most of the public appears more comfortable relying on the state to act as an intermediary for mediating relations with business.

International companies such as ArcelorMittal are, however, keen to publicize their CSR programs. In Ostrava, ArcelorMittal has reinforced its image as one of the region's primary employers by running a youth education program that trains young people in the basic operations of the steel mill. The company also engages in wide-ranging activities that situate it more broadly as a local benefactor, giving money to build parks, support children's reading programs, and promote the local beekeeping industry. The company's employees are photographed donating blood at the local hospital, and the plant has contributed an incubator to the local neonatal unit.

But perhaps the most widely publicized and controversial CSR program was ArcelorMittal Ostrava's donation of asthma inhalers to local children. Many viewed this as the height of hypocrisy and yet another indication of ArcelorMittal's unwillingness to put health before profit. As one local parent whose son suffered from acute asthma related, "If ArcelorMittal has made a profit, I'd ask them not to spend it on inhalers but on improving the environment" (Všelichová 2010).

Given the experiences of labor over the past twenty-five years of capitalist development as well as the enduring legacies of socialist perspectives on unrestricted capital, privately owned corporations cannot easily be recast as protectors of the interests of working people. For most Czechs, the issue at hand is thus not one of improving relations between industry and employees, much less between industry and the community, but rather of ensuring that the state does its duty of protecting Czechs against the activities of industry while recognizing the need for industry to provide employment.

There is, moreover, an added nationalist element to this call as ecologists, scientists, and activists frequently compare the Czech situation with Poland and suggest that while the Polish state may be content with even laxer emissions regulations, the Czech state must do what it can to protect its citizenry. The fact that ArcelorMittal's headquarters is in Luxembourg while its owner is originally from India but now lives in Britain further fuels nationalist sentiments calling on the Czech state to protect its own people.

But does the state care? Is it willing to protect its citizens?

The Nonreciprocating State

The focus of many of activists and scientists involved in these political debates is on recovering what they see as the deteriorating role of government in providing for and protecting its citizenry. In our conversations together, Professor Šrám paints the context of the Ostrava situation in terms of a country where free health care is being stripped away and the standards of medical services are slipping. Add to this a government that capitulates to industry and you have a situation in which it becomes increasingly difficult for those who are sick to survive, much less thrive, he tells me.

While the national government has implemented a series of initiatives to deal with some aspects of Ostrava's air pollution, both the boiler exchange program and the eco-friendly home initiative have been widely criticized as being ineffective. Nor has there been much traction from the EU's involvement. Although the EU has allocated funds to help alleviate Ostrava's pollution, these have been given to the Czech government to administer. The same goes for the EU's guidelines for emissions limits, which it is up to the Czech government to follow. Indeed, one public health specialist explained to me that in the Czech Republic, EU measures have "no teeth" when it comes to health issues or pollution. Perhaps out of recognition of this, in 2010 the EU even threatened to sue the Czech government if it did not rectify the pollution problem in Ostrava, but still tangible results have not been forthcoming.

There are many different suggestions for the route government should take, with the most heated battle being over the government's enforcement of reasonable emissions limits. The environmental law service EPS launched a legal case over ArcelorMittal Ostrava's Integrated Pollution Prevention and Control (IPPC) permits. According to EPS, the Ministry for the Environment and regional authorities incorrectly set up ArcelorMittal's IPPC permits, allowing the company to "run most of its installations under conditions that do not fully meet the Best Available Techniques criteria" (Peek et al. 2009, 12). The case resulted in increasing pressure on ArcelorMittal Ostrava to comply with legal limits and in August 2010 the Ministry for the Environment halted the reconstruction of one of the plant's facilities on the basis that it did not have sufficient antipollution measures in place and would therefore contravene existing emissions regulations. A few years later, in February 2014, the company announced it would take further steps to alleviate pollution levels by implementing new dedusting measures (4-Traders 2014).

But perhaps the most controversial attempt to force the national government into action has been the city of Ostrava's suit against the state. The unprecedented nature of a lawsuit by one level of government against another led many commentators to shrug off its seeming impossibility as mere "political comedy." Nonetheless, the case, which was heard in 2013, raised serious allegations about the state's unwillingness to support its citizens. Ostrava's claim was that the state is responsible for ensuring a "favorable environment" for its citizens. The city thus sued the overall national government, as well as the Ministry for the Environment and the Ministry of Transport, for not fully and effectively protecting the atmosphere in Ostrava and not creating a "functional system" for the enforcement of emissions limits.

In the end, the case was settled in favor of the state as the head of the court, Ludmila Sandnerová, explained that while the court was convinced that "the limits of polluted substances have been breached and that some illegal activity has clearly led to this," the city had not proven "that inaction or passivity on the part of the [state] is what led to this illegal outcome" (TV Nova 2013). Sandnerová then turned the tables and added that the city of Ostrava had not shown that it was doing all it could to improve the air quality, referring to the city's reluctance to establish no-emission zones.

Ostrava's mayor, Petr Kajnar, publicly responded, "We have done all we can, but the question is, what *can* we do? What is the point of having a no-emission zone of tens of kilometers squared, when there is two and a half thousand kilometers darkened by an [atmospheric] inversion [that holds in the smog]?"

According to Kajnar, the court did not have the "courage" to decide in the city's favor, as to do so would have meant taking on the government (TV Nova 2013). The fact that the judiciary would not stand up to the state did not, however, in Kajnar's mind, alleviate the state's responsibility to its citizenry. "The substantive issue," Kajnar declared, "is that people are dying here because the state is not acting" (TV Nova 2013).

For Kajnar, and for many others, the situation comes down to the state's legal and moral obligation to act. While many would agree that citizens should act in the interests of the wider collectivity, they may choose whether or not to do so. The state, on the other hand, must do so or its legitimacy is under threat. That the state may not, however, always uphold its side of the bargain is well known, and thus various steps in both legal and civic domains are used to attempt to lever it into acting on behalf of the citizenry.

But in addition to the legal courts, there is also the court of public opinion, and another way of attempting to force the state to take up its role is by shaming it, as Kajnar attempted to do in his public statement. In this court, the figure of suffering citizenry, and in particular of suffering children, has become a central trope in the political struggle.

Who Gets to Suffer? Labor, Gender, and Citizenship

The social contract requires that contributions be made by each side, as the state and the people engage in a reciprocal exchange with one another. Some citizens are, however, deemed more able to give than others. Historically, the most valuable contributions made in Moravia have been the bodies and labor power of men, primarily those of miners and steelworkers.

There is widespread acknowledgment that the working conditions in mines and steel mills can have profoundly debilitating effects. ArcelorMittal's own publications note that some workers have particularly physically and psychologically arduous jobs and are therefore entitled to more generous health benefits (ArcelorMittal Ostrava 2008).

Both mining and steelwork are culturally coded as masculine jobs, premised on the understanding that social well-being is reliant upon forms of masculine sacrifice.[4] In Ostrava, it is usually taken for granted that the lives of men who mine or work in the steel mill will be characterized by intense bodily labor in the midst of physically demanding conditions, be it the loud, hot, and cramped spaces of the coal mines or the equally physically onerous sites of steel production. During the state socialist period, miners in particular were held up as symbols of national progress. As the widely known saying "I am a miner, who is more than that" (*Já jsem horník, kdo je víc*) intimated, the Communist Party proclaimed that nothing could be more honorable than the mining profession. The miner or steelworker was thus known to go through great physical hardship but was honored for shouldering the burden of regional and national development. It was his suffering that enabled Moravia to prosper following the first blows of the steelworks' hammer.

During my visit to the ArcelorMittal Ostrava steelworks facility, the company's human resources representatives proudly spoke of the measures undertaken to make the industry as safe as possible. When, however, wearing the standard-issue blue jumpsuit, hard hat, gloves, and visor, I found myself struggling with the heat, noise, and overall intensity on the steelworks floor, the men whose daily working lives revolve around this labor laughed and told me of the extremes they encounter as the heat sometimes reaches as high as 55 degrees Centigrade (131 degrees Fahrenheit). The response to my suggestion that perhaps some of the novices might find the physical conditions initially difficult to deal with was met with more laughter, followed by the simple proclamation, "We are men" (*My jsme hoši*).

In contrast to the valor accorded to masculine sacrifice, there is a widely held public view that children are not supposed to suffer for the state, but rather should be collectively protected from harm. As Fassin (2013, 113) argues, the image of the suffering child is perhaps one of the strongest emotive symbols of twentieth- and twenty-first-century humanitarian discourse. Its political power rests on two assertions regarding children: "first, that they were innocent creatures who could not be held responsible for what happened to them, and second, that they were vulnerable beings and needed protection against the hazards of life" (118).

Another important feature of the potential to politicize children is their positioning both within and outside of social contracts, in the sense that the child receives protection without being required to reciprocate (yet). Reflecting the outer limit of individualization discourses, young children cannot be asked to take care of themselves. Families, however, are not always able to provide for children. As Fassin argues with respect to the AIDS epidemic in South Africa, families thought to be falling apart generate even more community or national concern over vulnerable children's fates.

In the Czech Republic, the specter is not of families falling apart, but of the family unable to protect its children in the face of rampant, foreign industry with the result being that the state must step in. The privileged role of the Czech state in protecting children is nothing new. During state socialist rule in Czechoslovakia, the child, whether part of a family or not, was in many respects under the guardianship of the state, which could demand certain forms of ongoing care regardless of parental consent, and regularly enacted a range of interventions from enforcing childhood immunizations to removing children from their parents if they were thought to hold politically undesirable opinions.

It is thus not surprising that some of the most stirring images and pronouncements about the need for the state to curtail the air pollution in Ostrava have involved children. One example is the widely reproduced photographs of children and their mothers wearing gas masks. Another is activists' claims that children, and not adults, are the ones who really matter in this dispute. One local father on a TV program characterized his family's struggle against ArcelorMittal by noting, "It is not about us"—referring to himself and his wife—"we will stick it out in our lives, but it is about our kids." He then added that the only one who can put a stop to their suffering is the government (Všelichová 2010).

If children are posited as innocent victims and labor is clearly coded as masculine, then where are the women in this story? Despite the fact that many Czech women work outside of the home, Czech society widely embraces what are referred to as "traditional" (tradiční) gender ideals, namely that women's primary role is the reproduction and nurturance of children (Trnka 2017; Trnka and Busheikin 1993). Usually, these activities are thought to be confined to the domestic sphere (Heitlinger and Trnka 1998), making mothers' entries onto the political stage particularly dramatic. Many of the photographic images that focus on Ostrava's women and children are thus reminiscent of the early protests by the Prague Mothers or the "ordinary mothers" of Teplice whose circumstances were so dire they felt compelled to publicize their very private, domestic struggles to keep their children healthy in order to garner the state's attention.

But politicking over children's asthma can also result in intensely emotive denunciations of the political mileage derived from the figure of the suffering child. When I mentioned that my research would consider the question of asthma and air pollution in Ostrava, one asthma sufferer (who lives in Prague) angrily declared, "Don't overemphasize the air quality issue. It is not so important. . . . We do *not* have such unusually high asthma in the Czech Republic. Those people who claim it is so high are . . . generating these asthma statistics for political purposes."

Indeed there have been some notable controversies with respect to Professor Šrám's studies and the role that his political commitments to the people of Radvanice and Bartovice might play in shaping his findings. Much of the scientific controversy has focused on issues of diagnosis. Professor Šrám's asthma rate of 37 percent was initially derived from a study of children under the care of Dr. Shallerová. This was later expanded through a series of larger studies involving close to 2,000 children under the care of ten different pediatricians: 37 percent of them were found to suffer from wheezing, which may or may not be due to asthma (Dostál, Pastorková, Rychlik, et al. 2013). Critics have, however, suggested that some of the children in the original sample who were categorized as having asthma may similarly suffer from other respiratory conditions and were misdiagnosed, thus inflating the figure of asthmatic children and gaining international attention through the claim that the district has the highest rate of childhood asthma in the world.

As one of the scientists who works in Šrám's team related to me, "I gave these results as part of a presentation and a well-known respiratory specialist tore them apart. . . . He said, 'You cannot tell if it is asthma or obstructive bronchitis [that these children suffer from], because you cannot do a spirometry [lung function test] on kids under the age of four and skin prick tests will turn up negative for kids under the age of two, so how can you know what is going on?'" The scientist being questioned defended the results on the basis that Dr. Shallerová had carried out "a very intensive check on these children." He also, however, proceeded to wave the controversy away in light of the larger political issues it threatens to overshadow. "When people told *her* that all of the children don't have asthma," he went on, "she retorted, 'My children [i.e., my patients] are *choking*, whether it is due to asthma or not.'" As these statements suggest, if the underlying issue is that air pollution causes respiratory illness, then the differentiation between asthma, chronic bronchitis, and other respiratory conditions can, on one level, be irrelevant. However, in the domain of scientific practice, ensuring reliable diagnoses remains a central concern, without which the epidemiological results regarding rates of childhood asthma would be meaningless.

Possibly a more troubling question that has been raised is how central a role air pollution plays in determining Ostrava's asthma levels. The team's own findings uphold the now increasingly accepted perspective that there may be no single asthma, but rather a variety of asthmas, some due to air pollution and others due to viral illnesses, pollen, cat dander, and so on (Pearce 2011). Multicausal models furthermore suggest that some asthma does not have a single factor but rather is provoked by a combination of factors, suggesting that industrial air pollution alongside other factors may be at play in Ostrava. Indeed, Professor Šrám's colleagues explained to me that they found a variety of factors contributing to the Ostrava children's asthma, implying that the steelworks may not be as singularly responsible for local rates of asthma as activists contend.

One team member, for example, determined that the high asthma rates are related to exposure to secondhand smoke as well as children's own smoking habits. Publication of this part of the study was held up due to statistical complications, its lead author explained, before adding that a research center devoted to demonstrating the causal links between industrial pollution and respiratory illness will hardly welcome findings that demonstrate the significant role that "individual habits" such as smoking may play. All of this complicates the rather simple story of the industrial giant that makes children ill and the political cost that the figure of the suffering child has been made to bear in this struggle.

Erasing the Roma

Smoking isn't the only thing that can disqualify children from being seen as innocent victims. In both activist and scientific discourses, the innocent party is always Czech, necessitating the erasure of yet another group of families and children who are breathing polluted air, namely the Roma.

Given the reluctance of many Roma to publicly identify themselves, it is difficult to get reliable statistics on the number of Roma currently in the Czech Republic. The European Roma Rights Centre estimates their numbers as being about 2–3 percent of the overall population. It is generally agreed that the Ostrava region has a high concentration of Roma who constitute between

10,000 and 30,000 residents, that is, 3–10 percent of the city's population (Sudetic 2013). Roma tend to be concentrated in the lower economic classes and are thus likely to live in areas most affected by air pollution.

Originally a nomadic people who once spoke the Romany language and today hold onto a range of distinctive cultural traditions, the Roma are widely scapegoated in Czech society for acting outside of Czech social norms. There are frequent descriptions of Roma as unproductive, social malingerers who are happy to consume state handouts and make little effort to contribute to the state or to society. For many Czechs, such depictions culminate in the sentiment that Roma are irrevocably Other.

There is no specific research that I am aware of on Czech Roma respiratory health, and in part this appears to be due to ethnic prejudices that pervade some of the medical and scientific establishment. A Czech public health specialist, for example, explained to me that Roma don't get asthma (or diabetes) because "they are completely different from us." Referring to them with the derogatory but widely used name of *cikáni* or gypsies, she told me, "Gypsies don't work. They receive state support for their children so they might have five children just so they can get more state support. They steal and move from one place to another to get away from the laws they have broken."

A Czech scientist, who is a member of Šrám's research team, similarly asserted that the Roma don't get asthma or allergies and explained how he removed them from his statistical computations. "In Ostrava there are a lot of Roma kids but they never get asthma, so you need to take them out of the sample so they don't confuse the statistics," he told me. "Once you remove them, then you get the figure of over 30 percent [of children in Radvanice and Bartovice suffering from asthma]. Before [they are removed], the statistics are lower." When I queried how he could be so certain the Roma never suffer from asthma or allergies, he explained that the Roma don't use medical services for these conditions, and that at least one local allergy specialist he knew in Ostrava had confirmed to him that he doesn't have any Romany patients. "I don't know why they don't have asthma, but they don't," he assured me.

This kind of prejudice as well as the fact that state statistics do not differentiate health conditions based on ethnic groups makes it difficult to get information on the rates of asthma (or other health conditions) among the Roma. However, a medical anthropologist who worked with Roma in Slovakia disputed such suggestions, asserting that her fieldwork experiences suggest the Roma suffer from high rates of respiratory conditions but refrain from seeking care from medical authorities due to racism.

Asthma is thus defined as a citizenship issue but, as is so often the case, citizenship itself is restrictively defined. While Czech Roma technically hold Czech citizenship, the wider Czech public considers true membership in the nation-state to be reserved for ethnic Czechs who are collectively viewed as upholding their end of the state-citizen exchanges. Responsibility here is viewed as inherently reciprocal, though with the acknowledgment of a generational lag; those who give to the state, or whose parents and grandparents have given to the state, have the right to expect a return, while those who are seen as not contributing are cast out of the equation.

Conclusion

While few would suggest that the Czech Republic is on the verge of another political upheaval of the size and significance of the 1989 Velvet Revolution, environmental pollution and its impact on children's health continues to constitute an issue of national political concern. Childhood asthma and, in particular, the suffering of Radvanice and Bartovice's children are actively held up as part of banners of protest and widespread calls for realigning relationships between citizens and the state. Asthma has become a contested political object in terms of both how causation is attributed (is it emissions by Arcelor-Mittal or something else that is making so many children in Ostrava sick?) and the ways in which different forms of personal and collective responsibility for mitigating respiratory distress come to be articulated. In stark contrast to the responses garnered by most children's health issues in the region, asthma has come to constitute the fulcrum of public debates and contestations over some of the most fundamental principles of contemporary governance.

What is at stake here is twofold, as the environmental crisis in Ostrava raises profound questions about what happens to the citizenry if the state does not hold up its end of the bargain, as appears to be the case, as well as what happens to the future of the state if the citizenry has been irrevocably poisoned. On both local and national levels, struggles over structural issues such as environmental degradation, poverty, unemployment, and the rising cost of medical care have been crystallized through the historically familiar battles between trade, industry, and the state but with growing concerns that this time, the state might have already divested itself of the responsibilities that the people have entrusted it to uphold. In this respect, the situation in Ostrava has become a litmus test of the relations between the state, the EU, citizens, and industry during twenty-first-century capitalism.

It is also a litmus test for how far the discourse of personal responsibility can be extended, as the company attempts to blame individuals while individuals, in turn, call upon a larger power than themselves (that is, the state) to be held accountable for their and their children's plight. Of particular significance in activist conceptualizations of responsibility is the breakdown of the dichotomy of personal versus collective responsibility. Instead there is an active interlinking between different levels of responsibility, as citizens are exhorted to take on more personal responsibility in order to force the state to recognize its obligations in solving what is envisioned as a collective, national problem. Activists, in turn, call upon the state to reciprocate the contributions of its citizens, demanding care and protection for Ostrava's residents and, in particular, local children. Companies are cast outside of the sphere of moral life, not out of some perceived inherent lack of ethical obligation but from a pragmatic recognition that labor will find little traction in invoking the moral responsibilities of management. Despite widespread skepticism and distrust, there emerges a politics of last resort through which the Czech state is being constantly reminded of, and publicly held to account for, its responsibility to mitigate harm, safeguard citizens, and uphold the possibilities—however slim—of achieving justice.

NOTES

1. PM10 is particulate matter up to 10 micrometers in size.

2. Contemporary views of citizen-state relations are not only strongly shaped by the socialist legacy, but also draw generously from the nation's long historical association with European and American liberal theory. For example, the political philosophy that guided the drafting of Czechoslovakia's first constitution and underpinned the perspectives of its first president, Tomáš Garrigue Masaryk, was largely shaped by American liberal theorists (cf. Pithart 2002).

3. Jarmila Veselá is a pseudonym. In contrast, all of the other interviewees in this chapter are well-known individuals who have granted the author permission to be identified.

4. While some forms of sacrifice are open-ended, my intention here is to invoke those that are predicated upon the anticipation of a return. For more discussion of sacrifice as part of anticipated exchanges, see Godelier (1999).

FOUR. Audit Culture and the Politics of Responsibility:
Beyond Neoliberal Responsibilization?

CRIS SHORE

The price of greatness is responsibility.
—WINSTON CHURCHILL

Most people do not really want freedom, because freedom involves
responsibility, and most people are frightened of responsibility.
—SIGMUND FREUD

Responsibility and Responsibilization

Responsibility is a concept that has fundamentally different meanings. For
Churchill, it was a corollary of statesmanship and importance (greatness),
a quality associated with political leadership and nationhood. For Freud, by
contrast, responsibility entailed a psychological disposition, one that provokes anxiety because of our apparent fear of freedom. Yet what both quotes
above highlight, albeit in different ways, is the complex and ambiguous relationship between power and responsibility and their entanglement with
forms of subjectivity. This is the broad theme that I explore in this chapter,
drawing on case studies from New Zealand and the United Kingdom. More

specifically, I focus on responsibility as a distinctly political project and the wider uses and effects of the rhetoric of responsibilization, or what happens when responsibility talk becomes institutionalized and mobilized for political and managerial ends. In this respect, my chapter adds a different dimension to this volume. Rather than focusing on the many different and competing forms of responsibility or the complex sets of obligation and interdependency in which individuals are enmeshed, my concern is to explore some of the mutations that have occurred around advanced liberal discourses on individual self-responsibility and what these reveal about changing power relations and contemporary forms of governance. As I illustrate below, the distinction between responsibility and responsibilization provides a useful lens for examining wider societal trends and dimensions of modern power.

Let me begin this analysis with some brief observations about language use and the different semantic fields that responsibility and responsibilization occupy. Over the past decade there has been an explosion of academic interest in the idea of responsibility. This is evidenced in the proliferation of new books, articles, and conferences on the subject and the complex legal, ethical, and political issues that they raise. Much of this interest reflects specific disciplinary concerns or policy issues, including responsibilities for health and care of the suffering (Olaru 2008), or philosophical debates over personal responsibility, free will, and determinism (Brown 2009; Fischer 2006), and the contribution of continental philosophers from Heidegger and Sartre to Levinas and Derrida on the "ontological origins of responsibility" (Raffoul 2010). But a substantial part of this literature, particularly in business studies, commerce, and management, also addresses the issue of corporate social responsibility (CSR). By contrast, if one searches for new books under the heading "responsibilization," very little appears on business studies and management, and almost nothing on CSR. What appears instead are scores of titles—largely from sociology, criminology, and policy studies—on topics that include deviancy, crime, youth offending, policing, community safety, prostitution, poverty, and individualization. At first glance, these two literatures seem almost totally unrelated, but as I will demonstrate, this disconnect highlights an interesting dimension of the way contemporary narratives of responsibility and responsibilization operate.

Beyond academia, the institutionalization of "responsibility-speak" has become a defining feature of contemporary societies—particularly in those countries that have gone furthest in embracing neoliberal policy agendas. Notions of responsibility now permeate all aspects of society and social policy, from social inclusion, deviancy, crime, and welfare, to ideas about parenting, taxation, insurance, and citizenship. Even in the areas of foreign affairs, trade, education, and the environment the term *responsibility* is mobilized to drive policy and endow government decision making with moral authority. How do we account for this increase in discourses of responsibility, and what are its effects? This chapter sets out to explore these questions by looking more closely at the way the concept is being put to work in the political sphere. I also want to examine the connection between responsibilization and the emergence of new regimes of auditing and accountability. I argue that responsibilization can be seen as a contemporary keyword (Williams 1975) that embodies both a political project and a mode of governing. If one of the effects of that project is to produce autonomous, self-disciplined, and responsibilized subjects, I suggest it may also be producing undisciplined and unaccountable financial institutions.

My chapter is framed around four main questions: How can the concepts of responsibility and responsibilization be used to shed light on contemporary forms of governance and power? Second, how are issues of responsibility and responsibilization linked to the practices of management and financial accounting, or what I term audit culture (see below)? Third, what does a closer analysis of this audit culture and its technologies of responsibilization reveal about wider social and political processes that are reshaping our world and ourselves? And finally, what are the limits of responsibilization as a political project? That is, what are the contradictions in these attempts to create responsibilized individuals? I illustrate my arguments by drawing on ethnographic examples from Britain and New Zealand that show how neoliberal ideas of responsibility have been deployed as technologies of governance. I contrast two case studies from the 1990s—one concerning a Thatcherite project to make council housing tenants in England responsible for managing their own estates, the other a government attempt to promote a code of social responsibility to reshape family behavior in New Zealand—with two contemporary examples from New Zealand. The first explores a university management and leadership program aimed at creating responsibilized academics, while the second examines issues of CSR following a major mining tragedy in 2010. Together, these case studies illustrate how projects of responsibilization have changed and deepened as a result of the expansion of financial accounting techniques. They also provide a tentative answer to the question of what comes after neoliberalism: in the case of New Zealand, it seems that neoliberal rationalities of governance are actually deepening and becoming more entrenched.

Responsibility: Master Symbol or Contemporary Keyword?

Typically, anthropological analysis begins by identifying the key concepts used in a particular society, mapping their meanings and uses, and examining the contexts in which they are deployed. Following Wittgenstein, I suggest that we look for the meaning of a word not in some fixed, a priori definition but in its uses. As Trnka and Trundle (2014) point out, *responsibility* is a polysemous term with multiple and sometimes contradictory meanings. It also incorporates all three of the defining properties of a key symbol: condensation of meaning, multivocality, and ambiguity (Kertzer 1987, 11). That is, it condenses and unifies a rich array of different representations; it has a spectrum of meanings that can be understood in different ways by different people; and it has no single or precise meaning. Depending on the context, responsibility therefore tends to be used in four distinct ways:

1 In the sense of being autonomous, free, or self-determining; the state of being in charge, important, or having control over
2 Being dependable, conscientious, trustworthy, loyal, and sensible (i.e., qualities you find in the Boy Scout code, of which we also see echoes in Levinas's theory of cosmopolitanism)
3 Being the causal agent for something
4 Being accountable, answerable, or obligated (e.g., to pay; to behave correctly as part of a job, role, or legal duty)

It is also useful to see responsibility as a contemporary keyword in Raymond Williams's (1975) sense of the term, that is, words that are embedded in social patterns of thought and argument and that create particular ways of thinking and arguing. Keywords are also concepts in which, and through which, we can track major processes of social and historical change.

Given the spectrum of meanings above, it is easy to see how responsibility, as a political term, can be a double-edged sword: that is, it is both a "weapon of the weak" (Scott 1985) for holding rulers to account and placing responsibility on the powerful to act more ethically, and also an instrument that the powerful can use to consolidate or extend their domination. In New Zealand, for example, trade unions often appeal to the Employment Relations Authority and to the courts to force companies to take seriously their legal responsibilities and obligations as good employers. Similarly, Maori groups will often invoke the idea of a fiduciary relationship with the Crown and its responsibilities to protect Maori interests under the Treaty of Waitangi in order to press for rights and settle land claims (Hayward 1997, 481–82). But equally, governments can demand responsibility of the weak and powerless and use the law in less ethical ways. A good illustration of this was immigration minister Scott Morrison's announcement on July 25, 2014, of an overhaul of Australia's system for processing asylum seekers. The new legislation makes it the responsibility of asylum seekers to prove their claim, and the Australian authorities will refuse protection visa applications for those who cannot establish their identity. While Morrison acknowledged that some asylum seekers, particularly stateless people, do not have official documents, he nevertheless insisted that "ultimate responsibility" for identification will lie with the asylum seeker (Barlow 2014).

The point here is that like the term *subject*, *responsibility* simultaneously evokes the idea of agency and autonomy and discipline and subjectification (Foucault 1977). This is what makes it such a potent word. Given its associations with ethics, autonomy, and personhood, it is very hard to oppose calls to act responsibly or be responsible. That is, one cannot easily make a moral argument for behaving irresponsibly; all one can do is argue about who should be responsible. Responsibility is therefore a highly normative concept, one steeped in notions of morality that become internalized and thus part of the way we come to measure and construct ourselves as political subjects.

Responsibilization and the Neoliberalization of Society

Returning to the question posed at the outset, how do we account for this rash of concern with the promotion of responsibility? To some extent it can be linked to increasing concerns over legal and financial liability and the rise of what sociologists have termed "risk society" (Beck 1992). As Tom Baker (2002, 33) observed, "The proliferation of risks produces a proliferation of responsibilities"—such as "fiscal responsibility," "managerial responsibility," "ministerial responsibility," and so on. More controversially, the identification of risk actually creates new kinds of responsibility, particularly in the burgeoning insurance industries, where risk management and internal audits have become major areas of profit and growth.

It is also linked to the politics of neoliberalism and government attempts since the 1980s to render individuals responsible for duties and risks that were previously considered responsibilities of the state or government authorities. This strategy was originally based on the neoliberal assumption that the welfare state had divested individuals of responsibility for governing themselves or looking after others reliant on them. According to the logic of 1980s British conservatism, responsibilization would have emancipatory potential. It would engender moral agency that, in turn, would enable individuals to better manage themselves and their own affairs. As Mrs. Thatcher famously argued in response to criticisms that her policies were leading to a more selfish and uncharitable society, the Good Samaritan was only able to act charitably because he was wealthy. This was an early iteration of what opponents of Ronald Reagan derisively termed trickle-down economics. It was in the late 1980s and early 1990s that the idea of individual responsibility as a political project first came to attention during what Peck and Tickell (2002) term the rollout phase of neoliberalization. Let me illustrate this with two ethnographic examples.

CASE STUDY 1. *Responsibilizing Council Housing Tenants in 1990s Britain*

Susan Hyatt (1997) carried out fieldwork among working-class women on a council housing estate in Bradford in the north of England in the early 1980s. This was the period in which the Conservative government under Mrs. Thatcher sought to naturalize its ideology of popular conservatism and economic liberalism as the new common sense. Having famously pronounced in an interview that there "is no such thing as society" and that "no government can do anything except through people, and people must look to themselves first," Thatcher introduced a raft of new political shibboleths and epithets that epitomized this new ideology. These included the terms *self-reliance, consumer choice, taxpayers' rights, active citizenship, citizen's charters*, the *property-owning democracy*, and *stakeholders*. At the heart of her project was an attempt to create a new regime of governance, one based on the idea of the sovereign individual, the minimal state, and the virtues of entrepreneurialism that would transform Britain into an "enterprise culture" (Keat and Abercrombie 1991). These market metaphors helped to reconceptualize the space to be governed, turning government itself into a form of enterprise organized through pseudo-markets. Schools, hospitals, health practices, housing estates, even railways were remodeled as free, independently managed, competitive, quasi-enterprises (but within state-funded systems subject to complex regulation) (Shore and Wright 1997, 32).

Individuals were offered the opportunity to take over the management of these areas that had previously been the responsibility of government, providing that subsequent audits and inspections judged that they were exercising their freedom correctly. At the time of Mrs. Thatcher's first election in 1979, some 30 percent of the British population still lived on council estates (Hyatt 1997, 222). Encouraging tenants to take on the management of their own housing estates was an idea that originated partly in the tenant activism of the 1970s. Paradoxically, it became the cornerstone of Conservative government policies for reforming what remained of the state's public housing stock (Hyatt 1997, 218).

While local authorities had their budgets savagely cut, central government provided special Section 16 grants, administered by the Department of Environment, to train residents in the skills of managing their own estates. The goal was to empower tenants by making them active citizens who would exercise choice in their own best interest and experience freedom through self-management. Council estates, once the epitome of the welfare state, had by the 1980s become so run down that many needed rebuilding. Faced with little alternative, many residents responded to the government's incentives to take over responsibility for managing their estates. Initially, this policy was seen as empowering: it gave women opportunities to become active citizens, to exercise choice in their own interests, and to experience freedom through self-management. As self-managing tenants, they acquired expertise and authority over their estates and gained confidence in their dealings with the council. However, the women discovered that they were being asked to take on more responsibility than they had bargained for. Not only were they shouldering the duty of managing their estates for their communities (as a voluntary workforce), increasingly they found themselves in the precarious position of being asked to police the estates (Hyatt 1997, 219–20). The effect was burnout and disillusionment among a section of the community already burdened by extreme poverty. In response, the women refused to collect each other's rents or monitor their neighbors' behavior, and they skillfully redeployed sections of the Tenants' Choice Act to push responsibility back onto government. To echo John Clarke (2005, 460), they became "skeptical subjects" who "refused to 'know their place.'" What this story exemplifies is the shift in emphasis that occurred during the Reagan-Thatcher era, from social improvement to the more individualized, therapeutic model of self-improvement. It also illustrates what Nikolas Rose (1999b) called "governing through freedom"—albeit in this case a failed attempt at creating responsibilized, self-managing neoliberal subjects.

CASE STUDY 2. *New Zealand's Code of Social Responsibility*

Towards a Code of Social and Family Responsibility was a discussion document sent out by the New Zealand government in February 1998 to all New Zealand households. The document and its genealogy have been extensively analyzed and critiqued by Wendy Larner (2000). Here I simply summarize the main points and implications of the story.

Following similar moves in the United States and United Kingdom—notably, President Clinton's Personal Responsibility for Work Opportunity Reconciliation Act (1996) and the Blair government's green paper *New Ambitions for Our Country: A New Contract for Welfare* (Department of Social Security 1998)—this document exhorted New Zealanders to become active subjects responsible for their own well-being—while threatening direct monitoring of those families and individuals who refused to comply. Driven by Prime Minister Jenny Shipley, it sought to address New Zealand's "social deficit" (Kelsey 1995b) by creating a new social contract that would put an end to the rising problems of dysfunctional families, substance abuse, illiteracy, and juvenile delinquency. Inspired by the U.S. model of workfare, the government replaced the concept of social capital with that of social responsibility, calling for a new social consensus that would shift the public discourse around rights to one of responsibilities. Like Thatcher's council estates policy, it was an experimental attempt to produce responsible citizens (Larner 2000, 251).

The government therefore delivered 1.4 million copies to households, supported by facts sheets that could be ordered from a toll-free number, and community groups were encouraged to organize group discussions of the document. The stated purpose of the code was to "make it clear how people are expected to meet their responsibilities," to "influence people," and to "set out guidelines for policy" on a range of subjects from how to look after children to "keeping ourselves healthy" (Larner 2000, 252). Those who refused or failed to take self-responsibility were pathologized. The punitive dimension of the document was disguised in seemingly innocuous questions like, "Should a person on a benefit long term who cannot take up part-time or full-time work be encouraged to do things such as community service" (New Zealand Department of Social Welfare 1998, 23). Other veiled threats included curfews and withdrawal of benefits for the undeserving. Public reactions to the code were overwhelmingly hostile: even conservative commentators criticized it, arguing that the state should not enforce morals.

Larner (2000, 261) argues that the code was not the embodiment of neoliberal governmentality but a hybrid assemblage of both neoliberal and conservative rationalities. In this respect, it shared much in common with Thatcherism and Tony Blair's so-called Third Way politics. But perhaps the most important point is that what these two case studies highlight is not so much the strength of responsibilization as a political project, but rather its weaknesses.

The Strange Nondeath of Neoliberalization

It would be good to end here and pronounce the death of neoliberalism as a coherent post–welfare state rationality. From an economic perspective, neoliberalism has been an abject failure and was largely responsible for the boom and bust and financial deregulation policies that precipitated the global financial crisis of 2008 and the subsequent Eurozone crisis. As Crouch (2011) and others have noted, neoliberalism was never particularly coherent as an ideology or program. Yet despite this, neoliberal economic ideas about the virtues of privatization and free markets, deregulation, flexible labor markets, consumer choice, and delegation to independent regulatory agencies such as banks and rating agencies have proved remarkably resilient. Thanks to the political power of corporations and financial institutions, not only have they survived, they remain dominant and virtually unchallenged throughout the Organisation for Economic Co-operation and Development (Crouch 2011; Schmidt and Thatcher 2013, 2014). Many of the processes of responsibilization they set in motion have continued, only in more subtle ways. Indeed, many have extended themselves and spread to colonize new lifeworlds (Habermas 1987a, 1987b). Like a virus, once introduced into a system, these processes tend to acquire a life of their own, often producing unanticipated and perverse effects. One of these is what we might term the increasing "managerialization" of personal responsibility. According to Grahame Thompson (2007, 28–29), "There is a coherent, large-scale 'responsibilization' process under way, led by governments and public authorities and experienced in their daily lives by citizens and employees." That process, he argues, "is fundamentally premised on the construction of a moral agency that accepts the consequences of its actions in a self-reflective manner" (28–29). It requires not compliance with rules or obedience to authority but rather "the un-coerced application of certain values rooted in the motivation for action" (30). In short, it mobilizes our agency and complicity in the governance of ourselves, a process that Thompson (2011, 481) elsewhere describes as the "'responsibilization' of agency." This is part of a wider trend toward new forms of "governance of the self" characteristic of modern societies, as Miller and Rose (1990; see also Rose and Miller 1992) noted long ago.

But what are the mechanisms through which this responsibilization of agency occurs? One key factor has been the application of financial accountancy techniques to the management of human relations. This is what Sue Wright and I (Shore and Wright 1999, 2015) have termed the "rise of audit culture." With its hallmark emphasis on scrutiny, inspection, surveillance, cost accounting, and compliance, audit has become a powerful technology for producing responsible subjects.

Audit Culture and Technologies of Responsibilization

The term *audit culture* refers not so much to a people or a society as a condition and corresponding set of behaviors: one shaped by the application of modern principles and practices of financial accountancy to contexts far removed from the worlds of finance and accounting (Strathern 2000a). Its key feature as a style of thinking is the use of financial accounting techniques as instruments for the governance of human behavior (Shore 2008). This entails the translation of human operations into a calculating rationality of measurable financial costs and benefits. These processes have a transformative effect on organizations as audits invariably reshape the environments into which they are introduced in order to render them auditable (Power 1997). What is distinctive about audits today is the scale of their diffusion and the extraordinary extent to which auditing principles and practices have proliferated. As Michael Power (1994) noted, under Britain's Conservative government an "audit explosion" occurred in which the logic of audit was applied to a vast range of new domains; everything from health and safety, the provision of public services, and the newly privatized utilities, to less tangible areas including environmental audits, democracy audits, corruption audits, and audits of well-being and stress. As argued elsewhere, audit has become a major organizing principle of contemporary society (Shore and Wright 1999, 2000). But auditing has also proved indispensable for new public management, where it has been linked to a second major technology of the self: measurement. Together, these political (and moral) technologies are radically reshaping our economy and society.

There is nothing particularly novel about the use of quantitative performance indicators as instruments of workplace management. Indeed, their origins can be traced back to World War I and to the rise of the scientific management movement and Taylorism in the 1920s and 1930s. However, what distinguishes audit culture from other forms of "governing by numbers" and from Foucault's notion of "biopower" (Foucault 1991; Rabinow and Rose 2006) is its close connection with finance and rationalities of commerce. It is not simply about how to introduce the principle of economy into the regulation of human conduct (Foucault 1991, 92), but rather the application of the principles of financial management and fiscal responsibility. What is also new is the way in which performance indicators have been combined with new clusters of words like *accountability, quality, efficiency, effectiveness, transparency*, and within new ideologies (Bruneau and Savage 2002, 12). Audit thus embodies a new form of ethics: it presents itself as a beneficial and virtuous practice, a technology not only designed to promote public trust and eliminate fraud, but one that will bring transparency and economic efficiency. Audits have thus acquired "a social presence of a new kind" as people and organizations have "become devoted to their implementation" (Strathern 2000a, 3). As well as reshaping the way people understand the world and themselves (as workers, professionals, citizens, or parents), audits reshape organizations in their own image, turn targets into measures, and transform people into self-managing subjects. The result is the creation of a new kind of individual: the "auditee," a political subject who embodies an "auditee mentality."

Once again New Zealand and the United Kingdom are among the countries that have developed these processes the furthest. New Zealand is well known for being a laboratory for neoliberalism (Kelsey 1995a; Larner and Le Heron 2005), but what is less acknowledged is the key role the New Zealand Treasury played in developing the theories of new public management (Boston et al. 1996). This is significant because audit culture is not simply an advance on neoliberalism; it also shares much in common with new public management and the so-called shift from government to governance. Notable features of that process include massive deregulation of the private sector combined with increasing auditing of the public sector; a refocusing of government on steering and arm's-length control through the creation of purchaser-provider splits and the expansion of contracts and performance measures; reduced funding for core services combined with a relentless drive toward outputs and efficiencies (rather than outcomes or social effectiveness); the transformation of parts of government departments into service providers competing for short-term contracts in quasi-markets; the growth of a new class of senior managers and administrators with freedom to manage combined with a deprofessionalization of the traditional professions; the substitution of professional judgment and trust with external scrutiny, performance criteria, and new forms of surveillance; and the use of performance appraisal and efficiency drives to create proactive workers with boundless capacity for innovation and self-improvement.

How then does audit relate to the theme of responsibilization? Issues of accountability and responsibility have become deeply entangled with techniques of accountancy and organizational processes (Neyland 2012, 845), but it is Peter Miller who best sums up how this process works. As a technology of government, he writes, "One of the principal achievements of management accounting is to link together responsibility and calculation: to create the responsible and calculating individual. . . . The calculative practices of accounting thus help to create the calculating self as a resource and an end to be striven for" (Miller 2001, 380–81).

This is what Rose terms the "twin process of autonomization plus responsibilization," or "opening free space for the choices of individual actors whilst enwrapping these autonomized actors within new forms of control" (1999b, xxiii). Instead of managing human behavior through extensive lawmaking and policing through authority, individuals are now controlled through the technologies of regulation—demanding self-discipline in all areas of social and personal life.

Two questions emerge from this discussion of audit culture and responsibilization. First, does this constitute a new form of governmentality that might be termed post-neoliberal? And second, where do we see evidence of these processes at work? One place where audit culture has become deeply embedded is in universities. The introduction of research assessment exercises such as the Research Excellence Framework in Britain and the Performance-Based Research Framework in New Zealand exemplify the way that introducing new systems for measuring and ranking research output and performance has transformed academic life. These ranking exercises have intensified competition between institutions, departments, and individuals, created new status hierarchies and anxieties, and introduced competitive league tables that bring prestige and extra resources for the winners, and shame and ruin for the losers (at least until the next research exercise). However, a more interesting example is the recent turn toward "leadership competencies" spearheaded by many university managers.

CASE STUDY 3. *The University Leadership Framework*

In 2013 the University of Auckland, following other aspiring world-class research-led universities, launched a new policy called the Leadership Framework. The stated aim behind the launch of this program was to "provide clarity and a shared vision of what leadership looks like at The University of Auckland." By redefining all academic and administrative work, including research and publication, as part of leadership, this new policy document sought to mobilize staff, especially academic staff, "to contribute their leadership skills to taking the University forward" (UoA 2013b, 3). To these ends, the vice chancellor, Stuart McCutcheon, announced he had made the Leadership Framework a feature of the university's new strategic plan for 2013–20 and that the framework would be "incorporated into all new position descriptions during 2013/2014" and used for academic performance reviews from 2014 onward (UoA 2013b, 5). In future, all staff would be assessed according to the behaviors and performance standards set out in the framework (UoA 2013b, 4).

What are these behaviors? According to the guide to the Leadership Framework, "personal leadership is at the heart of every role within our organization and is key to our success" and the goal is to foster "a culture of distributive leadership" in which "all staff play a leadership role" (UoA 2013b, 4, 6). The document identifies five higher-level dimensions of leadership, each of which is given a Māori name and logo, supposedly demonstrating the university's commitment to inclusivity and compliance with New Zealand's official policy of biculturalism. These five higher dimensions of leadership are exhibiting personal leadership, setting direction, innovating and engaging, enabling people, and achieving results.

Exhibiting personal leadership (or *rangatiratanga*) is symbolized by a silver fern, a classic icon often used as an emblem for New Zealand national sports teams. Key attributes of personal leadership subjectivity include: "displays integrity and professionalism, builds and demonstrates self-insight, adapts to change, shows personal courage and demonstrates University citizenship" (UoA 2013b, 7). The second dimension, setting direction (*mana tohu*, represented by the five stars of the Southern Cross) highlights the individual who "displays an understanding of the international and commercial context in which the University operates." Here the capabilities expected of senior leaders are distinguished from those expected of all employees. These extra qualities include: "*demonstrates an understanding of the competitive global environment and key market drivers* . . . and uses this understanding to *create and seize opportunities, expand into new markets* and deliver programmes . . . : displays behaviors of a leader who *demonstrates global and commercial acumen*; leads and inspires innovation, *pursues ambitious ventures* [and] advocates and clearly articulates the University's aspirations, objectives and values" (UoA 2013b, 8, emphasis added).

The personal skills of innovating and engaging (*whakamatara*, represented by a woven mat) include: "using an appropriate interpersonal style to advance the University's objectives; facilitates change and innovation, addresses barriers to resistance, [and for senior staff,] identifies strategic opportunities, formulates action plans, and leverages own areas' expertise to add value elsewhere in the University" (UoA 2013b, 9).

Enabling people (*hapai*, represented by a fantail) highlights the equity goals of the university (including collegiality, respect for others, and inclusiveness).

However, these are all aligned to "developing self, others and teams so they can realize the University's strategy and values." The fifth leadership dimension, achieving results (*whai hua*, symbolized by a canoe, or *waka*) emphasizes accepting "accountability for making decisions and taking action to deliver the University's strategy," targeting opportunities and establishing "stretch objectives/goals." The ideal achiever is someone who "sets high objectives for personal/group accomplishment, uses measurement methods to monitor progress toward goals, tenaciously works to meet or exceed goals managing resources responsibly, seeks continuous improvement" (UoA 2013a, 11).

Embodying an entrepreneurial disposition, it would seem, is deemed an essential quality for any academic seeking promotion. Another University of Auckland document provides guidelines on how to use the guide. "Consider the exploration of the guide as an on-going process rather than a one-off event," it suggests. "Try cutting and pasting suggestions from the Guide into your Outlook calendar as a regular 5–15 minute appointment with yourself. . . . Be sure to allow time to inspire yourself and to inspire and enable others" (UoA 2013a, 4).

As the Leadership Framework received little public exposure during its developmental phase and was implemented without much fanfare or even discussion, its existence at the time of writing was still not widely known. However, it has serious implications for university appointments, careers, and promotions as these criteria are now embedded in the university's new academic standards policy. As I subsequently learned during fieldwork interviews, some members of the Human Resources office were also privately skeptical about the inclusion of terms like "market drivers" and "commercial acumen," but they were apparently overruled by the vice chancellor.

What we see in the story of the Leadership Framework is the confluence of two different rationalities: a neoliberal emphasis on the autonomous, self-disciplined individual whose behavior is tailored to a program of continuous self-monitoring and improvement (what Mitchell Dean and others have termed neoliberal "reflexive projects of the self"), but combined with a financialized vision of the leader as a kind of Schumpeterian entrepreneurial hero: a dynamic, risk-taking go-getter (Dean 1999, 147). For senior staff the expectations are even greater. The achieving leader "translates strategic priorities into operational reality and drives high standards for own and others accomplishment, creates alignment to ensure activities produce measurable and sustainable results; tenaciously works to meet or exceed challenging objectives; maintains fiscal responsibilities and seeks continuous improvements at all levels" (UoA 2013b,11).

The University of Auckland's Leadership Framework, it should be noted, was mirrored on similar leadership programs that have been developed at other leading global university brands, including the University of Sydney at Melbourne, University of California at Berkeley, UCLA, McGill, Hong Kong, and Bristol. Many of these practices were first trialed in Australia and built on the work of Professor Geoff Scott, emeritus professor of higher education and sustainability and former pro vice chancellor for quality at the University of Western Sydney. Following publication of his influential report, *Learning Leaders in Times of Change* (Scott, Coates, and Anderson 2008), Scott was invited to New Zealand to run workshops on academic leadership and change management strategies for remaking university culture into a more managed corporate culture. Scott's report recommended that universities identify the "performance indicators and capabilities for effective performance," develop "cost effective ways of assessing academic leadership potential and the capabilities that count," and ensure that "change implementation in higher education be part of every orientation and development program" (xix). However, it also highlighted "emotional intelligence" and "empathising" as the most critical competences for academic leadership (xv, 69), qualities that receive little attention in the Leadership Framework documents.

Beyond Neoliberal Governmentality? Market Discipline and Responsibilized Subjectivity

As I have argued elsewhere, the Leadership Framework exemplifies what might be termed "post-neoliberal responsibilization" (Amsler and Shore 2015). The hyphen here does not imply a transcendence of the neoliberal rationality but rather its further refinement, entrenchment, and institutionalization and the inclusion of ever more authoritarian modes of governing. Responsibilization is thus no longer simply a "reflexive project of the self" that seeks to produce responsibilized self-managing subjects; instead it has become harnessed to the financial, bureaucratic, and managerial imperatives of the organization so that senior staff are rendered responsible for delivering the performance targets of those they manage. In short, the disciplinary technologies of the self are enjoined by more traditional modes of supervision and managerial oversight. This kind of system is not new: it was developed over twenty years ago in Britain and used extensively in private sector corporations like British Telecom. What is perhaps new is its introduction into the management of universities. University leaders are to be held responsible for the activities of those under their charge. This reflects a very different concept of the professional self: the new academic self is a subject who must follow externally imposed targets. This seems to contradict the claims about personal leadership, but perhaps the question that really needs to be asked is, what concept of personhood does this model entail?

The Leadership Framework is a manual for policing both the self and others. Its aim is to encourage staff to align their behavior to the commercial and managerial goals of the university (understood in its narrowest sense as the university management), by rendering their behavior auditable and visible to themselves and to external evaluators. What would Max Weber have made of this? It is not so much the iron cage of bureaucracy and the dead hand of rationalization as the transparent glass prison of auditability: the Camp Delta model of governance that seeks to render its proactive, self-driven workforce simultaneously individualized, totalized, and permanently auditable against the set of externally imposed performance indicators.

The Leadership Framework was drafted by external marketing consultants, which may explain its curious language and corporate tone, although the emphasis on commercial competencies, entrepreneurial skills, and measurable market capabilities, as I discovered during fieldwork interviews, was something that the vice chancellor had insisted on. But do these technologies of the self actually work, and how seriously do employees take them? Privately, the Leadership Framework provoked derision among many academics, or at least among those aware of its existence, as the policy had been introduced at a time when the university was embroiled in a major industrial dispute over the vice chancellor's attempts to impose a new academic standards policy. The academic union had successfully sued the vice chancellor in the national Employment Relations Authority, winning the right to retain their existing promotions procedures outlined in their national collective agreement. However, a further review of the promotions policy, coupled with changes to New Zealand employment law that no longer required employers to reach a collective agreement with employees in workplace disputes, resulted in a second decision in favor of the vice chancellor. Since the beginning of 2015 the capabilities and behaviors outlined in the Leadership Framework have been fully incorporated into the academic recruitment and performance process and have to be taken seriously. Indeed, in July 2016 Human Resources wrote to all academics encouraging them to sign up for a 90 minute workshop on how to incorporate the framework in their annual performance reviews. The e-mail also encouraged academics to complete an online self-assessment against the leadership capabilities included in the Academic Standards.

For anyone seeking continuation or promotion, therefore, noncompliance is not an option. And it is not only the University of Auckland where these continuing capability instruments have been introduced. I reviewed an application for promotion to senior lecturer by an academic at one of Australia's leading Group of Eight universities. The lecturer was asked to evaluate himself against a series of performance targets. Under "Evidence of Teaching Impact" he wrote, "I strive to continually improve courses and course materials based on student feedback. . . . I also continually innovate courses and course structures. My redevelopment of [Anthropology 101] to make it MOOC-ready underlines my commitment to continual improvement and innovation."

Under "Impact Measures," he continued, "My Academia.edu profile has had over 1200 views and over 750 document downloads; currently I have over 400 twitter followers." Under "Grants, Contracts and Bibliography" he declares that 'attaining grants is a continuous endeavor. I continue to be engaged in the process of applying and writing grants, tenders and making forays via personal relationships with government departments." Although seemingly banal, these academic promotion forms exemplify perfectly how the rationality of neoliberal audit, with its emphasis on productivity targets, self-monitoring, and continuous self-improvement, is institutionalized and translated into practice. While junior academics may privately dismiss these self-evaluation forms as bureaucratic nonsense, few can afford to ignore them.

To sum up, if the techniques and rationalities of financial accounting and neoliberal responsibilization were emergent in the 1980s and '90s, today they have become increasingly complex, refined, and more deeply embedded in institutional structures and practices, so much so that they seem to embody a new regime of governance, auditability, and power that is increasingly pervasive and influential in shaping the conduct of individual employees.

The Limits of Responsibilization;
or, Power without Responsibility

Let me return to the theme of responsibility and power raised at the outset. The Leadership Framework also exemplifies how "responsibilization" tends to empower some (usually corporate managers and employers) over others (employees). But what are the limits of neoliberal responsibilization as a political project? And what are the contradictions between responsibilization, autonomy, and empowerment? In their eagerness to demonstrate their business-friendly credentials, post-1990s governments in Britain and New Zealand presided over a period of deregulation and outsourcing during which private sector power without social responsibility grew at an unprecedented rate. At the same time the state heaped responsibility without power onto itself, particularly in the form of public-spending commitments. But once a state has divested power to private sector corporations, it is often difficult to enforce accountability and responsibility, particularly when they are able to evade the state's jurisdiction. Many large private companies are powerful enough to mount effective opposition to government attempts to responsibilize their behavior. They are content for governments to supplement their low wages, prop up failing transport systems, and come to the rescue when their actions threaten to bring about a catastrophe—as the 2008 global financial crisis demonstrated. But the idea that private financial institutions and companies will necessarily regulate themselves, or that the discipline of the market will guarantee corporate responsibility, is a dangerous fallacy. Let me illustrate these arguments with a final example from New Zealand.

CASE STUDY 4. *New Zealand's Pike River Mine Disaster*

On November 19, 2010, a gas blast occurred at the Pike River Mine in New Zealand's South Island, killing twenty-nine workers. This was New Zealand's worst mining disaster since 1914, and, given the highly irregular nature of the explosion, the government announced a Royal Commission inquiry to investigate the tragedy. To compound the tragedy, most of the miners had been working 1,500 meters from the mine's entrance and high methane levels made rescue work impossible. The mine shaft was therefore sealed and the bodies may never be recovered. Families of the miners accused both the private company, Pike River Coal Ltd., and government ministers of failing to meet their responsibilities to protect the health and safety of their workers. Initially, the police seemed to concur. Just days after the tragedy, police lawyer Simon Moore QC (now a High Court judge) announced that "the police were undertaking the biggest homicide enquiry in New Zealand's history" (Morris 2014). At the time of the tragedy, the company had fallen behind targets and was trying to speed up production.

The Pike River Royal Commission inquiry (PRRC 2012a, 2012b), which involved seventy lawyers and cost $10.5 million (Macfie 2014), published its report in October 2012, almost two years after the tragedy. It found that the "drive for production before the mine was ready had created the circumstances for the tragedy"; that despite knowing the risks of methane gas, Pike's directors and executive managers had not installed a system fit for the purpose of monitoring its major hazard; and that workers had been exposed to "unacceptable risks" on a daily basis (PRRC 2012a, 12). The report also criticized the Department of Labour, saying it did not have the "focus, capacity or strategy to ensure that Pike was meeting its legal responsibilities" (PRRC 2012a,12). Prime Minister John Key (2012) apologized to relatives of those who died because of the regulatory failures, but also lashed out at the company, saying that it had "completely and utterly failed to protect its workers." However, he dismissed as "ridiculous" the claim that profit-maximizing firms will always prioritize profitability over safety, unless the government, as regulator, ensures workers' safety. The Royal Commission's findings, however, suggest otherwise: "There were numerous warnings of a potential catastrophe at Pike River. One source of these was the reports made by the underground deputies and workers. For months they had reported incidents of excess methane (and many other health and safety problems). In the last 48 days before the explosion there were 21 reports of methane levels reaching explosive volumes, and 27 reports of lesser, but potentially dangerous, volumes. The reports of excess methane continued up to the very morning of the tragedy. The warnings were not heeded" (PRRC 2012a, 12).

A subsequent prosecution brought against Pike in the Greymouth District Court found the company guilty on nine charges relating to its failure to mitigate the risk of explosion and ordered it to pay $3 million in compensation to the families. However, a month after the disaster Pike had gone into receivership, its assets sold off to pay its creditors, and no funds remained to pay compensation to the families of the victims. The Royal Commission report made sixteen recommendations, which included an urgent review of the statutory responsibilities of directors (PRRC 2012a, 36) and a requirement that employers "have a comprehensive and auditable health and safety management system" (PRRC 2012a, 37). More controversially, although the word *responsibility* is used throughout the report (eighty-two times in total), the commission concluded that since the problems at the mine were "systemic," no specific officials should be held responsible, thereby exonerating the directors of the company and its owners (PRRC 2012b, 27). That decision provoked an outpouring of public condemnation but little action from government except for the resignation of Kate Wilkinson, the minister of labor, who said it was the "right and honorable thing to do," although her actions fell short of resigning her other ministerial portfolios (APNZ 2012). Defending her position, John Key apologized to the families of the dead men but said much of the fault lay with the mine's owner, Pike River Coal, as well as with successive governments (Vance, Watkins, and Levy 2012). Successive governments had indeed deregulated health and safety and relinquished powers to private companies who, in theory, were supposed to regulate themselves, but the uncomfortable lesson from Pike River was that having relinquished its regulatory power, government was powerless to force the private mining company to act responsibly: all it could do was accept moral responsibility for the tragedy. The minister did the dutiful thing by offering her resignation, but this was a resignation in both senses of the term as she was powerless to make the owners pay.

Conclusion: Responsibility, Responsibilization, and Post-neoliberal Governmentality

The Pike River disaster and university leadership case studies are important for our analysis as they highlight many of the issues at stake in debates over competing responsibilities. One of these is the analytical distinction between responsibility and responsibilization and the asymmetrical power relations that audit culture produces. What I have termed the rationality of post-neoliberal governmentality represents not a transcendence of neoliberalism but rather its extension and deepening through a new assemblage of market-oriented performance indicators and traditional techniques of managerial control. Workers and employees are increasingly responsibilized and ren-dered auditable, accountable, visible, and powerless, while senior managers of financial corporations and private company owners have responsibility but can evade responsibilization. Deregulation gives them the power to act re-sponsibly but also to avoid being held accountable. This asymmetry seems to have grown and become increasingly institutionalized as a result of successive neoliberal reforms. However, it is also often legally enshrined in employment laws, in the law of limited liability, and in the very idea of the limited liability company itself. Perversely, that limited liability status may encourage compa-nies to act irresponsibly by externalizing costs so that they are passed along to someone else, typically the general public, the state, or the individual em-ployee. The 1984 disaster at Bhopal in India is a good illustration of this: over forty tons of methyl isocyanate gas leaked from a pesticide plant, immediately killing at least 3,800 people. This was the worst industrial accident in history. The company, Union Carbide Corporation, immediately tried to dissociate itself from legal responsibility. Eventually it reached a settlement with the Indian government through mediation of that country's Supreme Court and accepted moral responsibility and paid $470 million in compensation, what many consider to be a derisory sum of money. The Deepwater Horizon oil spill in the Gulf of Mexico in 2010 involving the oil giant BP is a rare example of a major corporation being compelled by a government (in this case, the United States) to accept full legal and financial responsibility for the environmental damage resulting from its gross negligence.

Second, these case studies highlight the way that the shift from audit as a simple instrument of financial regulation to audit as technology of governance and management often leaves the private sector increasingly deregulated and unmonitored. This was one of the reasons why health and safety standards at Pike River were so compromised—and why the Royal Commission recommended legislative and administrative changes to "ensure that inspectors routinely consult workers and health and safety representatives as part of audits and inspections" (PRRC 2012b, 337). In an age of proliferating audits and increasingly individualized responsibility, it seems paradoxical and perverse that the idea of individual responsibility was rejected and that proper auditing procedures were removed from those areas where they are most needed. Significantly, the commission did not recommend a change to legislation to allow for a charge of corporate manslaughter, which is what families of the Pike River victims were calling for. Such a law was introduced in the United Kingdom in 2007 and allows companies and organizations to be found guilty of corporate manslaughter as a result of serious management failures, such as those found at Pike. Instead, a different solution was found. In December 2013, the Ministry of Business, Innovation and Enterprise dropped all charges against Pike River Coal's chief executive, Peter Whittal. The judge presiding over the case at the Christchurch District Court insisted that this was not a case of Mr. Whittal "buying his way out of a prosecution" (Bayer 2012). However, two months before that decision was taken, Mr. Whittal's lawyer wrote to Crown Law offering a "voluntary payment" of $3.41 million for victim compensation, conditional upon the Crown dropping its prosecution (Bayer 2012).

Finally, these case studies show how responsibility and responsibilization are linked to audit culture and to the new politics of accountability it promotes. To echo Strathern (2000b, 3), "audit is where the moral and the financial meet." Audit culture is producing a new kind of ethics, one that is characteristically shaped by financial imperatives and measurement, yet is curiously oblivious to the social and human costs that these processes produce. At a societal level, what is at stake here is nothing less than a new kind of social contract, one that combines auditing, performance measurement, and contractualism—three of the most powerful technologies of responsibilization—into a new disciplinary assemblage. But this harnessing of audit culture to neoliberal projects of responsibilization may have contradictory and perverse effects that include a culture of compliance, cost cutting and managerialism, the centralization of control and decentralization of accountability, health and safety violations, and institutional incentives to ignore corporate responsibility. None of these elements helps to produce autonomous, socially responsible subjects. It seems rather worrying, therefore, that vice chancellors and government ministers should be seeking to promote these same disciplinary technologies and rationalities in order to forge new versions of enterprise culture within their own universities and ministries.

FIVE. From Corporate Social Responsibility to
Creating Shared Value: *Contesting Responsibilization
and the Mining Industry*

JESSICA M. SMITH

Corporate social responsibility (CSR) has become a standard feature of the global mining industry's discursive practices, management strategies, and public reporting. Major transnational corporations as well as junior firms generate policies and publish reports assessing environmental and social performance alongside more traditional financial accounting, and trade groups such as the International Council on Mining and Metals (ICMM) seek to standardize a panoply of best practices through codes, reporting guidelines, and case studies of lessons learned. Corporate social technologies—directed corporate efforts to shape social and cultural life—expand beyond formal CSR programs (Rogers 2012) and take on a variety of terms. Yet CSR remains an umbrella term (Blowfield and Frynas 2005; Frynas 2009) used by industry practitioners and academics alike to refer to policies and programs that seek to reconcile the pursuit of profit with the well-being of the environments and people impacted by business.

Corporate social responsibility comes under fire from a range of points across the political spectrum; many fiscal conservatives follow a narrow interpretation of Milton Friedman's economic philosophy in arguing that the sole responsibility of corporations should be to produce profits for shareholders, while some academics and community organizations argue that CSR is corporate greenwashing that seeks to preempt more stringent regulation from governments and neutralize critique from civil society groups. Though "there is no agreement among observers on why the concept of CSR has risen to prominence in recent history" (Blowfield and Frynas 2005, 500), the majority of social scientists concur that the intense public criticism leveled against mining projects prompted the industry to play a leading role in the development of global CSR discourses, institutions, and practices in the 1980s and 1990s. Indeed, the rise of CSR in mining during that period coincided with the industry's highly contentious expansion into "greenfield" territories— areas without established extractive industries—in the Global South that were home to indigenous and agrarian communities who protested, delayed, and sometimes halted mining operations (Davis and Franks 2014; Kirsch 2006, 2014; Szablowski 2007). The financial cost of local disapproval made managing social risk a key goal of CSR strategies.

Despite the current predominance of CSR, there is no single definition of CSR even within the mining industry that encompasses all of the policies and programs implemented in its name, inspiring two key scholars in the field to argue that the term has "become so broad as to allow people to interpret and adopt it for many different purposes" (Blowfield and Frynas 2005, 503). This chapter analyzes what kind of responsibilities animate the policies and programs implemented under the banner of CSR in the mining industry, with special attention to the significance of the word *responsibility* being dropped in the current, growing, and contested move in favor of the term *creating shared value* (CSV). As implemented in many mine sites, CSR programs facilitate the transfer of many state responsibilities to corporations and attempt to responsibilize (Rose 2006) targeted communities into entrepreneurial subjects. Yet many community members trouble these activities, using the language of responsibility instead to hold corporations accountable for local development through long-term connection and financial patronage. The new era of CSV maintains and perhaps accentuates these programs' focus on generating economic value while dispersing potential calls for accountability among a wider net of actors—rather than being a corporate responsibility, economic, social, and environmental well-being is officially cast as a shared one.

CSR and State Responsibilities

Perhaps the most widespread critique of CSR is that it extends neoliberal governance throughout the social order. With few exceptions (e.g., Welker

2014, 71), critics argue that CSR erodes the authority of state government and reduces its role in providing for citizens and regulating industry, all the while cultivating enterprising, risk-taking subjects who assume responsibility for their actions (e.g., Gond, Kang, and Moon 2011, 644; Shamir 2008). This section and the next take up those two critiques in the same order, beginning with the proposed shift from government to governance.

In many ways, mining companies are taking on many activities otherwise associated with states. They increasingly find themselves expected to build and maintain infrastructure and provide social services in the locations where they operate. They also influence the creation of the regulations to which their operations will be held. Scholars trace this reorganization to two interrelated developments. First, the expansion into greenfield areas in the Global South meant that companies began operating in places with weak political institutions—due to the long-term neglect of peripheral territories by national governments, the influence of extractive industries over political life, or a combination of both—making it necessary for them to fill the gaps in state governance in order to function (Blowfield and Frynas 2005, 508; Szablowski 2007, 59). Second, increasing resistance to mining projects created a need for companies to garner a *social license to operate*, a term favored by industry to designate social acceptance of mining projects (Owen and Kemp 2013). Building much-needed roads, schools, and hospital clinics is a popular strategy for shoring up community support, and vibrant photographs of these fill the pages of CSR reports as tangible evidence of a company's commitment to CSR. Like CSR initiatives in general, however, infrastructure projects can also reinforce hierarchies between companies and communities and set limits on the purview of CSR, as evidenced by strict demarcations between the relatively luxurious town sites built by companies to house employees and the surrounding communities (Appel 2012; Rajak 2011; Welker 2014).

The assumption by corporations of responsibilities previously held by the state has weakened some state structures and sovereignty, a development that is particularly concerning for the issue of enforcing mining regulations originally designed to protect employees, communities, and workers. The CSR premise that corporations voluntarily regulate their own practices and go above and beyond the requirements of law raises multiple challenges for corporations, governments, and civil society. While there are numerous voluntary international standards for best business practices, there is little standardization in corporations' reporting on CSR metrics in their publications, especially related to outcomes rather than simply expenditures on programs (Frynas 2009; Yakovleva 2005). Moreover, the guidelines, principles, codes of conduct, and standards that increasingly replace or exist alongside laws, rules, and regulations "do not necessarily enjoy the coercive backing of the state" (Shamir 2008, 7).

Though the large-scale devolution of governmental authority from states to self-regulating corporations fits neatly within the "age of responsibilization" (Shamir 2008) framework, other research cautions that scholars not so hastily lament the retreat of the state. States can play a variety of active roles in CSR, by facilitating, coordinating, and mandating self-regulation by industry as a "feature of wider regulatory strategies" (Gond, Kang, and Moon 2011, 643; see also Auld, Bernstein, and Cashore 2008; Rajak 2011, 129, 232). Welker's (2014, 71) ethnographic study of the practice of CSR in an Indonesian mining region makes the strongest argument against a simplistic characterization of the neoliberal state withdrawing from the social field, finding that advocates of sustainable development within Newmont actually sought an expanded role for the state in ensuring the well-being of the communities closest to the mine.

Though states may continue to play active roles in relation to corporate governance, the largely voluntary nature of corporate community development, self-reporting, and self-regulation does raise fundamental questions about the participatory models underlining CSR. Corporate social responsibity programs and publications conspicuously avoid the language of rights or obligations more characteristic of state governments and international declarations (Aaron 2012; Coumans 2011; Doane 2005; Gilberthorpe and Banks 2012; Rajak 2011). The absence of rights-based language and programs reinforces the neoliberal ideal of self-managing subjects at the same time as it circumscribes the ability of those subjects and communities to shape programs and policies stemming from CSR models. "Despite rhetorical acceptance that the industry needs to 'do something more' to gain the acceptance of society in the new global political climate, the position demonstrated by existing corporate-driven certification institutions is that the questions of 'what' and 'how' ought ultimately to be decided by industry" (Szablowski 2007, 86). The frequent framing of CSR projects as gifts—and corporations and their personnel as beneficent givers—is one mechanism that entrenches corporate power in the midst of discourses of community empowerment and participation: individuals and communities must appeal and be deferential to corporations rather than utilizing democratic processes and making rights-based claims of citizenship on them (Rajak 2011).

The industry's use of the term *social license to operate* can have the ironic effect of similarly entrenching corporate power at the expense of more democratic decision making. While the term raises the profile of social concerns in mining firms, the term itself remains outside of critique and can be interpreted as an "effort to disguise or silence opposition" (Owen and Kemp 2013, 31). Furthermore, the social license to operate falls well short of the "free, prior and informed consent" established in international law for indigenous populations (Campbell 2012; Coumans 2011; Kirsch 2014; McGee 2009; Slack 2012) and endorsed by the ICMM trade group. Social licenses to operate are informal, intangible, and comparatively more difficult to analyze, enforce, and revoke, especially given the vast inequalities in power between major multinationals and the places where they operate in the developing world. For example, BHP, Rio Tinto, and Newmont each have higher market values than the GDPs of Papua New Guinea, Madagascar, and Ghana, the countries home to their major operations, respectively (Hilson 2012, 133).

These limitations lead to the frequent argument that for CSR to be effective, it must be complemented by strong state regulation and democratic processes (Blowfield and Frynas 2005; Frynas 2009; Hilson 2012; Slack 2012). The primary challenge is that the concept itself originally emerged in the United States and western Europe, where it complemented relatively robust labor and environmental regulations, but is being implemented in very different political contexts.

CSR and Responsible Subjects

The second key mode through which CSR is argued to reinforce processes of neoliberal governance is through the responsibilization of its community participants. Corporate social responsilibity is "presented as a universal good that can be embraced by different sections of the political spectrum" (Blowfield and Frynas 2005, 505). Yet specific programs are steeped in a universalizing vision of development hinged upon the creation of neoliberal capitalist subjects, even if that vision is imperfectly realized in actual practice (Li 2015; Rajak 2011; Welker 2014). This vision of development stresses self-reliance and entrepreneurship to help people help themselves. In contexts where this economic ethos collides with nonmarket economies, even well-intentioned CSR programs can transform cultural and social structures that provided economic security, replacing them with heightened economic inequality and community divisions (Gilbertthorpe and Banks 2012; Welker 2014).

Ethnographic research reveals that the responsibilization of the subjects of CSR is contested and often incomplete. At a mine in Peru often held up by industry and social scientists as using best practices in community engagement, the attempted cultivation of entrepreneurial subjects was partially foiled by the differing cosmologies and expectations of industry held by surrounding indigenous campesino communities. When Federico Helfgott and I conducted research there in 2009 (see Smith and Helfgott 2010), when the mine was still in full operation, the mine conducted community development activities through a foundation that locals viewed as being coterminous with the company even if it was organizationally distinct. The foundation built a dairy, which allowed campesinos to pasteurize their dairy products, and thereby encouraged them to sell alpaca milk, yogurt, and cheese at markets at greater distances. Local religious leaders and campesinos alike critiqued the dairy for centralizing control.

The foundation also sponsored a greenhouse program in six of the communities, aimed to teach locals more modern, scientific techniques for growing vegetables and raising guinea pigs, ideally for market. The foundation's representatives described the greenhouses as having failed due to the disorganization of the communities, alleging that people volunteered to take care of them but then failed to follow through. They planned to follow a different model in which the families would put up the walls themselves, leaving the foundation to provide the glass. The justification offered was that locals would therefore have a personal investment in the project. Local farmers, however, remained skeptical of the greenhouses and the new cultivation techniques, which the foundation interpreted as ignorant superstition rather than critique. Foundation representatives dismissed locals as irrationally believing that greenhouse vegetables caused cancer, asserting that the true danger came from vegetables imported from the coast that were raised using fertilizers and pesticides. Such variegated and contradictory local uptake of responsibilizing CSR programs underscores the importance of distinguishing "projects or rationales of rule" from "the messier practices of rule" (Welker 2014, 130).

In contrast with the mine foundation's capacity-building activities, the campesinos demanded more traditional philanthropic aid from companies, such as school facilities, scholarships, and donations to community groups and events in addition to the fees the company paid directly to the local government. In asserting demands on the company based on its status as a powerful benefactor (rather than as a disingenuously equal partner in development), the campesinos reanimated and transformed older patronage relationships in order to establish a more enduring and direct relationship with mining companies (see also Babidge 2013; Gardner et al. 2012; Welker 2014). These patron-client relations can also be (albeit unintentionally) cultivated by CSR practitioners to shore up their own authority. Dinah Rajak, for example, finds that CSR practitioners in the South African platinum industry identify suitable targets of their empowerment or capacity-building programs in Victorian discourses of the "'deserving' and 'undeserving poor' . . . on the one hand the 'deserving' who have earned their status as beneficiaries by demonstrating their will and capacity for upliftment and conversion to the entrepreneurial spirit; and on the other the 'undeserving poor,' who are rendered dependent and idle through social welfare" (2011, 217).

The reinvention and redeployment of older relations of patronage observed in a variety of global contexts of extractive activity illustrate a broader pattern of community desires for increased connection with, rather than independence from, mining companies. Underlining CSR's definition of sustainable development is a "process of disconnection: the donor withdraws and the good works continue" (Gardner et al. 2012, 173). Though ensuring that the economic and social health of communities continues beyond the life of a mine is a laudable goal, communities may understand the obligations of corporations from a different perspective. The corporate ethic of detachment documented in Chevron's Bangladesh operations resonates with similar developments in mining. Chevron did not fulfill their promises of jobs or development to the local community, which subscribed to a model of assistance based on patronage by landowners and wealthy villagers visiting from abroad. What local people desired from Chevron was not sustainability predicated on distance, but connection: "not just to officials who might act as patrons, but to the long term benefits of global capitalism and the modernity it is supposed to bring" (Gardner et al. 2012, 174). Together, these cases suggest that the ostensibly neoliberal elements of the responsibility cultivated by CSR exist alongside and in tension with other models of responsibility grounded in connection and care, even when paternalistic (Trnka and Trundle 2014).

Responsibilizing the Corporate Person

If communities in Peru, South Africa, Indonesia, and Bangladesh were like many others in seeking to hold mines accountable for their actions, and enmesh them in enduring ties of obligation, what kind of responsibility were they seeking from the companies operating them? Does CSR responsibilize corporations as corporations seek to responsibilize the subjects of its outreach (Welker 2014, 131)? After all, the primary discursive focus of CSR is ostensibly the heightened responsibility of corporations, not chiefly citizens or communities. Answering these questions, however, raises another, more fundamental one: for whom or what is the corporation being held responsible?

An argument could be made that the profit-driven corporate person is the entrepreneurial subject par excellence, the template for the risk-averse entrepreneurial subject at the heart of so many CSR programs. This reading would lend support to assertions of the increasing economization of public domains that accompanies the moralization of markets (Shamir 2008). In this case, CSR would very much figure as a responsibilization of the corporation, as CSR ideally involves companies internalizing social and environmental harms rather than simply externalizing them (Auld, Bernstein, and Cashore 2008; Crouch 2006). The fact that companies with robust CSR programs continue to externalize these harms, perhaps most infamously demonstrated by the catastrophic failure of "Beyond Petroleum," BP's Deepwater Horizon drilling rig and the company's attempts to avoid compensation payments to the locals it harmed (Bond 2013; Kirsch 2010a), frequently serves as evidence for critics arguing that CSR is a smokescreen for continued business as usual rather than a fundamental shift in corporate practice. At the Peruvian mine discussed above, for example, one of the communities is engaged in an ongoing dispute over heavy metal contamination of local water and soil, which they believe is to blame for increasing farm animal deformities. Though multiple studies found elevated levels of aluminum, arsenic, copper, iron, lithium, and manganese in samples, the company explained them as the effect of natural background mineralization.

Yet even though corporations are ascribed a unitary legal personhood and frequently portrayed monolithically by academics and activists, they are internally variegated and characterized by multiple, competing interests. Institutionally, CSR and community relations teams are often cordoned off from the technical units dedicated to engineering and production within mining companies, and these divisions can be strongly gendered—the technical hard teams that do the actual mining and the soft side of creating and nurturing social relations (Kemp and Owen 2013; Rajak 2011; Welker 2014; see also Shever 2010 on the oil industry). Moreover, competing visions and practices of CSR can also coexist within a single division within a company. Whereas the manager in charge of community relations at Newmont's Batu Hijau mine fostered symbiotic relationships between the corporation and community that approximated patronage, the community development manager sought to disentangle the company from the community and encourage stronger relationships between the community and the state, all in a model of sustainable development (Welker 2014, 68–71). The latter model fits the framework of responsibilization more closely, since it positions responsibility for community welfare with the community itself, rather than the company.

Viewing the corporation not as a "natural, fully realized, discrete, unfettered, self-present, and self-knowing liberal individual" but one that has a "partible, permeable, and composite dynamic" (Welker 2014, 1, 18; see also Ho 2009, 173; Mollona 2009, 21) illuminates the challenges for communities seeking to hold the companies who actually produce and practice CSR responsible for their own actions. The mining industry's critics invoke responsibility in a way that involves answerability and dutiful response (Trnka and Trundle 2014). But who answers for a corporation? Who responds?

While the corporation as a whole can be held responsible in a legal realm, the more mundane arena of everyday interactions, negotiations, and disputes is much murkier. Though communities may seek to hold individual corporate personnel accountable for the larger company's actions, those individuals may have very little influence on the actual actions undertaken by other people and groups who enact the corporation in a different manner. At a more basic level, changeovers in mine ownership and management complicate efforts to hold one company, let alone a tangible person, accountable for a company's actions. For example, a grassroots activist I came to know during research in the Pacific Northwest, who was successful in halting an open pit mine and then negotiating a settlement for the underground mine that eventually opened on the same site, was chagrined that he had outlasted every single environmental manager or community outreach official the headquarters had sent to deal with him. What he called the "revolving door" of corporate personnel frustrated his efforts to hold the company accountable, since the persons enacting the company had little institutional memory of previous agreements and arrangements and could distance their own selves from the corporation they represented (Rolston 2014; see also Luning 2012). The corporation he sought to responsibilize was infuriatingly intangible, even as it had concrete, deleterious effects in his mountain home.

Creating Shared Value

If holding corporations accountable for their impacts was difficult within the framework of CSR, what is the significance of the word *responsibility*—and its wider implications of answerability through an obligated, dutiful response (Trnka and Trundle 2014)—being dropped in the current discursive move toward creating shared value? Since 2010, the concept of CSV has migrated from the academy and consulting agencies to major corporations, at times existing alongside more conventional CSR discourses and practices, and other times replacing them. In an influential 2011 article in the *Harvard Business*

Review, business strategist and Harvard professor Michael Porter coined the term with Mark Kramer, a venture capitalist and managing director of the consulting firm that spearheads the Shared Value Initiative. Porter and Kramer define CSV as "policies and operating practices that enhance the competitiveness of a company while simultaneously advancing the economic and social conditions in the communities in which it operates" (2011, 6). Rather than considering social and environmental problems as external pressures that impinge on a firm's financial performance, it treats them as opportunities to both grow business and serve the greater good, thus recognizing the "interdependence" (7) of successful businesses and successful communities. Initiatives for CSV center heavily on making supply chains more efficient and thus more environmentally responsible; creating marketable products or services that address key societal needs, such as "health, better housing, improved nutrition, help for the aging, greater financial security, less environmental damage"; and building industry "clusters" to support companies (7).

Though Porter and Kramer go to great pains to distinguish CSV from the CSR they and their consulting group aim to supersede, both industry CSR practitioners and academics contest the difference between the two concepts. Porter and Kramer (2011, 6) argue that in contrast with CSR, CSV is an internally generated strategy to enhance a firm's overall competitiveness and profit, rather than a response to external pressures that is separate from the larger business activities of the firm in both spirit and budget, thus generating economic as well as social value. Distinguishing CSR and CSV in this way, however, rests on the creation of a straw man CSR, cut in the outdated mold of philanthropy, that does not acknowledge entire bodies of research and practice that align CSR with the core business activities and strategic (including profit-generating) goals of corporations (Crane et al. 2014; see also Auld, Bernstein, and Cashore 2008).

Porter and Kramer's view of the relationship between CSV and state regulation also shares much in common with more mainstream CSR. Similarly, CSV rests on an idealistic view that social and economic goals, and the interests of businesses and communities, can almost always be reconciled without trade-offs (Crane et al. 2014). Porter and Kramer posit that CSV must be accompanied by state "regulations that enhance shared value, set goals and stimulate innovation" as well as "limit the pursuit of exploitative, unfair or deceptive practices in which companies benefit at the expense of society" (2011, 14). Yet they also assume compliance with these regulations, stating that "creating shared value presumes compliance with the law and ethical standards, as well as mitigating any harm caused by the business, but goes far beyond that" (Porter and Kramer 2011, 15). Though this acknowledgment of the active role of the state may seem different from mainstream CSR, which is commonly portrayed as superseding or eroding state power, CSR exists alongside and within larger state governance structures (Auld, Bernstein, and Cashore 2008; Gond, Kang, and Moon 2011). Even a brief perusal of mining company CSR reports reveals consistent acknowledgment that they work within the constraints of state regulation—chiefly in terms of environmental and safety management—and in concert with federal and state agencies that regulate and seek to improve performance in those arenas.

In conversation, CSR practitioners in the mining industry who work for or with companies that jumped on the CSV bandwagon express healthy skepticism, if not outright denial, of the uniqueness of CSV in relation to CSR. An analysis of the reports of companies that use the term CSV reveals a similar conclusion. The content of Xstrata's 2011 "Creating Shared Value" sustainability report is virtually indistinguishable from more conventional CSR reports. It is cast in an informal font, with bright colors, vaguely indigenous designs, and graphics that present information and stories as clippings on a bulletin board or a paper-clipped stack of weathered documents. These representational techniques are a mainstay of CSR reporting and aim to informalize and level the relationship between the corporation and the reader (Livesey and Kearins 2002). The dedicated "Creating Shared Value" section focuses on Xstrata's financial performance: devolved authority means that mines can act "nimbly" with an "entrepreneurial spirit"; diversified assets reduce the corporation's risk; and an "industry-leading approach to sustainable development" means that they can "gain access to new resources [and] maintain a social license to operate" (Xstrata 2011, 5). The value created for local communities is cast in terms of employment and revenue sharing. The section "Growing Economic Benefits" also includes local sourcing of goods and "a range of community initiatives to improve living standards." With the exception of living standards, these "values" are all economic.

In a manner similar to Xstrata, the diamond giant De Beers focuses on economic values in its 2010 Report to Society, which defines CSV as "sustainable economic growth that will endure beyond the life of existing mines" (De Beers 2011, 19). Their partnership with host governments is said to be designed as one that "maximizes the economic value of our production, reduces our operating risk, and helps support the creation of skills and capacities for a diversified post-mining economy" (De Beers 2011, 20). They also profess to engage in local sourcing and enterprise development to support economic development in the places where they operate. For both Xstrata and De Beers, shared value both during the mining process and after its halt is primarily economic. This focus on economic value is in line with the business case argument for CSR as a tool for reducing financial liabilities through managing social risk and for creating enterprising capitalist subjects who support their own development.

Though Newmont is a prominent partner in the Shared Value Initiative, the company's 2013 report, "Beyond the Mine," is notable for integrating the language of both CSV and CSR, and for providing more specific details of some of the social values they seek to foster. For example, the company commits itself to providing "meaningful, long-term benefits," which includes local employment and procurement practices, as in the cases of Xstrata and De Beers. Yet unlike the other two companies, it also includes "better access to clean water, energy and underlying conditions required for healthy economies" (Newmont 2013, 6). The wording of the last sentence is significant in placing seemingly noneconomic values of human and environmental health within the larger context of economic health. The opening letter from the CEO also justifies their sustainable development efforts in terms of producing profit for shareholders, stating, "Newmont has an important role to play as a catalyst for sustainable development, and we need stability to justify investing our shareholders' money in timeframes that span—and affect—generations" (Newmont 2013, 6).

Despite the dropping of the word *responsibility* in the term CSV, if not in the actual discursive repertoires of company employees, the concept and its attendant field of practice might emphasize the responsibilization of subjects even more than CSR does. The value that CSV initiatives seek to create is seductive because it is potentially expansive and polysemous. Porter and Kramer argue strongly for social as well as economic value, such as improving the health and well-being of communities. Yet as implemented by the mining companies noted above, CSV is primarily considered in terms of profit creation for companies and economic growth for individuals and communities.[1] Indeed, the five case studies promoted by the Shared Value Initiative (2014) as exemplifying the creation of shared value in the extractive industries each place the purported social values within an overarching economic one. According to the report, AngloAmerican's water treatment plant in South Africa makes a profit providing 12 percent of the local municipality's daily water requirements and treating water from the nearby BHP Billiton coal mine. AngloGold Ashanti's malaria program in Ghana reduced disease incidence by 72 percent, which the report heralds as reducing worker absenteeism and increasing mine productivity. BHP Billiton's local procurement program in

Chile is praised for generating over $120 million in cost savings for the company while providing opportunities for thirty-six suppliers who employed more than 5,000 people. And Newmont's apprenticeship program in Ghana is commended for reducing operating costs for the company and providing transferable skills for other kinds of employment.

While more standard CSR is also often justified in terms of the business case for increased profitability, it also more readily incorporates values that are not entirely or primarily economic in nature, such as human health and cultural heritage. Though the mining company and foundation in Peru sought to cultivate entrepreneurial subjects through the dairy and greenhouse projects, for example, they also engaged in activities that exceeded the creation of economic value: nutritional support for children and pregnant mothers; education and illiteracy mitigation programs; summer camps celebrating artistic creativity through arts, handicrafts, and dance; and cultural heritage contests. Though the health, education, and culture of surrounding communities can be clearly implicated in the creation of neoliberal subjects, and though a business case can be made indirectly for them increasing financial stability by reducing company risk, they cannot be solely or primarily justified in terms of generating economic returns for companies.

If the value produced by CSV is primarily economic, CSV is similar to CSR in grounding and reframing "socio-moral concerns . . . within the instrumental rationality of capitalist markets" (Shamir 2008, 3; see also Rajak 2011). Yet the more limited focus of actually existing practices of CSV, aimed at creating shared economic value, brings it closer in line with Rose's notion of responsibilization, despite CSV conspicuously lacking the term *responsibility* itself. The mismatch between the responsibilization of subjects, manifested the most clearly in CSV programs, and the broader understandings of responsibility as enduring obligation and answerability, as articulated by the communities in Indonesia, South Africa, Bangladesh, and likely elsewhere, signal more fundamental tensions in the practice of contemporary capitalism. In conversations about CSR with mining industry professionals, many express a distaste for the term CSR not simply because it is too broad or has become equated with philanthropy. They argue that it unfairly focuses responsibility on the corporation and obscures the responsibilities that communities and governments also have for ensuring economic, social, and environmental well-being. For them, responsibility should be shared among those actors, whereas communities seek instead to signal the heightened responsibility of powerful corporations.

Conclusion

Asking corporations to take more responsibility for regulating themselves and contributing to community development is said by critics to represent a change in focus for institutions otherwise dedicated to the pursuit of profit. For them, CSR implies that the "very corporations which, for years, freely polluted and contributed minimally to the communities where they operated, have suddenly morphed into philanthropic organizations" (Hilson 2012, 132). By positioning corporations with the responsibility to both define and solve social and environmental problems associated with its practice, CSR raises the specter of allowing "business to appropriate the meaning of ethics" (Blowfield and Frynas 2005, 512). Critics argue that CSR is a strategy for corporations to neutralize criticism through co-opting concepts originally used to critique the industry, such as sustainable mining (Kirsch 2010b), as well as the missions of civil society groups (Baur and Schmitz 2012). To wit, mining corporations often choose to work with what the business community calls "light greens," environmentalists who view the market as the solution to environmental problems, rather than "dark greens," those who view the market as part of the problem and remain critical of corporate claims to social and environmental responsibility (Kirsch 2010b, 2014; Rajak 2011; Welker 2014; see Rolston 2014 for an exception).

In contrast, proponents of CSR point to the business case for responsible practice, arguing that environmental stewardship and positive community relationships actually enhance profitability by minimizing risk. Proving the business case is difficult, and more research is needed to tease out if firms that invest heavily in CSR are more profitable or if profitable firms are those who are able to invest heavily in CSR. Even the foundational, industry-sponsored Mining, Minerals, and Sustainable Development report warns, "Win-win solutions are not always possible; voluntary approaches alone are insufficient where there is a compelling priority but little or no business case to justify the additional expenditures needed to meet it" (IIED 2002, xxiii). Better understanding these cases is crucial for wrestling with the opportunities and challenges of CSR, as they pose the greatest challenges to reconciling profitability against social and environmental well-being (Aaron 2012; Auld, Bernstein, and Cashore 2008; Hilson 2012, 132).

Rather than falling into polarized debates about CSR serving as either a hallowed solution for reconciling markets with morality or as mere greenwashing, critical appraisals of CSR must consider the kinds of responsibilities its current frameworks presume and seek to promote, and at the expense of what alternatives, such as rights and obligations. If responsibility, in contrast with responsibilization, minimally implies safeguarding the well-being of communities impacted by mineral development, do CSR policies and programs address the structural root causes of underdevelopment in general (Blowfield and Frynas 2005; Campbell 2012; Crane et al. 2014; Fleming and Jones 2013), as well as the insecurity of the boom-bust cycles of the mining industry in particular (Luning 2012; Rolston 2014)? What kind of institutions—and relationships between corporate, government, and civil society groups—are required to enhance the responsibility desired by the communities impacted the most by this development? And perhaps most significantly, how do the language and ontological frameworks of CSR and CSV, which emerged from and remain faithful to the business community's focus on profitability (Fleming and Jones 2013), constrain the ways in which corporate, community, and other actors configure their responsibilities among each other and their ability to imagine alternatives?

NOTE

1. Kirsch (2010b) observes a similar phenomenon in the "emptying out" of the word *sustainability* in the mining industry, from an ecological to an almost wholly economic sense of the term.

Part III. Violence

SIX. "The Information Is Out There": *Transparency,*
Responsibility, and the Missing in Cyprus

ELIZABETH ANNE DAVIS

Everything that can be said about responsibility in relation to the Cyprus Problem seems to be said in a four-minute sequence toward the end of *In This Waiting*, a documentary film by Anna Tsiarta screened at the Lemesos International Documentary Film Festival in August 2011. In the sequence, one person after another—each one a relative of a missing person lost in the violent conflicts of the 1960s–70s; each one identified at the beginning of the film by a first name and an ethnonational label—sits in the same cracked red leather chair in the same dark study, surrounded by books and old furniture in blurry shadow, facing the camera from the same angle, sight line directed slightly off-camera toward the same silent, invisible interviewer. Although each of these speakers is alone with the film crew, the sequence is edited to summon up a conversation among them. They question and contradict one another:

> ANDREAS ("Greek Cypriot"): You can't easily say to somebody: "Here. . . . This is your brother, this is your father, this is your son." And you place a flag on that box and you send a letter and it's considered closed? I really don't get it. Where was that person? Where did we find him?

What happened? These are questions that need answers. And from the moment that these people began serving this state, the state became responsible for providing these answers. . . . War is war. War is an ugly game. People from both sides have their reasons as to why they fight. But war has rules. And one of the rules is that, from the moment one surrenders, or is unarmed, you are responsible for him. And it doesn't matter if he is your enemy.

LEYLA ("Turkish Cypriot"): If Ahmet is dead and this is definite and official, I would like to know this, and indeed, if his killer is alive, I would like to talk to him. Why did he do this? And now what does he feel about what he did? If he could face me.

AGNI ("Greek Cypriot"): I'm not interested in finding out. Why find out? What good will it do me? What, will he come and apologize to me? Or will I go and harm him? No.

NEOFYTOS ("Greek Cypriot"): I do feel angry sometimes: why have these people not been punished?

AGNI ("Greek Cypriot"): Punished, yes. But the one who pulled the trigger, it wasn't his fault. . . . It was the others who made him do it. If a soldier killed them, someone ordered him to kill them. They were just instruments. . . . They were ordered to kill. That was their job.

SEVILAY ("Turkish Cypriot"): I don't know. Perhaps he needs to ask for my forgiveness. But I still need to think about it. The best thing is to do is to commit him to God's judgment. Let God forgive him. This is what I think and feel at this moment. I don't know.

ANDREAS ("Greek Cypriot"): Since all of us in Cyprus . . . all of us have a relative, a friend . . . all of us have this question: why? And this demand: we want justice. So as to think they were not lost in vain.

The cognates of justice named in this staged conversation—punishment, vengeance, apology, explanation, forgiveness, God's judgment—are as multiple as the subjects of responsibility, individual and collective: enemy, killer, soldier, instrument, those who give orders, "these people," the state, "all of us in Cyprus." Some of the remarks are propositions; others are antipropositions: open questions, statements of not knowing or not wanting to know. Despite the diversity of their inchoate judgments and desires, however, the contributors to this conversation are united in the implicit premise that knowledge—

what happened, why, and who—exists; that answers can be given that would compose a more coherent story of responsibility than any told as yet. At this point in the film, it has already been disclosed that some of these relatives have recently received the remains of their missing persons, found and identified by a bicommunal forensic agency some thirty-five to fifty years after their deaths. But the remains are not enough.

In this chapter, I trace multifarious attributions of responsibility for the missing in Cyprus. Drawing from fieldwork I have been conducting in Cyprus since 2007, I connect two sites where the negotiation of responsibility has become entangled with the production of forensic evidence. First, I appraise suspicions of secrecy surrounding the forensic investigations currently being conducted into the missing, and the discourse of transparency with which those suspicions are dynamically aligned. Second, I examine juridical conceptions of responsibility that have emerged in right-to-know litigation undertaken by relatives of the missing (see Bryant 2010; Demetriou and Gürel 2008; Kovras 2008; Kyriakou 2011, 2012a, 2012b; Sant Cassia 2005; Yakinthou 2008). These two sites, where the fate of the missing is undergoing distinct processes of determination, are united by the conviction among relatives that more could be known about what happened to their loved ones. In the speculation opened by this conviction, I discern resistances to thinking about both personal and collective responsibility for the history of violence in Cyprus.

A Purely Humanitarian Issue

Since 2007, I have been visiting and working in Cyprus, a country still divided by the so-called Green Line, a de facto cease-fire line dating to 1974. A coup backed by Greece in July of that year and the subsequent invasion by the Turkish military compelled the evacuation of Greek Cypriots to the south and Turkish Cypriots to the north of the island.[1] This division put a provisional end to revolutionary, intercommunal, and state violence that began during the anticolonial struggle of the 1950s and continued throughout the 1960s and early 1970s. Although a political settlement for reunification has persisted as the dominant issue in Cyprus since 1974, the Green Line remains in place today.

My research in Cyprus is situated in more recent events of apparent opening in this history of closure: from the opening of checkpoints between north and south in 2003, to the European Union's opening to Cyprus in 2004, to the opening of new unity talks between Greek Cypriot and Turkish Cypriot authorities in 2008, 2010, 2012, 2014, and 2016. These events appear—at least to some Cypriots—as a radical break in their fraught history of hostility and opacity across the divide. But this history is not only one of entrenched divisions between Greek-Cypriot and Turkish-Cypriot communities and authorities. It is a history animated as well by suspicions of secrecy on the part of states and statelike entities: the Republic of Cyprus; the Turkish Republic of Northern Cyprus, unrecognized by the international community, with the exception of Turkey; the "parent" states of Greece and Turkey; the proxy agencies of the United States and United Kingdom; and a range of Cypriot parastate and paramilitary agencies. Many Cypriots suspect these entities of colluding with foreign powers, sponsoring and concealing violence against civilians, surveilling and suppressing journalists and activists, censoring the press and school curricula, and preserving the stalemate over reunification in the service of hidden motives. These forms of secrecy are being countered in Cyprus today by individuals and organizations who demand government transparency, in line with the new horizon of European integration and peaceful coexistence between Greek Cypriots and Turkish Cypriots.

Transparency is by no means a priority in all areas of governance in Cyprus. Many problems remain notoriously opaque—such as human trafficking, undocumented labor, black markets for weapons and drugs, offshore banking, and the political activities of religious institutions. But what is known as the Cyprus Problem—that is, the division of Cyprus—is one area where transparency is valorized and actively pursued by Cypriots, perhaps because it has so thoroughly determined the structure and operations of government since the founding of the republic in 1960 (Constantinou 2006; Demetriou and Gürel 2008). Residents on both sides of the Green Line have long accused the Greek, Turkish, and Cypriot states of fomenting and perpetrating violence in the period from independence in 1960 to the division in 1974. Few members of the police, military forces, and paramilitary groups active at that time have been tried for their crimes. It is said that some of these people enjoy prominence as politicians and wealthy businessmen today, a public secret that helps to account for the persistent impasse in reunification. During my time in Cyprus, I heard many times of a truth-and-reconciliation investigation undertaken in the 1990s by a parliamentary committee in the republic in order to determine the scope of the atrocities and the identities of those responsible; the findings, I was told, had been deposited in a closed file inside parliament.

Suspicions of state secrecy in Cyprus raise the question as to what kinds of evidence might either substantiate or refute them. In this chapter, I explore some of that evidence, produced in the domain of forensic science. The evidence is drawn primarily from fieldwork I conducted in 2011–12 with the

Committee on Missing Persons in Cyprus (CMP), a bicommunal, Greek-Cypriot–Turkish-Cypriot agency established in 1981 under UN auspices to investigate over two thousand cases of Greek Cypriots and Turkish Cypriots—civilians and combatants—lost in the violence of the 1960s–70s. Since 2004, teams of Greek-Cypriot and Turkish-Cypriot archaeologists, physical anthropologists, and geneticists have been conducting investigations: exhuming remains on both sides of the Green Line, analyzing them, and confirming their identity with DNA testing. Once a missing person's identity is confirmed, the remains are returned to the person's relatives, who also receive, if they wish, psychological counseling and financial support for burial.

These activities have been widely publicized in Cyprus, starting from investigative reporting on the missing in the 1990s by journalists such as Andreas Paraschos in the south and Sevgül Uludağ in the north. Today, reporters routinely cover exhumations and funerals of the missing, as well as the many scandals at the CMP. The CMP has its own public information office and regularly issues press releases in English, Turkish, and Greek, to newspapers in both the north and south—where they are often mobilized for radically different political messages—and on its own website, where all its press releases are archived.

Thus, despite the history of secrecy surrounding the fate of the missing, the CMP has received a great deal of media coverage in Cyprus in recent years. The forensic teams have also featured in a number of television broadcasts and documentary films. Images of scientists working with bones have become as commonplace as those of grief-stricken relatives in representations of Cyprus's violent history. This imagery originates and circulates in a very different way from the forensic photographs produced in the process of investigation and stored in the CMP's confidential archives. These very public photographs and films of scientists at work participate in a genre of representation that is well established outside Cyprus—in places like Spain, Argentina, Chile, Guatemala, and Bosnia-Herzegovina, where, as in Cyprus, forensic investigations of the missing and disappeared have become a public forum for witnessing and memory recovery (see Arsenijević 2011a, 2011b; Crossland 2000, 2002; Ferrándiz 2006; Ferrándiz and Baer 2008; Nelson 2009; Renshaw 2011; Sanford 2004). Along with the forensic training and the infrastructure of investigation contributed to Cyprus by international agencies comes this genre of publicity, which Ferrándiz and Baer (2008, 5), documenting exhumations of leftists killed in the Spanish Civil War, describe as a "global pool of images of repression, loss, terror and violence." This genre features images of mourning women—the Mothers of the Plaza de Mayo in Argentina, for example, mirroring the Mothers of the Missing in Cyprus—as well as images of forensic teams working with bones in a scenario of grim science that Whitehead (1990, passim) calls "forensic theater."[2]

The Cypriot audiences addressed by this publicity are "organized" in a "space of discourse," as Warner (2002, 413) defines "a public" (as distinct from "*the* public"), noting that the discursivity of this space may well be visual rather than textual, as with ubiquitous images of the forensic scene in Cyprus. This public—a group with shifting membership, crossing all lines of community, language, and citizenship—is summoned not only as the audience but also, in a sense, as Sant Cassia (2005, 209) suggests, as the chorus for the tragic drama of the missing, as this history is often described in the press. They are the public of public secrecy: those whose "knowing what not to know," as Taussig (1999, 6) distills this logic, describes both their complicity with state secrecy and their drive to seek the truth.

Although global in its reach, the forensic theater of postconflict investigation is not performed on the same grounds in all of its locations—nor does it display the same kinds of scenes. In many postconflict sites, such as Argentina and Spain, exhumations of missing persons were initiated by grassroots organizations and conducted by volunteer forensic teams, who worked directly with relatives and witnesses and maintained open access for the public to their excavation sites and forensic findings. In both cases, excavations became sites of memorialization as well (see Crossland 2000, 2002; Renshaw 2011; Ferrándiz and Baer 2008). In Cyprus, by contrast, the CMP—not a grassroots organization but rather a hybrid state agency hosted and funded by the United Nations—conducts its confidential investigations outside the public eye. Although excavation sites are not hidden, and indeed are quite visible to people living and working nearby as well as to the journalists who report on them, their locations are not publicized; access is restricted by safety tape and mesh fences, and sites quickly fall back into invisibility once excavations are complete, backfilled and unmarked by signs or plaques. The CMP's anthropological laboratory, likewise, is located in a protected UN site without public access; even invited guests and press representatives require special permission and a UN escort to enter.[3] The extensive critical coverage in Cypriot newspapers of scandals at the CMP, and complaints about the speed, effectiveness, and correctness of its investigations, signal doubt and suspicion on the part of Cypriot publics. There is no sense of grassroots initiative at the CMP, no place for relatives or others invested in the investigations to play an active role in shaping their objectives or procedures. The visibility of field and lab work is tightly controlled, even as the CMP engages in its own strategic self-promotion—a peculiarly synergetic dynamic of secrecy and publicity.

It is with this dynamic in mind that I see the controversial mandate of the CMP. According to its terms of reference, laid down in 1981, "the committee will not attempt to attribute responsibility for the deaths of any missing persons or make findings as to the cause of such deaths." This mandate is grounded in the expectation that confirming the deaths of the missing, and returning their remains to their families, will suffice to heal the wounds of the past and clear a path toward reunification. The CMP's mission of closure and healing fosters an ethos of service to the families of the missing among the scientists who work on their cases. Yet the publicity surrounding the CMP's activities creates a structural tension between service to families and respect for their rights—especially their right to privacy and their right to know. I learned about these tensions first from H., an investigator for the CMP who positioned himself as a somewhat oppositional figure within the organization.[4] It was from that position that he extended help to me, arranging for me to work at the lab, to visit excavations, and to attend viewings—as if despite the wishes of the CMP, although I had been granted formal permission to do this very work. In our conversations, H. often criticized the CMP's attempts to control information. "This is all for show," he said to me when we first met at the lab, gesturing toward the scientists working at computer terminals and tables of bones. "If you ever want to get the real story, come talk to me."

H.'s politics of transparency were tied to his politics of responsibility. Despite appearances, he told me, the CMP was an entirely political organization, a "public relations operation" staged for the cameras. Its interest lay not in determining the truth about what had happened in the past, but rather in bolstering Cyprus's international reputation as a peaceful democratic regime invested in human rights. He condemned the CMP's silence about responsibility for the deaths it investigated, since relatives of the victims never learned what they most wanted to know—namely, how and why their loved ones had died: "No responsibility means no justice. No findings as to cause of death means no truth." He took the position that the CMP's work should be part of a justice process that would ultimately attribute responsibility for the deaths of the missing. "It's hypocrisy," he said. "The politics of human rights are the dirtiest politics of all. You can't be selective with rights!"

In his insistence on the right to know vested in relatives of the missing, H. aligned human rights with a particular conception of justice, denigrating the proceduralist ideology of transparency promoted by the CMP for contributing to the political foreclosure of responsibility in Cyprus. The conception of responsibility he invoked was juridical, referring to war crimes and human rights, and thus, at least implicitly, a national or international system of criminal justice. A number of cases regarding the missing in Cyprus, structured by this conception of responsibility, have been brought against both the Republic of Turkey and the Republic of Cyprus in the European Court of Human Rights (ECtHR) since the 1980s, usually originating in claims lodged with the CMP that, unsatisfied by the CMP during its decades of inactivity, were then referred to the ECtHR.[5] These cases include the interstate case *Cyprus v. Turkey*, brought in 1994 and decided in 2001, in which Turkey was found to have violated the rights of several Greek-Cypriot claimants to know the location and disposition of their relatives, missing in action since the war in 1974. In *Varnava and Others v. Turkey*, a case brought by a group of Greek-Cypriot claimants in 1990 and decided by the ECtHR in 2009, the court found in favor of the claimants on most counts. However, two cases brought by Turkish-Cypriot claimants against the Republic of Cyprus in 1989, *Karabardak and Others v. Cyprus* and *Baybora and Others v. Cyprus*, were rejected by the ECtHR in 2002 on the grounds of the claimants' ostensible failure to adhere to the six-month rule governing cases of enforced disappearance.[6] In the domestic space of litigation, several civil cases have also been brought by Greek Cypriots against the Republic of Cyprus—for example, *Palma v. Cyprus* and *Passia v. Cyprus*, both decided in favor of the claimants by the Supreme Court of Cyprus in 2012.

In some of these cases, the right of claimants to know the fate of their missing relatives was connected with other questions produced and sustained by political division, including the right of refugees to return to their homes on the other side of the Green Line and their right to the property they had left behind. In this light, the historical unfolding of the problem of the missing in Cyprus can be seen as part of "the process by which human rights have been used to translate political claims in legal language" in Cyprus, as Demetriou and Gürel (2008, 26) describe this history of legal innovation, enhanced by the occupation of Cyprus by the United Nations since 1964 and especially by the accession of Cyprus to the European Union in 2004. The question of the missing thus cannot be disaggregated from the emergence of the litigating subject as a social-political form in Cyprus. Cypriot litigants do not necessarily hold a specific concept of legal or criminal responsibility in mind when they bring cases against the state, be it Cyprus or Turkey, but such a concept persists as precisely that form of responsibility foreclosed by the CMP investigations and its rhetoric of transparency. In all the court cases named above, the knowledge relatives sought under the rubric of their right to know concerned the location and disposition of the remains of their missing person—not the circumstances of the person's death, nor the identity of the killer. It is a profoundly restricted kind of knowledge, matching exactly the kind of knowledge produced by the CMP, whose investigations since 2004 have come to obviate additional such litigation.

But more has been opened by these lawsuits than a forum for making and satisfying demands for knowledge of death. I recall here Nicole Loraux's (2002) focus, in *The Divided City*, on lawsuits in ancient Athens as the most threatening kind of memory prohibited by the amnesty after civil war, since the bringing of evidence (in the form of memory) to sue for justice (in the form of punishment) could only nourish and amplify conflict in the city. In the shadows cast by the forensic investigations in Cyprus lie murky but intense yearnings for justice where it has been rendered unspeakable in forensic terms. In the lawsuits, the remains of the dead stand in for knowledge about the deaths of the missing that the CMP is prohibited from disclosing. Suspicions that more could be known are given voice in court, even if the framework of agreement between the two regimes does not permit such knowledge to surface there. In this sense, right-to-know litigation in Cyprus has helped to reinforce secrecy as a position maintained by the defendants in these lawsuits—that is, the governments in the north and south. At the same time, this litigation has opened up an imagination of responsibility as a kind of claim made on the state by its citizens, on both sides of the divide.

In becoming litigants, grieving relatives of the missing have retained the symbolic authority of their losses authorized by the state, while transforming the state's withholding of information into a position of victimization by the state. Their right to know has become a right to sue. This emphasis on rights and harms may indicate a broader process of judicialization in Cyprus, as Demetriou and Gürel suggest—a process in which, as Comaroff and Comaroff (2006, 22, 25–26) put it, "politics itself is migrating to the courts," part of the growing "culture of legality" or "fetishism of the law" coinciding with the rise of violence and lawlessness in postcolonial societies, though not only there. Judicialization, in their telling, represents a new reckoning of the responsibility and accountability of the state itself that is emerging through litigation undertaken by citizens, often in class actions combining elements of criminal law, human rights law, and tort law (Comaroff and Comaroff 2006, 27). This reckoning is particularly urgent and compelling, they note, in states where jurisdictions are multiple, unclear, or in the process of being "remap[ped]"—not only in places where the vertical sovereignty of the state is redistributed across or contested by the "horizontal, partial sovereignties" of corporations, criminal organizations, and religious, nationalist, or otherwise communal groups, but also in places, such as Cyprus, where courts with supranational jurisdiction supplant or supplement state courts (Comaroff and Comaroff 2006, 33, 40).

For critics of judicialization, one of its inherent dangers is the reduction of conceptions of harm, responsibility, and entitlement to the bodies and claims of individual litigants, thus obscuring structural harms, collective responsibilities, and social reciprocities that would, in theory, be properly and more effectively addressed in the field of politics. Thus, for the Comaroffs, judicialization marks a "displacement" into the juridical domain of conflicts that, in other times or places, would properly be pursued and mediated "in parliaments, by means of street protests, mass demonstrations, and media campaigns, through labor strikes, boycotts, blockades, and other instruments of assertion" (Comaroff and Comaroff 2006, 3, 26). Right-to-know litigation in Cyprus invites a reconsideration of such idealization of politics as the proper field of justice. This litigation may well signal a trend toward the judicialization of politics; after decades of ineffectual public protests, the demands for knowledge brought to court by relatives of the missing in Cyprus, articulated in terms of human rights and harms, do indeed risk the occlusion of other victims of the conflicts, and other forms of harm besides the loss of a relative. Yet the excess suffering, longing, and suspicion expressed by right-to-know litigation—conditioned by the impossibility of tying responsibility to forensic evidence in court—convey an understanding among relatives that politics in Cyprus remain both determinant of justice and mired in secrecy.[7]

What You Know and What You Don't Know

The CMP's mission to promote healing and closure while refraining from politics corresponds to an understanding of mourning as an individual psychological process. When a missing person's remains are identified, a psychologist from the relatives' presumptive ethnonational community is dispatched to counsel them and prepare them for a viewing of the remains. Viewings take place at the CMP's anthropological laboratory, where relatives can see the bones and artifacts, meet the scientists who have worked on their case, and ask questions. This event is the culmination of a lengthy process of investigation, during which relatives have little if any direct communication with the scientists working on their case. Their first contact is usually the viewing, where scientists can convey what they know—or some of what they know—and relatives can come to reframe or translate in forensic terms their grasp of what happened to their missing person. Although these viewings are designed to yield closure, they sometimes yield conflict instead. A., an anthropologist, told me that interacting with relatives was sometimes difficult, because they often had questions that were "not scientific" in nature, or that scientists could not answer for other reasons. "Some family members are okay," she said. "Some are angry; some cry; others don't; some accept the death, others don't. The atmosphere can get tense when they're suspicious of us. You just have to stay calm and keep explaining what you know and what you don't know."

I saw these dynamics of suspicion and transparency between relatives and scientists play out in one of the viewings I attended at the lab. Three missing people had been identified: two teenaged brothers and their uncle, killed during a raid on their village in August 1974. At the viewing, the remains of the three people, mostly small bones and fragments, were arrayed as far as possible in the shape of bodies on three separate tables. Another table held the artifacts associated with the individuals, in clear plastic bags: some scraps of clothing, buttons, shoelaces, a cigarette case. Three small wooden boxes, like coffins, were stacked in another corner of the room; when the viewing was over, the remains would be wrapped and placed in these boxes, then transferred to the CMP office in south Nicosia to await the funerals a few weeks later. Next to the boxes, along the back wall of the room, a sort of family shrine had been assembled, with framed photographs of the three victims, a lit oil candle, an incense burner that would be lit when the family entered the room, and icons of Mary and Jesus. K., one of the anthropologists, told me she always felt strange setting up these shrines, lighting the candles, putting the photographs of the victims in the frames, bringing the boxes with remains into the room: "There's nothing scientific about it! It's much too personal. It makes the viewing feel more like a funeral." She thought it was inappropriate for her to be involved so intimately in the family's grief. But the CMP psychologist, who had worked with the relatives as the case unfolded and arrived at the viewing before them that morning, insisted it was important for the family to begin the process of mourning when they first encountered the bones: "The symbolism matters," she said.

Sixteen members of three generations of the victims' family attended the viewing, including the widow of the adult man, who was also the aunt of the two young brothers. The chief investigator on the case introduced himself and the scientists who had worked on the case, and explained the purpose of the viewing to the family. "Our mission is purely humanitarian," he said.

"We don't do political work or pursue criminal justice. The role of the forensic teams is very limited; their sole purpose is to find the remains of the missing and determine their identity. We do not investigate the manner of death or attribute responsibility. The purpose of our meeting this morning is for the scientists to explain the investigation, to present their findings, and to answer any questions you have."

The presentation of archaeological findings began with witness information that had led the team to a site near the victims' village, which they had excavated over a period of several months. The team leader gave a PowerPoint presentation with satellite maps pinpointing the grave site and a series of photographs of the excavation itself. She described the progress of the dig, as they had located layers of irregular soil and bone fragments and then continued to the bedrock level to ensure they had found everything. The bones and bone fragments were small and very dispersed, she explained; the archaeologists had had to dig slowly and carefully, mostly with hand tools rather than machines, so as not to miss anything. They had ultimately found the bones of at least ten individuals, of whom three were the relatives of the people in the room.

During the presentation, one of the relatives asked the team leader a series of questions about the burial. Could they tell if the soil had come from somewhere else? Could they tell if all the bones had been buried there at the same time? Did they know how many people were buried there? Did the presence of so few bones mean that all the people murdered that day in August 1974 were not killed at that site? The team leader was circumspect in her responses. She replied that they could not know for sure, but the most likely scenario was that all the villagers had been killed and buried at this site at the same time, and then at some later time — "No, we can't tell when" — the bodies had been moved elsewhere, and all that was left were these small bones and fragments. No, they couldn't test the soil to date the different types more precisely; tests could be done on the soil to determine this, but the CMP did not conduct those tests. Later, the archaeologist told me she suspected this relative had been trying to elicit scientific evidence that he could use to bring a court case. "I could tell he was skeptical," she said, so she had tried to be very careful in explaining what the team could and could not determine about the grave on the basis of their excavation. "The most difficult part is when there's nothing else to say," she told me, "but the family just keeps asking for more."

After the presentation of archaeological findings, K., a physical anthropologist who had worked on the case, presented her findings. She explained the basic process of establishing age and sex, the analysis of bone pathologies, and the hard work of associating fragments. This family's missing relatives were three of ten people buried at this site whose identity had been confirmed by DNA analysis; there could be other people represented by the remains, she said, who could not be identified by DNA. A geneticist from the Cyprus Institute of Neurology and Genetics explained that, after a preliminary identification of the remains had been made through anthropological analysis, bone samples had been sent to the genetics team for blind confirmation using DNA samples provided by family members. He told the family, "The results were double-checked. It is 100 percent certain that these bones are yours." The widow of the adult victim began to weep, and then others, as well.

The chief investigator then explained the next steps to the family. After the viewing, the remains would be taken from the lab to his office, where he would issue documents confirming the deaths of the victims that the relatives could take to the municipality to acquire death certificates and make funeral arrangements. On the day of the funeral, if they wished, soldiers would escort the coffins to the church. At that time, they would be given a file on their relatives with information about the investigation, two summary reports with the archaeological and anthropological findings, a photograph of the gravesite, and a photograph of each person's bones. The skeptical relative asked if the reports would show cause of death, and mumbled something I could not follow when the investigator said no.

After the presentation of findings, the family was invited to the next room to see the bones. They milled around, looking at the arrays on the tables. The widow continued to cry, comforted by others. Another relative, an elderly man, picked up one of the finger bones, stroked it, compared it with his own, put it back on the table. He counted the bones on each table, shaking his head as if in disbelief. The widow stood in front of her husband's bones, repeating, "We sent them as men, and they came back in pieces!" Then, gesturing to the array in front of her, "Those aren't his bones!" I heard her words as a refusal, although it is ambiguous what exactly she meant when she disclaimed her husband's bones—or, too, why exactly the elderly man shook his head as he counted them. An archaeologist I met in the field, who had attended a number of viewings, told me that family members "always ask for skulls," which were found in only about 10 percent of cases. Skulls, he explained, gave relatives more of a "sense of a person" than other bones; they felt they could see their person by looking at the underlying structure of the face. In the viewing I attended that morning, the relatives, faced with nothing but fragments, did not accede so easily to recognition of the remains. The parallel scientization and sacralization of bones did not suffice to connect the people their relatives remembered to the remains they saw, thirty-eight years later.

Indeed, what I have seen and heard of encounters between forensic scientists and relatives of the missing suggests that closure remains elusive for many. Some relatives did seem relieved to receive the bones of their loved ones and to go through the process of burying and mourning them. T., an archaeologist on a field excavation where I worked, told me that a viewing would go badly only if the forensic team gave a bad presentation. He described his presentation of archaeological findings in a difficult case where they had found only a few bones. "I spent a long time talking to the family," he said. "I showed them pictures; I told them all about the methods our team used. We were six or eight people, sifting and wet-sieving, and we looked for months, and this was what we found. The family just kept saying, 'Thank you, thank you'—they were very grateful, not suspicious at all." Relatives in other cases, however, had greater difficulty recognizing and claiming the bones. The case files contain many stories like this. They include complaints to the CMP written by relatives after a viewing, accusing the scientists of hiding evidence—often, signs of gunshot or knife wounds—or of making an erroneous identification. However familiar the forensic images of bones might have been to Cypriots, after almost ten years of publicity surrounding the CMP, relatives of the missing did not recognize the remains in these cases. They doubted the identification of their person and suspected the scientists of incompetence or fraud.

I discussed this disparity in the persuasiveness of forensic evidence with V., an anthropologist at the lab who had dealt extensively with relatives. "There are the angry ones, the cynical ones who think we're withholding information from them," he explained. "There are the upset ones, who ask questions we can't answer. There are the ones who are over it, who are going through the process but came to terms with the death long ago. Then there are the ones who take a small piece of information and run wild, speculating a whole chain of events and not really listening to us—like the fact that the clavicle was shattered in a certain way, and they come up with the idea that the person must have been shot through the neck, even though there's no indication of a gunshot wound." He pointed out that, unlike forensic investigations in other postconflict areas, like Rwanda, the CMP investigations were designed to return as much of the missing person's remains as possible to the families for proper burial. This set up a strange encounter between families and scientists, he said, where remains—sometimes very scant—were treated as bodies, and their return to relatives became an emotional and symbolic event.

The first few times he had met with families at viewings, V. told me, he had gotten upset. "It was very intense," he said. "But now, I understand the process. I know what has to happen, and I don't feel anything. I had to learn to anticipate the reactions of family members and not allow them to push me into saying things they want me to say. It's very personal—it's not like giving forensic testimony in court." In his training, he had studied osteology alongside forensic anthropology, including a course in legal frameworks. He had learned in that course how to give precise evidence without exceeding the bounds of what he actually knew from his own analysis. "With forensic testimony," he said, "the judge makes a finding and then puts the case away; he doesn't think about the testimony of the anthropologist after that. But what you say to families, you know they're going to take it and carry it with them for the rest of their lives. This will be the information they tell themselves over and over again, whenever they think about the person who died, and that's a heavy burden for us. I feel it very much."

We All Have Darkness in Our Hearts

Mistrust reverberated in such failures, or refusals, by relatives to recognize the remains of their missing persons, expressing deeply embedded disposi- tions of suspicion among these victims of political violence. But this mistrust may also speak of what remained unspoken in encounters between relatives and scientists: namely, the relatives' own experience of violence, which was not always limited to victimhood.[8] The same people who assembled for a viewing of bones might themselves be keeping secrets about what they saw years ago, or what they did. M., an archaeologist, raised this issue in telling me about a difficult excavation in north Nicosia on which she had worked a few years earlier. The case involved only one individual, buried in 1974 near an olive tree in the backyard of a house at the edge of the buffer zone. Inves- tigators had gathered conflicting information from witnesses, who identified the victim as either Turkish Cypriot or Greek Cypriot. The house belonged to an elderly couple who lived there with their daughter. According to M., they were a wealthy family and had lived in the house since the early 1960s. "They were the least cooperative people I've ever dealt with," she said. "When we're excavating in a village or a town, people in the neighborhood come by all the time to watch, and they tell us how they admire the work we're doing. They compete to bring us things—water, snacks, coffee." In this case, how- ever, the old couple resisted. They had grudgingly given permission to the CMP to excavate the lot next door, which they also owned, but the team had not found any remains there. A witness had pointed out the olive tree in the backyard of their house, but the old couple did not want the CMP to excavate there. "They said they didn't want their yard ruined," M. said. "They didn't like us being there—they didn't let us into the house at all. People usually welcome us in. We're allowed to use their bathrooms and kitchens, and they do it gladly! Not in this case." Thinking the old woman might feel accused by the CMP, M. told me, the members of the team repeatedly assured her that she was doing a good thing by letting them do their work—that it was an honor for her, that she was not in any trouble. But she kept saying it was impossible that someone was buried there. "She was just ashamed," M. said. "They must have been there when the body was buried, since they lived there at the time. They paved the driveway right over the grave."

In the end, the team found remains quickly and were able to excavate an entire body belonging to an elderly man. Several of his bones were sampled for DNA testing, but no matching relatives were found in the data bank. His remains were never identified and ended up being stored in the lab annex.

"The information is out there," an investigator told me. "We haven't gotten very far in the last forty years, but it's not because no one knows anything. People know things. Knowledge is everywhere. But there there's no political will to bring it out." Yet the sort of resistance to opening up the graves of the missing that M. had encountered in the old couple was dynamic, rather than fixed. The same investigator told me that the relatives he worked with had often been holding on to their pain for so long that they had become "hardened," an existential state that sometimes entailed extreme political views—virulence against people from "the other side" and resistance to reconciliation. At the moment when their missing relative was found, however, and they were preparing to bury the person at last, they would sometimes "soften," he said, and "want to connect with 'the other' on a basic human level." They would become willing to acknowledge the violence done to the other side, and talk about what they knew. At moments like that, relatives had shared information with the investigator about possible locations of a burial site in their village, or, even if they said they did not know anything, they suggested the names of people who might. "Maybe for them it's a catharsis," he suggested. "They've been living for so long with what they did that it's a relief to say it. We talk to all kinds of people—killers, rapists, fascists, Greek Cypriots and Turkish Cypriots. I try to find the cracks in them and see some light shine through. We're all killers—we all have darkness in our hearts, and we're all capable of these things, under the right circumstances."

The diffuse responsibility for the violence of the past indicated to me by this investigator is obscured—must be obscured—by the narrative framing of healing and closure promoted by the CMP, and by the sacralization of bones that fortify that narrative symbolically. The recovery and reburial of missing persons has been displaced in Cyprus from the political register of collective responsibility, public accounting, and criminal justice, and entrenched instead in the psychological-therapeutic register of mourning and healing within the family. Public accounting and private mourning are not intrinsically incompatible processes; indeed, they might reinforce and supplement each other. It is possible, too, to oppose the priority placed by the CMP on mourning over accounting without assuming that a public accounting process—such as a truth and reconciliation commission (TRC)—would necessarily promote recovery and reunification in Cyprus. Many TRCs have been criticized for failing to yield peace, justice, and healing, especially in cases where amnesty has been transacted for testimony, as in postapartheid South Africa (see Mendeloff 2009; Payne 2008; Scheper-Hughes 2007). If TRCs foreground truth, it comes in the form of individual narratives; victims, perpetrators, and witnesses tell their stories and, in theory, are relieved of pain and guilt in the process. The investigations of the CMP might seem to take the opposite course, obstructing such narratives and thus prioritizing mourning over truth. Yet the truth production administered by TRCs entails its own distinctive forms of silence. As H. said to me, "TRCs are about individuals, not about structures. They don't touch the structures. They aren't about truth, so they aren't about justice. They're a joke." By "structures," he explained, he meant the planning and coordination of violence on a large scale, and the concealment of evidence afterward—processes that he saw occurring "dialectically" on the local level, the state level, and the international level. The TRC model of reckoning with violence indeed constitutes a different approach from the closure model of the CMP, but, as H. indicated, the distinction between these models does not turn on revealing versus concealing truth; rather, it turns on the different parameters these models place on truth, and the different possibilities for mourning they open up.

Conclusion

When I visited Cyprus in April 2014, more than a year had passed since the republic had entered the company of Eurozone states in crisis. In March 2013, banks had closed, foreign capital had withdrawn, corruption scandals had erupted, and parliament had been presented the forced choice of a European bailout (known as "the haircut"). A new era of austerity began, in which the gift of membership in the European Union—from which the north had largely been excluded, in practice if not in policy—turned out to be poisonous. Austerity had come to the north several years earlier, when Turkey imposed tax increases and massive cuts in public sector salaries. After the crisis of 2013, the south appeared to be swiftly catching up, transforming from the comparatively developed and prosperous side of the island into a site of economic stagnation, political volatility, and dependency on foreign patrons.

During my visit, I spoke with B., a Cypriot friend who worked in a real estate company in Nicosia that was on the verge of bankruptcy. She told me that "all the trouble" had begun with the former president of the Bank of Cyprus. He had long been aware of the coming debt crisis, B. said, but he made no public announcements: "It was election season and it wouldn't have served anyone's interests to disclose this information." The EU was offering emergency liquidity aid at the time, but the bank president took no action and failed to warn depositors. "The politicians knew what was coming," B. told me, "and people connected to the high-ups at the bank. They were able to get their money out. But the poor people knew nothing, and they lost all their savings in the end." Charges of fraud and corruption were brought against the bank president by the government when the crisis hit, but when the new administration took power a few months later, he was granted immunity, given 300,000 euros, and allowed to leave the country. "The big shots here want him out of the way, since he knows all their secrets," B. said. "What do you expect? This is Cyprus. We had an invasion here, and no one paid! We had a coup and no one paid!"

It was a short step for B. to take from the debt crisis of 2013 to the coup and invasion, thirty-nine years earlier. This step was facilitated by a deceptively straightforward conception of responsibility, holding that murderers and bank presidents alike should pay for their crimes—a reckoning of criminal responsibility in which secrecy has played an integral role over the long historical *durée*. The chronic persistence of such crimes without redress has given rise to a seemingly boundless sense of responsibility, at least in my friend's accounting, which extended well beyond individual persons to corporations, to states, to global systems of security and capitalism. Neoliberal governance by the Troika in the era of austerity mixed with the Cold War–era geopolitics of nationalist conflict and division. The one site where responsibility was not reckoned here was in the self.

In this chapter, I have tried to map the coordinates of this roving imagination of responsibility in Cyprus, focusing on its articulation around the issue of missing persons. I have not examined the discourses and techniques of personal responsibility associated with neoliberal governance, often glossed as responsibilization. Instead, I have explored the silences and desires circulating around responsibility in the juridical and forensic domains, which operate within a neoliberal political economy in Cyprus but with distinct and perhaps incommensurable conceptions of responsibility. The CMP's mandate not to attribute criminal responsibility to individual or state actors has certainly helped to foster suspicions among relatives of the missing that the CMP is hiding evidence and participating in state secrecy. By the same token, however, the desire to know what the CMP cannot disclose has fueled a certain fixation on criminal responsibility as the problem to solve. This way of envisioning the history of violence in Cyprus may impede any reckoning with the collective responsibility Cypriots bear for the conflict, and for the persistence of the division today.

Through its mandate to conduct politically neutral, purely humanitarian investigations, the CMP projects, against an opaque screen, a particular relationship between the present and the past, and between subjects and the state. The opacity of that screen describes the many obverse facets of transparency—secrecy, privacy, confidentiality, censorship, silence, ambiguity, ghostliness, classified status—confronted by Cypriot scientists and others seeking to know what happened in the past. Studies on audit culture are relevant to forensic knowledge production by the CMP, especially studies of bureaucratic self-scrutiny and self-documentation by which states prove their good governance to international auditors and media publics (Strathern 2000a). That such proof is undertaken by states under suspicion attests to an ideological supposition of a "double reality," a "duplicity" in the very operations of government, as Nelson (2009, 27) points out, connecting anticorruption campaigns to state terror through the ideology of transparency. Yet audit circumscribes knowledge too radically to account adequately for the work of the CMP. The proliferation of self-descriptive documentation and quantifying accounting practices associated with audit may well conceal a range of informal practices, and foreclose important questions about the unintended functions of institutions—thus producing certain forms of opacity or secrecy—but these processes nevertheless apprehend knowledge production as the analysis of institutional procedures linking explicit aspirations to measurable outcomes. While the rhetoric of the CMP may be reduced to proceduralism, in this sense, its knowledge production cannot be, as attested by the indeterminacy of recognition in encounters with forensic evidence by relatives of missing persons. Nor are the publics imagined and addressed by the CMP coterminous with the political constituencies or international patrons of audit—not least because these publics, in Cyprus, include the dead, those spectral subjects of historical violence.

I have therefore worked with a different notion of transparency, here, to grasp the dynamics of knowledge production about the missing in Cyprus— an aspirational orientation to responsibility, materialized in knowledge about the past that presumes duplicity on the part of the state but exceeds the responsibility of whichever governments happen to be in power in Cyprus at any given moment. Cypriots who demand transparency from their governments recognize knowledge in many nonveridical forms yielded by violence and terror—forms of knowledge such as haunting, rumor, and public secrecy, which confront and subvert the stabilization of the past by veridical knowledge in the present (see Navaro-Yashin 2012; Sant Cassia 2005). Attempts to challenge the secrecy in which recent Cypriot history is embedded must accommodate the synergetic dynamic of secrecy and transparency: the ways in which some knowledge is rendered visible while other knowledge is left or kept unseen. If secrecy thus expresses power, it may also denude and erode it—and it is at the intersection of these processes that the CMP stands in its arbitration of responsibility.

ACKNOWLEDGMENTS

I am very grateful to the members of the Committee on Missing Persons in Cyprus and their assistants, who facilitated my research on field excavations and at the anthropological laboratory in 2011–12. I am especially indebted to the archaeologists and anthropologists on the forensic teams of the CMP, who shared their thoughts and experiences with me and tolerated my presence in the midst of their work. Many thanks go to Susanna Trnka and Catherine Trundle, for inviting me to join in the workshop "Rethinking Responsibility" and seeing this project through to publication with such imagination and perspicacity, as well as to the other workshop participants for their thoughtful questions and comments. Finally, for their close attention and valuable feedback on some of the material in this chapter, I am grateful to João Biehl, Peter Locke, Michael Fischer, and my comrades in the 2013–14 Ethnography and Theory working group convened by Didier Fassin at the Institute for Advanced Studies in Princeton. My research in Cyprus in 2011–12 was supported by a Stanley J. Seeger Hellenic Studies Sabbatical Research Grant. Writing was made possible by a Richard Stockton Bicentennial Preceptorship at Princeton University and a membership at the Institute for Advanced Studies, Princeton.

1. This line of division (known by some and not others as the border) first marked the separation of Greek-Cypriot and Turkish-Cypriot municipal authorities in Nicosia in 1958. It was designated as a UN cease-fire line following devastating episodes of civil and paramilitary violence in 1963 and became the permanent de facto partition line after the invasion in 1974.

2. See Dorfman (2006), Gordon (1997), and Gandsman (2009) on the Mothers and Grandmothers of the Plaza de Mayo. See Arsenijević (2011a) on the global omnipresence of the forensic scene.

3. Renshaw (2011, 38) notes that, although relatives of the dead attended and actively participated in the exhumations in Spain, they were largely excluded from the anthropological analysis conducted in forensic labs, as in Cyprus.

4. Names and identifying features of my interlocutors in Cyprus have been changed to preserve their anonymity.

5. See the European Parliament's nonbinding Written Declaration 369 on the Work of the Committee on Missing Persons in Cyprus, adopted June 9, 2011. See also the International Convention for the Protection of All Persons from Enforced Disappearance (CPED), which was opened for signature by the UN in 2007 and entered into force in 2010. CPED article 24(2) states, "Each victim has the right to know the truth regarding the circumstances of the enforced disappearance, the progress and results of the investigation and the fate of the disappeared person. Each State Party shall take appropriate measures in this regard." Kyriakou (2012a, 87; 2012b, 35) notes the range of the definition of victim, here, "as not only the person who is subjected to enforced disappearance, but also any other individual that has suffered harm as the direct result of an enforced disappearance," including, but "not necessarily," relatives.

6. See Kyriakou (2011) for a detailed critical reading of these decisions.

7. In this, I have in mind the argument about the indeterminacies of judicialization developed by Biehl and Petryna (2011). Noting the overdetermination of subjects engaged in right-to-health litigation in Brazil by the evidentiary and identitarian coordinates of the judicial system, they nevertheless see "open[ing] up," in the intersections of pharmaceutical markets and judicial processes, "new spaces of ethical problematization, desire, and political belonging" (381).

8. See Bryant (2006, 2010) on the everyday complicity of Cypriot civilians with acts of violence in the 1960s–70s.

SEVEN. Justice and Its Doubles: *Producing Postwar Responsibilities in Sierra Leone*

ROSALIND SHAW

In 2002, at the end of a devastating civil war, Sierra Leone became a laboratory for transitional justice. For the first time, a truth and reconciliation commission (TRC) and an international criminal court (the Special Court for Sierra Leone) would produce their different kinds of responsibility—one primarily historical, the other criminal—side by side. Before this, many advocates of truth commissions had regarded TRCs and criminal trials as incompatible (Rotberg and Thompson 2000). For the international legal specialists who disagreed with them, the concurrent operation of Sierra Leone's TRC and Special Court represented an opportunity. By depicting this situation as an experiment, they lent scientific authority to their claim that truth seeking and trials produce compatible, not competing, responsibilities (e.g., Schabas 2003). This experiment was not, then, the outcome of experimental design, but of a struggle among different interests in a changing international climate.

Sierra Leone, recast as a laboratory, would authorize a view of trials and TRCs as not only compatible, but also ranked. The experiment was located within an expanding process of judicialization, manifest in the proliferation of international criminal trials after the Cold War, in which the norms of criminal justice reconfigured international relations (see, e.g., Hazan 2010;

Oomen 2005). In a judicializing global reality, responsibility for mass violence was redistributed through a focus on criminal individuals, within which historical and institutional explanations are subsumed (Clarke 2010, 2011; Kelsall 2013). This process has engendered new moralities, movements, and policies: "the rule of law," a "culture of human rights," the "fight against impunity," "no peace without justice."

If responsibilization denotes a mode of neoliberal governance through which individuals accept responsibilities previously assumed by the state, then judicialization forms its counterpart as a mode of global governance (Clarke 2009; Kelsall 2013). With its emphasis on individualized responsibility and its de-emphasis on the state, it upholds, as Kamari Clarke argues, "particular knowledge fields within which liberalist capitalism circulates" (2010, 645). These knowledge fields are especially visible in models of international peace building for the Global South. They underwent a shift, after the Cold War, from a "politics of pardon" in which amnesties were exchanged for peace to a judicialized "politics of punishment" (Hazan 2010) in which the production of individual criminal responsibility became a requirement for peace. Sierra Leone's transitional justice experiment, arising at a watershed moment, was made to produce the new knowledge on which this "politics of punishment" is based.

As this volume's editors observe, responsibilizing processes are always enmeshed with competing forms of responsibility. In this chapter, I explore how Sierra Leone's justice experiment entangled responsibilities in the TRC and Special Court, not only with each other, but also with a process of national "lawfare" (Anders 2014) and the (re)integration of ex-combatants.[1] These entanglements decoupled the responsibility-generating machinery of the Special Court and TRC from the model of liberal peace building on which they were based. But finally, these entanglements were erased through the production of experimental results to create a universal—and internationally transportable—fact. Afterward, legal elites would affirm, with David Crane, first chief prosecutor of the Special Court, that "the Sierra Leone model is the right model. A plus B equals C. Truth plus justice equals sustainable peace" (Nichols 2005).

Laboratory Life in Sierra Leone

By defining an African nation as a laboratory, international legal specialists evoked a history of scientific colonialism. Colonial Africa was recurrently described as "a magnificent natural laboratory" (Tilley 2011, 2) for the production of temporalizing projects of state building that were envisaged as opening a civilizing trajectory of progress. After independence, programs of nation building through international development in Africa—funded as part of Cold War strategies of bipolar allegiance (e.g., Grubbs 2010)—reproduced the colonial logic of experiments, this time in the service of a promised modernizing convergence with the West (Ferguson 2006). But when this promise evaporated with the International Monetary Fund's austerity measures in the 1980s, and when the collapse of the Soviet Union reduced Africa's strategic importance for the United States and western Europe, the development model crumbled (Ferguson 2006).

Yet a new temporalizing project arose. When, at the end of the Cold War, repressive regimes fell in Latin America, eastern Europe, and South Africa, many states endeavored to create a new beginning that would establish a democratic era by dealing with the past. These successor states sought to produce accountability for violent state abuses through trials, truth commissions, the purging of officials, reparations, and official apologies. Through the interactions of lawyers, legal specialists, human rights activists, policy makers, political scientists, and others, the field of transitional justice emerged (Arthur 2009). When several armed conflicts (including Sierra Leone's) and two genocides (in Srebrenica and Rwanda) then arose from the shifting post–Cold War terrain, the model of transitional justice was extended from postrepression to postconflict states (Shaw and Waldorf 2010). By 1999, when Sierra Leone's Lomé peace talks began, transitional justice was becoming a normalized response to armed conflict (Teitel 2003).

Grounded in political liberalism, transitional justice offers a teleology of redemption through an idiom of accountancy. It claims, as Pierre Hazan writes, "that mass crimes constitute a blood debt that one part of society owes another. This blood debt must be paid to break the cycle of vengeance and violence. The debt, by the act of recognition it creates, builds a bridge between the past and the future. It constitutes this time of transition that, through recognition, leads to the establishment of a state of law, democracy, and, in the end, the guarantee of nonrepetition. . . . The damages of history are thus collectable" (2010, 53–54).

Transitional justice creates this recognition by mobilizing different kinds of responsibility. Through truth seeking, truth commissions establish a primarily historical and institutional responsibility, which they translate into accountability by publicizing a historical account of violations. Criminal prosecutions instead produce individual legal responsibility, which they convert into accountability by enacting legal retribution. Through such means, they promise, the debts of the past will be settled.

As transitional justice underwent a shift of focus from postrepression to postconflict states, the responsibilities it produced shifted too. During the 1990s, Archbishop Desmond Tutu successfully promoted South Africa's TRC as a therapeutic mechanism that would heal the wounds of both individual and nation through a cathartic revealing, enabling national reconciliation through "restorative justice" (Wilson 2001). But as the new millennium approached, Tutu's therapeutic model was eclipsed (although never entirely displaced) by the growing dominance of criminal justice norms. Instead of the citizen's therapeutic responsibility to reveal through truth telling, the norms of the Nuremberg tribunals, in which a small number of individuals were held legally responsible for the abuses of others through the concept of "command responsibility," became the gold standard (Clarke 2009; Kelsall 2013). This judicializing of transitional justice changed the currency in which history's debts could be collected.

In the Sierra Leone experiment, then, responsibilities did not compete as equals. This experiment, as I describe in the next section, privileged one kind of responsibility over others and underwrote its value through the imprimatur of science.

The Birth of an Experiment

Sierra Leone's civil war, which cannot be adequately described here (see Abdullah 2004; Keen 2005; Richards 1996), arose from the convergence of economic crisis, generational conflict, and opposition to the long kleptocratic rule of the All People's Congress (APC) regime from 1968 to 1992. Although it had ethnic dimensions, it was not an ethnic conflict. It was rooted in multiple layers of violence, including political violence (Fornah 2003; Reno 1995), the structural violence of social and generational exclusions (Peters 2011; Richards 1996), and a history of violent forms of extraction that reach back to British colonial rule and the Atlantic slave trade (Abdullah 1992; Ijagbemi 1968; Shaw 2002). And it was mobilized through transnational networks connecting to Liberia, Libya, Lebanon, Israel, and beyond (Abdullah 2004; Keen 2005).

In the 1980s, a group of young men, alienated by deepening exclusions and blocked opportunities under the APC, received training in Libya and support from Charles Taylor in Liberia. They formed the Revolutionary United Front

(RUF), adopting a revolutionary ideology but attacking civilian communities when they entered Sierra Leone from Liberia in 1991. When the Sierra Leone Armed Forces failed to halt the RUF (and sometimes collaborated with them), communities in the Mende-speaking south and east formed civil defense committees that armed their young men. In 1996, politician Sam Hinga Norman organized these young men, who took on the identity and ritual practices of Mende hunters (*kamajoisia*, anglicized as Kamajors), into a progovernment militia. In 1998, Norman became deputy minister for defense; he renamed the Kamajors the Civil Defense Forces (CDF) and expanded them to form a national force (Hoffman 2011).

Under President Kabbah, the government armed the Kamajors/CDF and favored them over the national army. Angered, junior officers from the Sierra Leone Armed Forces ousted Kabbah in a 1997 coup, established themselves as the Armed Forces Ruling Council (AFRC) junta, and invited the RUF into Freetown to join them. Meanwhile, an AFRC splinter group, the West Side Boys, formed outside Freetown in early 1998. After nine months of occupation, the AFRC and RUF were driven out of the capital city in February 1998 by Nigerian troops from the regional Cease-Fire Monitoring Group of the Economic Community of West African States. In retaliation, the ex-AFRC, together with the RUF, launched their devastating Operation No Living Thing in the rural provinces, and brought it to Freetown in January 1999, until Cease-Fire Monitoring Group troops again expelled them. Following this January 1999 invasion, the UN, United States, United Kingdom, and several West African leaders pressured President Kabbah to negotiate with the RUF (Keen 2005, 250; Rashid 2000).

Three months after the invasion, peace talks began in Lomé, Togo. But by then, the norms of criminal justice were reshaping the conditions of possibility for peace negotiations. The question of blanket amnesty, which facilitated peace agreements but foreclosed the establishment of individual legal responsibility, was pivotal. It polarized different interests, with war-weary Sierra Leoneans on one side, international human rights and justice advocates on the other, and national civil and political leaders in the middle. The Sierra Leonean public was open to a blanket amnesty as a condition of peace. They were desperate to end the war, and viewed the state, in any case, as sharing culpability with the RUF and AFRC. As Priscilla Hayner writes, "The public . . . believed that the war was the product of decades of bad governance, which reduced hatred of the rebels. The public support of forgiveness for the rebels unexpectedly strengthened in the face of continued human rights abuses, which the government could not stop or control. Statements like 'Give them what they want as long as they agree to stop killing us' were common at the grassroots level" (2007, 7).

Not all Sierra Leoneans felt this way. Political leaders, traditional leaders, and civil society actors in a consultative conference in April 1999 supported amnesty, but within a frame of historical accountability. They proposed that those who had committed serious human rights violations should go before a national TRC. A coalition of Sierra Leonean and international human rights advocates, meanwhile, opposed amnesty altogether, arguing for a truth, justice, and reconciliation commission that would "recommend judicial prosecutions for some of the worst perpetrators" (Article 19 and Forum of Conscience 2000).

When the Lomé peace talks began, negotiators agreed on a blanket amnesty. This had formed an uncontroversial part of a previous agreement, the 1996 Abidjan Accord (Hayner 2007). Besides, the government's military weakness gave its representatives little choice in the matter. But this was not 1996: international criticism was immediate (Amnesty International 1999; Takirambudde and Weschler 1999). The UN, which a few months earlier had encouraged President Kabbah to negotiate with the RUF, now sent an internal cable to all its representatives, telling them that the UN could not endorse amnesty for genocide, war crimes, and crimes against humanity. When the Lomé Peace Agreement, with its general amnesty, was signed shortly afterward in July 1999, UN Special Envoy Francis Okelo appended a handwritten disclaimer. But while the UN and human rights actors condemned the blanket amnesty, the Sierra Leonean public was far more offended by a power-sharing arrangement that gave RUF and AFRC leaders lucrative ministerial posts, including the vice presidency (Hayner 2007, 22; Rashid 2000, 32). Forgiving terrible abuses may have been an acceptable price to pay for peace, but rewarding those abuses with political power and mineral resources was not.

The Lomé Agreement also established Sierra Leone's TRC. For international human rights organizations, this was inadequate: a TRC, they stated, would be valid only as an adjunct to justice, which they equated with criminal trials. "It is important," stated Human Rights Watch, "that such a body emphasize justice as well as reconciliation" (Takirambudde and Weschler 1999, 1). Amnesty International claimed, similarly, that "there can be no true reconciliation if the truth about the gross human rights abuses which have occurred in Sierra Leone is not established and those responsible held accountable" (1999, 2).

But the Lomé Agreement did not, in any case, end the conflict. When the UN was slow to deploy its new United Nations Assistance Mission in Sierra

Leone (UNAMSIL) peacekeepers, the RUF, suspecting a lack of international commitment to Lomé, were reluctant to disarm (Hayner 2007, 24). In May 2000, the RUF took five hundred UN peacekeepers hostage in the provinces, while RUF leader Foday Sankoh's security guards fired on a crowd of protestors in Freetown. Foday Sankoh was promptly arrested, and a few months later President Kabbah asked the UN for a war crimes court to prosecute the RUF and AFRC. The UN, eager to undo the Lomé Agreement's blanket amnesty, responded by establishing the Special Court for Sierra Leone. This would prosecute not just the RUF and AFRC, as Kabbah had wished, but those from all combatant groups—including the Sierra Leone Armed Forces and the progovernment CDF militia—who bore "the greatest responsibility" for war crimes and crimes against humanity. But the TRC was kept in place. So began the Sierra Leone justice experiment.

There is more to say, however, about Kabbah's request for a war crimes court. Since 1998, the Kabbah government had used the law as a vehicle for political attack. The Special Court—and therefore the justice experiment—"has been presented," writes Gerhard Anders, "as standing . . . outside the national political landscape, but in fact it was the product of a violent conflict in which the RUF, and later the AFRC/West Side Boys were marginalized and ceased to play a decisive role in national politics" (2014, 539). In a series of human rights violations enacted through the national justice system, the government imposed a state of emergency and carried out hundreds of arrests and detentions without trial between 1998 and 2003. It also conducted treason trials, courts-martial, and, in 1998, the public execution of twenty-four combatants by firing squad on Goderich beach, near Freetown. The Sierra Leone experiment, then, arose from a landscape of "lawfare," "the resort to legal instruments, to the violence inherent in the law, to commit acts of political coercion, even erasure" (Comaroff and Comaroff 2006, 30). The responsibilities established by the TRC and Special Court would compete in a national political context in which individual legal responsibility could get you killed.

Reintegration and Responsibilities

First, however, I examine a different kind of postwar responsibility. Sierra Leone's justice laboratory was coterminous with the nation-state. It included ordinary rural and urban communities, in which people's lives were structured by preexisting practices of social morality that were also forms of responsibility. I now turn to some of these forms—obligations, entitlements, duties, dependencies, and reciprocities—through which ex-combatants and noncombatants renegotiated their postwar lives together.

Many combatants—probably most of them (Peters 2011; Richards et al. 2003)—did not go through Sierra Leone's national Disarmament, Demobilization, and Reintegration (DDR) program. Some had no firearm to hand in during the disarmament phase; others were left off the list compiled by their commanders; and others again wanted to avoid the stigmatizing status of ex-combatant. For those who did go through formal DDR, reintegration was treated as an individualizing process through which they would become self-reliant through skills training. Sierra Leone followed a standard security-based approach to DDR that Knight and Özerdem (2004) characterize as "guns, camps, and cash." Combatants handed over weapons, were cantoned in camps, and received photograph ID cards, six months of vocational skills training, tools, and a reintegration stipend (many of which failed to arrive) as part of their DDR package. Formal reintegration corresponded, in other words, to a loose process of responsibilization that gave ex-combatants little or no preparation for their reentry into civilian communities.

For the TRC, however, reintegration could be accomplished only by "truth telling," the narration of past acts of violence. "It was the view of the Commission," states the TRC Report, "that the acknowledgment of past wrongdoing could foster reintegration" (Truth and Reconciliation Commission, Sierra Leone 2004, vol. 3, ch. 7, para. 50). Only by doing so, according to the commission, could ex-combatants take responsibility, conceptualized in terms of the individual ownership of one's actions.

But ex-combatants usually faced a different set of expectations from the communities in which they sought to settle. "Ahmadu," an ex-AFRC combatant I met in 2003, had successfully met them. After DDR, he had settled as a stranger in a large Temne-speaking village I call Ma-pet, in Port Loko District, and worked on a construction project run by an international nongovernmental organization (NGO). A small man in his thirties, Ahmadu comes from Kambia District to the northeast, where his wife and three children still live. In 1998, he told me, he had been digging diamonds near the eastern town of Koidu when he fled into the bush with his friends to avoid attack by the AFRC. But at 4:30 AM, AFRC troops found and captured them: "They asked us, 'To join us or to cut [amputate] your hand, which one do you want?' We said, 'We will go with you.'" Ahmadu listed a succession of towns to which he was forced to travel over the next few months, carrying heavy head loads ("We carried their bundles, their wives' things") before his group was disarmed: "They called for a cease-fire, twentieth July, 1999. We moved from

Makeni to Kabala. Then UNAMSIL arrived in Kabala. The UN gave disarmament tags to all those who had disarmed."

Ahmadu's narrative had many silences. Absent, for example, was any mention of fighting. "Did the AFRC train you?" I asked. "No." "Did they give you a gun?" "No." Since bringing a weapon was the usual requirement for disarmament, it is unlikely that he would have been able to register for DDR without one. Like Ahmadu, many ex-combatants narrated brief accounts that emphasized their capture, their conscription, their forced labor, and eventually their escape or demobilization. Such ex-combatant narratives were formulaic. This does not mean that they were untrue: although many combatants joined voluntarily, thousands were indeed captured and conscripted. But Sierra Leone's civil war was a gray zone: many of those who were abducted and abused went on to commit abuses themselves. Then, during postwar reconstruction, local reintegration practices required a reinscription of clear boundaries. Ex-combatants who wished to settle needed to locate themselves as moral persons.

They did so through what I call narratives of subsumed agency, constructing a moral personhood affirming that their "hearts" (Temne, *ta-buth*) are not the "warm" (angry) hearts of fighters. They were not acting for themselves: their agency was subsumed by their commanders. These narratives draw upon local models of personhood, power, and agency, in which "big people's" (in this case, combatant leaders') power is manifest in their capacity for acting through the vehicle of subordinates (Ferme 2001)—whose actions, therefore, are not really their own. For the TRC, with its emphasis on individual responsibility through verbal acknowledgment, narratives of subsumed agency were abdications of responsibility.

Ex-combatants also assumed moral personhood through social forgetting. In Sierra Leone Krio and Temne, *reconciliation* becomes "cool/settled heart" (Krio, *kol at*; Temne, *ka-buth ke-thofel*). When the heart is cool, it is not warm or resentful. It does not cause one to think too much about painful memories. Most people expressed this in terms of forgetting: "I try to forget the war." By emphasizing his abduction and coercion to join the AFRC, Ahmadu affirmed that he was a moral person with a cool heart who represented no threat. To be responsible meant to forget the war, not to narrate its detailed memory.

After demobilization, Ahmadu learned masonry in a DDR skills-training program. In 2001 he found a job with an NGO that was building a school near Ma-pet and sought to settle in the village. "I met the people who own this town," he told me. "I told them, 'I am a stranger here. Now, [the NGO] has brought us here to work, to build houses. Please help me to find a place to sleep.' They said, 'Fine, we are glad.' They gave me the place." Here Ahmadu described the landlord-stranger relationship, which has a long ancestry in Sierra Leone. He maintained this relationship by giving a small amount of cash to his landlord out of every paycheck, and by providing labor when his landlord needed it.

"Now that I've got work," Ahmadu told me, "I'm satisfied. I want to forget. This work enables me to feed my wife and my children." His engagement in productive work formed a crucial basis for his integration in Ma-pet, not because it established him as the autonomous, self-reliant neoliberal individual valorized in DDR skills training, but because it confirmed that he was a useful person. It meant that he could support his family and participate in the reciprocal exchanges through which social personhood is built up. It meant, in other words, that he was responsible.

In Ma-pet, the "people who own the town"—the headman and senior men—did not ask Ahmadu about his wartime actions. "They told me the rules of the town," he told me. "No cursing, no stealing, no using your neighbor's woman. When anyone offends you, lodge a complaint—don't fight. That's it." His integration was based on his enactment of social morality, especially his humble acceptance of civilian authority: "He is not a scattered man," Ma-pet's headman told me. "He is so humble. First, he came to us and explained his situation. So after exploring this, we accepted him. Above all, we accepted him because of his good behavior." To be humble was to embody a contrast to the actions of combatants during the war. At the same time, Ahmadu's humility also meant deference to local authority structures and integration into preconflict hierarchies—thereby, as Utas (2005) described it, casting reintegration as remarginalization.

Ma-pet's headman was less interested in the verbal acknowledgment of past abuses than in moral practice in the present. He was aware of the formulaic nature of the accounts ex-combatants told him, but accepted them anyway. He told me:

HEADMAN: Some, they explain all their ordeals. How they carried heavy loads. I ask them, "Did you join voluntarily, or were you seized?"

RS: Do you ask them about bad things they've done?

H: No, and they don't tell me about this. All of them said they had been abducted. They say, "I was captured." Some, they explain, "We have escaped from the rebels." Some say, "We thank God to find ourselves here." And they beg for mercy. . . . We normally watch them for one or two weeks to see if they have really come to stay. Maybe their group is waiting in the bush. We watch for their character.

RS: What do you watch for?

H: One of the things we watch for is whether he will smoke ka-thai [cannabis]. We watch whether they drug themselves, whether they drink a lot, for these things inflame them. Even when they go from one part of the village to another, we watch them.

By asking ex-combatants if they had joined voluntarily, the headman cued them to adopt a position of subsumed agency. Once they did, however, he showed no interest in questioning their stories, allowing the past's moral grayness to remain quietly layered beneath a surface narrative of compulsion. Neither the headman's response nor ex-combatant narratives of subsumed agency, then, were signs of responsibility's absence, but rather of its presence in a register different from that of discursive verbal narration. Instead of being a product of telling the truth, responsibility emerges as a set of dispositions embodied in present actions—self-control, humility, productive work, usefulness, and a cool heart—through which moral personhood is manifest.

"Let's Go and Tell the Truth"

When the TRC arrived in 2002, it sought to create certain kinds of subjects. Sierra Leone's Truth and Reconciliation Act states that the TRC should "create an impartial historical record of violations and abuses of human rights and international humanitarian law related to the armed conflict in Sierra Leone" (Truth and Reconciliation Commission, Sierra Leone 2000, part III/6/1), thereby producing historical accountability. But in order to accomplish this, the commission's responsibility had to become the public's responsibility. Thus telling the truth before the TRC was cast as the citizen's responsibility to the state. "It is the responsibility of every citizen," states the TRC's report, "to make the process a nationally-owned process and to realize the importance of their contributions and participation" (Truth and Reconciliation Commission, Sierra Leone 2004, vol. 3b, 489). Soon after it was established, the TRC launched a sensitization campaign that urged people to become truth-telling subjects in order to realize justice, reconciliation, and national peace. Posters in Freetown and major provincial towns announced: "*Truth* hurts but *war* hurts more"; "Disarm your *Mind*! Tell the *Truth* to the TRC"; "Truth Today . . . Peaceful Sierra Leone Tomorrow"; and (in Sierra Leone Krio), "Tru at fo tok, but na im nomo go bring pis" (The truth is hard to tell, but only this will bring peace).

The TRC also sought to establish individual responsibility for human rights abuses. With the rising emphasis on criminal responsibility as the gold standard of transitional justice, truth commissions themselves became judicialized. They retained the examination of histories and institutions for which truth commissions are known, but have also become a "justice-supportive machinery" (Stahn 2001, 954) that shares certain features with criminal prosecutions. They emphasize the production of individual responsibility, not only by naming names but also by engendering individual admissions of violation. They have also been given more judicial and investigative powers: Sierra Leone's TRC, for example, was endowed with powers of subpoena, search and seizure, and cross-examination. Although it could not establish criminal responsibility, its hearings had a strongly prosecutorial character, especially when ex-combatants were aggressively cross-examined by the commissioners and a "leader of evidence." Despite repeated assurances by the commissioners that the TRC was not a court, it often had the appearance of one.

In order to encourage ex-combatants to testify, the commission targeted them in its sensitization campaign. It held workshops for them, in which it emphasized its independence from the Special Court (Truth and Reconciliation Commission, Sierra Leone 2004, vol. 3, ch. 7, para. 50) and asserted the claim that taking responsibility for past abuses would facilitate reintegration. Another part of the TRC's sensitization program was a series of skits broadcast on national radio and television. Titled *Let's Go and Tell the Truth* in Sierra Leone Krio (*le wi go tok tru*), these consisted of minidramas that conveyed responsibilizing messages about truth telling.

One skit featured an ex-combatant named Musa, who had just had an argument with his mother over his refusal to go to work. He could no longer face his workmates, who had stigmatized him, calling him a rebel. Angry and dejected, he sat on the steps outside his mother's home. When his friend T-Boy, another ex-combatant, arrived, Musa complained that his chest felt tight: the name calling at work had beaten him down. T-Boy explained that people suspected them because of their involvement in the war. The solution, he told Musa, was to "talk to the TRC." After allaying his friend's concerns about a connection between the TRC and the government, T-Boy explained the commission's process of truth telling and apology, and—in an echo of the South African TRC's message of healing through revealing, described the healing that would follow:

T-BOY: We who fought, we mingle with those who were hurt by the war. And they [the TRC] just give us the chance to explain what we did, and to apologize. [Wi we fet, mix wi di wan de we di war ombog. En dem jis gi wi di chance for explen wetin wi do, en mek wi beg padin.]

MUSA: I'll go to the commission, and will talk and apologize. I think after that, I'll feel light after I've talked. [Mesef go go na di Commission, en go tok en beg padin. I fil se afta dat, I go fil lait afta a don tok.]

The skits ended as they began, with an upbeat TRC jingle that framed these dramas within a trajectory of national peace that truth telling before the commission would help establish:

Come blow your mind
Come clear your chest
Truth and Reconciliation
De Commission we kam for hep [The commission that comes to help]
Make peace sidon na Salone [Make peace stay in Sierra Leone]
Make peace sidon na Salone

Justice Doubles

The skit told a story of anxiety—especially, but not only, among ex-combatants—about competing forms of responsibility, even as they modeled its resolution. When we think of competing responsibilities, we normally think of a play of incompatibilities, contradictions, differences, and dilemmas. But in the Sierra Leone justice experiment, the court's and the commission's productions of responsibility were objects of concern because of their resemblance to each other.

When the TRC and the Special Court both arrived in 2002, the same year as the official end of the civil war, they worked concurrently but (ostensibly) separately. International law expert William Schabas, who strongly promoted the idea of the Sierra Leone experiment as a model for the future, argued that their relationship was synergistic (Schabas 2004b), naturalizing this relationship through such analogies as "conjoined twins" (Schabas 2004a) and the building of a house: "The Truth and Reconciliation Commission is the plumber, and the Special Court is the electrician. The two trades work in different parts of the house, on different days, at different stages of the construction, and using different tools and materials. Nobody would want to live in a finished house that lacked either electricity or plumbing" (Schabas 2003, 1065).

But in fact, the court and commission produced forms of responsibility that were too similar: both produced individual responsibility for wartime abuses, and both did so through formal verbal testimony with the support of judicial powers. At the same time, the consequences of this individual responsibility were too divergent. They translated into sharply contrasting forms of accountability—one nonpunitive, enacted through apologizing and publicizing, and the other legal and retributive, implemented through sentencing and long prison terms.

Sierra Leonean concepts of the "double" (*thoma* in both Temne and Mende) offer a different view of the relationship between the commission and the court. Objects, plants, animals, and people are paired with doubles that may bear no resemblance to them and possess quite different powers, but nevertheless share an intimate connection. They may even switch positions. This idea has profound consequences for our capacity to infer reality from appearances, as Mariane Ferme describes:

> [It] creates a world where it is difficult to distinguish the simulacrum from the real, the benign from the dangerous, and the powerful from the weak. The effect of these simulacra . . . is to undermine any stable notion of which of two (or more) possible scenes of interpretive action must be brought to bear in particular circumstances. The plainly visible is not all it appears to be and may conceal invisible potency that is known only to a few. . . . The underlying logic . . . is that everything may have a double reference or use that is not immediately knowable, or visible. (2001, 211)

Ferme draws upon Mbembe's (2001) famous essay on doubles, in which he argues that the "capacity for proliferating substitution"—images, fakes, replicas—in urban African cultural forms makes everyday life unreadable. He locates the shifting boundaries of reality and appearance within experiences of political repression and economic crisis. We may also locate them in experiences of armed conflict, which in Sierra Leone (as elsewhere) were shaped by performance, rumor, masking, and spectacle (e.g., Hoffman 2011; Richards 2005). But it was especially the violence of the state that "undermine[d] any stable notion of . . . interpretive action," as the government of Sierra Leone's President Kabbah initiated wave after wave of mass arrests, political detentions, and executions from 1998 to 2003 (Anders 2014), using the national justice system to unmake the boundary between war and postwar.

Sierra Leone's justice experiment generated insuperable problems of interpretability. Planted in a terrain of national lawfare, "in which the legal and the lethal animate and inhabit each other" (Comaroff and Comaroff 2006, 31), the experiment doubled the relationship among testimony, responsibility, and accountability, turning truth telling before Sierra Leone's TRC into an act of unpredictable and dangerous potential. For TRC and Special Court staff, this was merely an administrative matter, to be resolved by official agreements and public announcements about information sharing. But repeated statements asserting that the TRC was not a court, that it was separate from the Special Court, and that testimony before the TRC would not be used for prosecution, became signs of a treacherous underlying reality rather than of reassurance.

Popular rumors divined hidden connections and redrew the relationship between the apparently innocuous commission and the powerful court, often routing this relationship through experiences of lawfare and public executions. The TRC, I was told, was "the child of the Special Court," "a feeder court for the Special Court," or "a 'witch-hunt' agency for the Court" (see Apori-Nkansah 2008, 175)—the latter evoking chiefs' use of witch-finding techniques during the Atlantic slave trade (Shaw 2002). Friends and relatives warned ex-combatants that talking to the TRC—or just to white people—could lead to their arrest and execution (Coulter 2009, 174, 179). When the TRC began to collect statements in late 2002, the rumors had preceded it. In Port Loko District, the site of the first TRC district hearings, only two ex-combatants in the whole district gave statements. In two towns, ex-combatants drove the statement-taking team away, some of them pelting the TRC vehicle with rocks. "Do you think we don't know the Special Court sent you?" ex-combatants shouted as they threatened to smash the windshield. After this, these statement takers felt safer when they covered up the TRC logo on their vehicle and left their printed TRC T-shirts and caps at home. Not for nothing does Mbembe call rumor "the poor person's bomb" (2001, 158).

When the TRC hearings traveled from district to district, ex-combatants usually left town or lay low. According to a senior NGO staff member, ex-combatant attendance for DDR skills training workshops in Port Loko plummeted from over one hundred to around thirty during the Port Loko District Hearings. Not a single ex-combatant testified in those hearings. When I attended the hearings in Bombali, Kambia, Moyamba, and Tonkolili districts, ex-combatant participation was either very low or was increased only by substantial door-to-door persuasion by TRC staff.

As a foreign white researcher conducting fieldwork on the TRC, I was folded into this doubling. In Lunsar, ex-combatants assumed that I worked for the TRC. They warned each other, "If you talk to her, you will hear your name on Radio UNAMSIL!" (the radio station on which Special Court indict-ments were announced). When I visited an ex-combatant in Ma-pet, his fam-ily denied that he lived there. "The white woman works for the TRC!" I heard someone exclaim inside the house. Shortly afterward, the ex-combatant rec-ognized me and invited me in. Other researchers working in different parts of the country in 2003 shared similar experiences (Coulter 2009, 273; Richards et al. 2003, 23).

"Rumors," observes Sverker Finnström, writing about northern Uganda, "link the personal with the political, and the local with the national and even global" (2008, 167). Rumors about the Sierra Leone experiment not only con-nected the TRC and Special Court, but also linked them to the state, the in-ternational community, and the government's waging of lawfare. The TRC headquarters' initial address in Pademba Road, Freetown, near the Pademba Road prison, notorious for its appalling conditions, materialized a connec-tion between the commission and the hundreds of ex-combatants detained behind prison walls.

When the TRC headquarters were later moved to the former Brookfields Hotel on Jomo Kenyatta Road, a kilometer away from the site of the new Spe-cial Court building on the same road, stories developed of an underground tunnel connecting the two. This image of the tunnel condenses both the material infrastructure and the concealed link between the doubled mecha-nisms. "Once you gave information to the TRC, it was channeled through the same tunnel to the Special Court," Apori-Nkansah (2008, 174) was told by one of her informants. For decades, Sierra Leone had functioned as a "shadow state" (Reno 1995), its formal appearance a simulacrum that masked extrac-tive connections among politicians, businessmen, foreign companies, and foreign aid. By invoking a shadow justice beneath the surface of the court and commission, people expressed the political realities they lived in.

Those who ran the TRC and Special Court interpreted these rumors as products of "confusion" (e.g., TRC Final Report 2004, vol. 2, 111, para. 591) or "illiteracy." William Schabas, a TRC commissioner, for example, consigned Sierra Leoneans to an implicitly racialized rural irrationality: "Most Euro-pean law students have trouble explaining the distinctions between the Euro-pean Court of Human Rights and the European Court of Justice," he observed before concluding, "Who can really expect uneducated, illiterate peasants in the countryside of Sierra Leone to do better?" (Schabas 2003, 1064–65). At issue, of course, was not a lack of knowledge (aside from Schabas's own, re-garding the country in which he served) but an excess of it, derived from accumulated experiences of political violence and lawfare.

The rumors turned out, in any case, to crystallize an important reality. Those who worked for the two transitional justice mechanisms had a great deal of informal contact with each other. They often socialized together: "It was common to see representatives from the Court and the TRC lunching together in Freetown," as Kelsall (2005, 381) observes. And at a time when the values of judicialization were dominant, some staff and officials were more committed to the values of criminal justice than to accountability through truth. A senior individual within the TRC was alleged to have declared to several colleagues that if he came across evidence useful to the Special Court, he would pass it to the court "under the table," because "justice is justice."

Then, of course, the Special Court represented an important source of employment for many TRC staff as the commission approached the end of its time. When the Special Court recruited TRC investigators, they inevitably drew upon what they had learned about specific ex-combatants while employed by the commission. Allegedly, the court used some as prosecution witnesses (Jalloh 2014, 493). One former TRC investigator was caught in the act even before the commission had ended:

> A Commission research team working in the vicinity of Magburaka Township . . . came across [a former TRC] investigator [recruited by the Special Court] while proceeding to a follow-up interview with a Commission witness. It turned out that the investigator had led a Special Court investigation team to the same witness, known as "Base Marine." Only a few weeks earlier he had been in the area under the auspices of the Commission. . . . The investigator's return to the Magburaka area to visit the witness on a second occasion, this time wearing a Special Court cap, served to deepen suspicion in the minds of residents. (Truth and Reconciliation Commission, Sierra Leone 2004, vol. 3b, p. 377, para. 54)

In the end, then, rumors about the TRC and Special Court as covert doubles not only spoke to the landscape of state violence in which the experiment was set, but also anticipated the court's capacity to capture the TRC's production of individual responsibility and drive it down its own path of criminal accountability.

Three Apologies

While those rumors revealed the dangerously divergent potential of individual responsibility in the machinery of justice doubles, some ex-combatants managed to adjust that machinery, transforming the production of individual responsibility itself. Through their participation in the TRC, they retooled the commission's practices of truth telling and apology, producing an alternative form of responsibility: one less like that of the Special Court and more like that of Ahmadu in Ma-pet.

Toward the end of the TRC's Bombali District Hearings in Makeni on May 30, 2003, the commissioners introduced the closing ceremony in the town hall. On the stage sat four figures of civilian authority: the paramount chief of Bombali Seborah chiefdom, the senior district officer for Bombali District, the chairman of the Makeni Christian Council, and the regional chief imam. Here, three former RUF commanders would undergo a reconciliation ceremony.

Only three out of the seventeen people who testified before the Bombali District Hearings were ex-combatants. These three ex-combatants had given fairly formulaic narratives describing the RUF's internal organization and politics, its ideology, its strict laws against harming civilians, its good treatment of civilians, accounts of troop movements, attacks, retreats, ambushes, their own successes within the movement, and their encounters with RUF leaders. Markedly absent was any verbal acknowledgment of responsibility for specific acts of violence.

After five long days of hearings, the concluding reconciliation ceremony was typically a brief event, conducted just before the tired TRC staff and commissioners headed back to Freetown. Central to these events were public apologies given by the ex-combatants, followed by their blessing by civilian leaders. In the closing ceremony of the Bombali hearings, none of the three senior ex-combatants acknowledged any specific personal wrongdoing, but the first two were clearly moved by the event. The first, Abdulai, fell to his knees before the audience and declared (in Sierra Leone Krio), emotion in his voice:

> I mean to say, what I have done, for the rest of my life, from '94 until this point, I believe it was a bad thing. . . . But if you my family don't leave me, God will not leave me. . . . If you forgive me, if you bless me, then God will put a blessing on my work. God will forgive me. But if you don't forgive me, if you don't bless me, the ending of my work, I will become zero, [until] the ending of my life. ["It's true!" audience members around me whispered.] So please, I beg you, for what I have done, I kneel down. I beg pardon for what I have done.

He moved to the table at which sat the four civilian leaders. When he dropped to his knees again and bowed his head, they laid their hands on him as a sign of blessing. Applause was forbidden, but noises of approval rose from the audience.

The second ex-combatant, Mohamed, was a former RUF Military Police investigator. His words were even more equivocal, but he too fell to his knees and seemed genuinely affected by his participation in the ceremony: "This is war. War is trouble. War is destruction. I am here to apologize to the community of Makeni and environs. I was an office holder, but I belonged to a group that did these crimes. People, please forgive me for what we have done. So I apologize. But please remember that I forgive. Let my brothers come and give testimony and get that everlasting blessing." He knelt before the four leaders and was blessed, the audience murmuring approval.

The third ex-combatant, Ibrahim, notorious for his brutal treatment of civilians, had not known of the reconciliation ceremony until he heard it on the radio. He swaggered up to the stage in shorts, a white T-shirt, a red baseball cap, and fashionable sunglasses—a legacy of a wartime eye injury. Remaining on his feet, he addressed the hall: "I am trying to make you understand that it was war. War enters into a country because of God. I am asking everyone to forgive and forget. What happened will never happen again. If I have done anything wrong to people here in Sierra Leone, they should forgive and forget. We should open a new page. What happened will not happen any more." Turning to the four leaders at the table behind him, he remained standing, gave them a perfunctory bow, and shook the hand of each in turn. "Eh!" the shocked audience exclaimed, following up with a chorus of angry teeth sucking.

According to liberal definitions, an apology involves a statement of individual responsibility and contrition based on truth (e.g., Minow 1998, 117). None of these three ex-combatants' avowals corresponds to this ideal-type apology. "To apologize," writes Tavuchis, "is to declare voluntarily that one has no excuse, defense, justification, or explanation for an action (or inaction)" (1991, 17). The TRC commissioners were often frustrated by ex-combatants' "ambiguous half-hearted confessions" (Truth and Reconciliation Commission, Sierra Leone 2004, vol. 3, ch. 7, p. 450, para. 92) before the hearings.

But as Kelsall (2005) argues for the Tonkolili District Hearings, these apologies had an efficacy that cannot, given their equivocations and ambiguities, be attributed to the power of truth telling. Abdulai's and Mohamed's apologies were popularly accepted. As with Ahmadu's integration into Ma-pet, their verbal acknowledgment of specific abuses was less significant than their embodied performance of a change in their hearts. Unlike Ibrahim, who continued to act like a big man, Abdulai and Mohamed no longer behaved like commanders. "I am an ordinary soldier who says, 'Yes sir,'" declared Abdulai, who had been inducted into the new Sierra Leone army as a private.

This performance of moral transformation was confirmed by blessings. Abdulai addressed the audience as "my family" and told them that only their blessing could open the way to God's blessings for him. Mohamed likewise encouraged his fellow ex-combatants to "come and give testimony and get that everlasting blessing." For Abdulai and Mohamed to beg the (civilian) audience in the TRC for forgiveness and blessing was an expression of their humility—their recognition of debt—to those over whom they had once presided through force. This was underscored by their physical postures and gestures of subordination, kneeling in front of the audience and the representatives of civilian authority.

Together, Abdulai, Mohamed, and the audience drove the TRC's reconciliation ceremony along a different path from that envisaged as a product of truth telling. First, by avoiding the explicit verbal narration of past actions, they evaded the dangerous doubling of individual responsibility in Sierra Leone's justice laboratory. Second, the apologies they gave and the blessings they received transformed these two ex-combatants as moral subjects in ways that had little to do with the liberal model of verbal responsibility. Like Ahmadu in Ma-pet, they apologized with their bodies, which worked in a different register to enact a different kind of responsibility: their obligations to others in the form of humility and a cool heart. It was through these embodied dispositions, their changed basis for moral relationships, that the audience accepted Abdulai's and Mohamed's less than explicit apologies. Their retrofit effectively disarmed doppelganger justice by more clearly distancing the TRC from the Special Court, while at the same time connecting them to the community in which they wished to integrate.

A year later, Abdulai was still in the army. After his public testimony and apology he gained celebrity as a poster child for the TRC. Television coverage of the Bombali District Hearings repeatedly showed him kneeling in a gesture of deference, begging the audience with his right arm extended in supplication. He currently appears in that position on the home page of the TRC website (TRC 2016). Mohamed became the personal assistant of the vice chairman of Makeni's city council: his TRC apology impressed the vice chairman so much that he offered Mohamed a job. Ibrahim, however, fled Makeni soon after the TRC, fearful of being sent to the Special Court.

Concluding Thoughts

After I returned from Sierra Leone in 2003, I was surprised to read that the justice experiment had been a great success. "As the TRC hearings progressed during mid-2003," wrote William Schabas, "many perpetrators came forward to tell their stories to the Commission and, in some cases, to ask pardon or forgiveness of the victims. They did not appear at all concerned about the threat of prosecution by the Special Court" (2003, 1051). Schabas argued that the relationship between the TRC and the Special Court was not merely complementary but synergistic: "This may well be a case of 2 + 2 = 5" (2004a, 1099), he concluded. This position emerged as a new fact, reshaping the international landscape. "It is now generally recognized," stated former UN secretary-general Kofi Annan in his influential 2004 report on the rule of law and transitional justice, "that truth commissions can positively complement criminal tribunals, as the examples of Argentina, Peru, Timor-Leste and Sierra Leone suggest" (United Nations 2004, 9).

But more than one form of knowledge emerged from the competing responsibilities of Sierra Leone's justice experiment. International legal elites recycled their canon of complementarity as "results," naturalized it through simple arithmetic logic ("A plus B equals C"; "2 + 2 = 5"), publicized it through international media, scholarly journals, and expert networks, and translated it into policy through the UN. Sierra Leonean activists and the TRC itself told a different story, disseminated through unpublished reports, of conflicting justice mechanisms and colliding responsibilities (TRC Monitoring Group). And members of the Sierra Leonean public spread popular stories recasting the court and commission as hidden doubles that worked together to draw ex-combatants into a lethal trap. These rumors situated the experiment within the state's waging of lawfare through mass arrests and executions. Some ex-combatants, however, modified the production of individual responsibility in the TRC by practicing embodied rather than verbally discursive apologies. They thereby disarmed the commission as the Special Court's double, effectively blocking the tunnel from the commission to the court. Both the apologies and the rumors disconnected the Special Court from the temporal trajectory drawn in judicializing models of liberal peace building.

Like other forms of responsibilization, the international judicializing imperative that gave rise to Sierra Leone's justice experiment created a political field shaped by a normative nexus of individualism and neoliberalism. In this imperative, however, the production of individual responsibility becomes a criminalizing process that depoliticizes armed conflict, facilitates states' pursuit of lawfare, and authorizes international intervention. It also reveals the temporalizing dimensions of responsibility, in which competing responsibilities imply competing temporalities. In Sierra Leone, the Special Court's judicializing norms contended with processes of ex-combatant reintegration that prioritized present moral dispositions and responsibility to others over verbal accountability for the past. More broadly, judicializing processes have moved transitional justice away from models of past trauma, present catharsis, and future reconciliation in TRCs. Instead, they locate responsibility for a nation's violent past in criminal individuals, and claim that individual legal accountability, once established, will launch a timeline toward future global frameworks of rights and nonrecurrence. Yet, as the Sierra Leone experiment demonstrates, the project of judicialization is always subject to interruption by competing responsibilities and temporalities.

NOTE

1. This chapter is based on four periods of multisited ethnographic fieldwork in Sierra Leone from 2001 to 2004: in Freetown (2001, 2002, 2003); Kabala, Makeni, and Port Loko (2002); "Ma-pet" (2002, 2003); Lunsar (2003); Makeni (2004); and in the TRC's Bombali, Kambia, Moyamba, and Tonkolili District Hearings (2003).

Part IV. Intimate Ties

BARRY D. ADAM

Responsibility is largely a question of who has the wherewithal to hold whom accountable for what. In the relatively short history of the HIV epidemic, first identified in 1981, a crowded field of contenders has sought to encode the epidemic with its favored discourses, which have inevitably allocated responsibility, if not guilt and innocence, in the spread of HIV. As a completely new entity in the history of disease, HIV was an open field in the 1980s into which rushed a series of institutional actors to make sense of a syndrome that fell most heavily on populations far from the levers of power. In these early days, at least in countries like the United States, Canada, and the United Kingdom, HIV was taken up by moralizing forces in the culture wars over changing visions of gender and family. Later in the 1990s, HIV became more the province of biomedical and legal regimes that purvey discourses marked by prevailing notions of citizenship in a society often conceived as a marketplace. These more recent constructions of HIV are more consistent with the neoliberal ethic that has so preoccupied social scientists in recent years and as such function in many of the same ways as neoliberal governance functions in other spheres of life. Responsibility becomes largely the domain of individuals most likely to face HIV management in everyday life, whether prevention or treatment, while the state and corporate sectors alternately help and hinder an optimal response to the epidemic.

As Joseph Gusfield (1963) pointed out in his classic study, *Symbolic Crusade*, symbolic politics can play a primary role in determining the direction of the accusatory finger of responsibility. *Symbolic Crusade* showed how the early twentieth-century temperance movement allowed self-righteous white, Protestant, nativist Americans to wield alcohol control as a symbolic assertion of their dominance over suspect immigrant classes of Catholic Irish and southern Europeans. Temperance also became caught up in the gender dynamics of the era as the early women's movement sought to control male domestic violence and discipline men to fulfill the demands of the breadwinner role through alcohol control. By the late twentieth century, the symbolic politic had become reconfigured around drunk driving, where the state and corporate interests combined to locate the problem of vehicular accidents in individual drivers, exculpating themselves from the marketing, promotion, and profit from alcohol sales. This paradigm in the social construction of social problems has much to recommend in casting light on the politics of responsibility in HIV. In the 1980s and early 1990s, the political dynamics of HIV responsibility were located in the identification of HIV with gay men when state and religious actors were eager to discipline and rehegemonize the patriarchal family as the solution to HIV. Medical and legal discourses have risen to the fore in the 2000s to construct responsible individualism consistent with contemporary neoliberal precepts.

The Early Phase

HIV made its appearance in the early 1980s in the midst of a contentious political environment marked by conflicts over the place of women and lesbian, gay, bisexual, and transgender (LGBT) people in Anglo-American societies. With the Republican Party ascendant in the United States throughout the period in the Reagan and Bush administrations along with the Conservative Party in the United Kingdom, the Christian right enjoyed an inside track in setting the moral tone of the era. Rather traditional moral precepts, promoted through the particularly fundamentalist cast of right-wing American Protestantism, led to governmental responses ranging from neglect to active blockage of pragmatic strategies in the face of the new epidemic of HIV. Safe sex messaging, innovated through community responses to the AIDS crises, met resistance in official and institutional circles, lest people be allowed (or encouraged) to have sex outside the nuclear family, through the propagation of what Simon Watney (1987, 124) called a "discourse of punitive fidelity." The U.S. Congress moved to suppress federal funding for "educational projects or materials that promote or encourage, directly or indirectly, homosexual sexual activity," a provision intended to suppress community-based attempts to educate gay and bisexual men on how to protect themselves from HIV transmission. Britain took a similar measure in the passage of Section 28 in 1988, a law intended to censor favorable speech about homosexuality that remained active until repeal by a later Labour government in 2003 (Adam 1989). The attribution of responsibility remained largely embedded in a semiotic framework that predetermined the moral status of vulnerable populations. Gay men, nonmonogamous women, men of color, and foreigners have long been designated the always already guilty infectors held responsible for HIV transmission in Western societies while women as mothers, children, and hemophiliacs were placed on the innocent victim side of the moral binary in a pattern reproduced from news coverage through court prosecutions (Altman 1986; Elford 1987; Patton 1990, 1996; Persson and Newman 2008). While this politic of responsibility has subsided over time, it has scarcely gone away, remaining a cultural bedrock upon which subsequent constructions of responsibility have been layered in later years.

Even in the early phase, the moralist frame was not the only contender for making sense of responsibility in HIV. At a time when medical science was struggling to identify a causal agent for this unprecedented epidemic, conspiracy theories abounded that invoked CIA labs intent on destroying populations that had long been vilified by the Republican Party and its Christian right allies, along with theories that proposed a wide range of biological and lifestyle causes (Epstein 1996). In the 1980s, before the identification of HIV as the causal agent of the AIDS epidemic and then for some years before the invention of an HIV test, the populations named by epidemiologists as the most affected by HIV responded in various ways in the face of this new and unprecedented threat. The early triad of epidemiological categories, dubbed the 3Hs—homosexuals, Haitians, and hemophiliacs—at the time provoked responses ranging from denial to alarm. By the end of the decade, the 3Hs had evolved into a categorical hierarchy now standard in HIV epidemiology: men who have sex with men, injection drug users, recipients of blood products, heterosexuals from HIV-endemic regions (primarily sub-Saharan Africa, the Caribbean, and Southeast Asia), other heterosexuals, plus now very small numbers of HIV infection from perinatal transmission and occupational exposure. Each affected population typically moved through its own internal process of allocating blame—at first so-called fast-lane gay men were targeted—before it became all too evident that the extent of infection and the devastating impact of disease on friends, lovers, and community figures becoming gravely ill stimulated a more collective sense of everyone being at risk and in need of care. Gay male communities, and in some places injection drug users, were among the first to develop an organized response as HIV came to be seen as a collective tragedy. Community mobilizations arising out of populations most directly affected by HIV sought to create practical measures of HIV avoidance while affirming the right to pursue sex and affection. They also created networks and social services to meet the needs of HIV-positive people at a time when institutional responses were slow or antagonistic. Communities affected by HIV that were most strongly reliant on religious language and organizations for making sense of the epidemic, and for a collective response to it, remained longer in a politics of blame that individuated responsibility for HIV among the immoral. The consequence of religious framing of the epidemic was to silence and abandon those who were infected, deny the extent of infection, and slow an organized response to prevent transmission and support the infected.

For all affected communities, taking responsibility was a fraught and treacherous undertaking. Gay and bisexual men and people of color, whose communities were most strongly affected by HIV, faced powerful institutional actors who were quick to fan the flames of homophobic and racist hysteria by advocating punitive measures and the suspension of the limited civil rights gains that had been made up until that time. At a time marked, for example, by Proposition 64 to quarantine all HIV-positive people in California (ultimately defeated by voters in 1986), affected communities were faced with insoluble dilemmas in the politics of responsibility: embrace responsibility and seemingly confirm the punitive rhetoric of their opponents or deny it and confirm the institutional neglect that already characterized the official response that was resulting in a lack of research, lack of treatment, and lack of education on how to prevent HIV. Gay communities attempted to navigate through these tensions with an ambivalent policy of "de-gaying AIDS" by, on the one hand, petitioning for state support for community-based organizations for HIV prevention and for care of the infected and, on the other hand, publicly arguing that anyone can get AIDS in an attempt to convince the public and politicians to admit some degree of responsibility in addressing the widening pandemic. The symbolic logjam was ultimately broken only when innocent victims of AIDS began to attract major press attention. Ryan White, an appealing (white) thirteen-year-old boy who acquired HIV through infected blood products and was thrown out of his school in 1984 in

Kokomo, Indiana,[1] became a face of the injustice caused by the AIDS panic. The U.S. congressional bill that first appropriated funding for AIDS research, treatment, and care continues to bear his name, namely the Ryan White CARE (Comprehensive AIDS Resources Emergency) Act. The 1985 revelation of the HIV infection of an iconic Hollywood actor, Rock Hudson, and the 1991 announcement by celebrated basketball star Magic Johnson, helped give HIV a human face and diminish the otherness of gay and African American men with HIV. These high-profile media events began to resonate with the day-to-day work of community-based organizations that were already seeking to displace AIDS panic by a discourse of safe sex and compassion through engagement with local groups, institutions, and professions.

HIV Responsibilization in a Larger Context of Neoliberalism

The language of medical science gained increasing prominence in constructing HIV, especially with the 1996 discovery of the protease inhibitors and triple combination therapies that ushered in a new era of much more effective treatment for HIV. Medical advances added to a process of defusing the energy in the moralist and conspiratorial frameworks of the early phase. Over time, public health and community-based AIDS organizations arrived at a reframing of the HIV epidemic and HIV responsibility that shared many of the premises circulating in advanced Western societies of the late twentieth and early twenty-first centuries. The rhetoric of grassroots AIDS movements embraced an individualized notion of shared responsibility exhorting affected communities to protect themselves and each other. Originating as a self-help strategy in the face of social and governmental neglect, if not hostility, the message of AIDS organizations throughout the English-speaking world was to emphasize that everyone must take responsibility for their own health and, in an analogy to defensive driving, to protect themselves from external perils, presuming sex partners to be potential sources of infection. AIDS service organizations (ASOs) found themselves carrying forward the philosophy of community self-governance as the way to meet the life-threatening challenge of HIV. As they became increasingly dependent on government funding, this philosophy dovetailed nicely with the increasingly dominant ideology of Western governments in the 1980s and 1990s of individual responsibilization as ASOs called on gay and bisexual men to remake their sexuality as responsible citizens practicing safe sex (Adam 2006; Weeks 1995). The public health sector adopted a similar discourse, compatible with a long-standing tradition of biomedical individualism, relying on a paradigm of people as rational, calculating actors in a field of risk (Davis 2002). Whether addressing smoking cessation, exercise, or defensive driving, public health typically called on people to reform their own behavior as the primary solution to health challenges (Lupton 1999).

This stress on individual responsibility meshes well with the leading discourses of contemporary neoliberalism, which postulate the "calculating, rational, self-interested subject" (Smart 2003) as the fundamental subject-citizen of liberal democratic states and the consumer in capitalist marketplaces (Habermas 1987b). This ascendant discourse of responsibilization helped move HIV into the realm of medical normalization and away from the religious and panic-stricken rhetorics that preceded it. It succeeded in creating safe sex as a normative expectation among gay men, thereby bringing down infection rates through the 1990s and, where needle distribution became standard practice, bringing down rates among injection drug users as well. It also helped diminish the overt stigmatization of people living with HIV. All the same, the neoliberal paradigm has its blind spots, partialities, and even cruelties in HIV, just as it has in other realms of governance. Typical of other regimes of governmentality, it generates new categories of irresponsibility as it instantiates the responsible subject and it limits, if not shields, responsibility as an attribute of the state or corporate sectors.

The Limits of Reponsibilization

The always already fully adult, rights-bearing, contract-making citizen and consumer presumed by liberal democracy and the capitalist marketplace tend to be the subjects taken for granted by and postulated in the speech of business and government. They circulate as the basic common sense of corporate mass media and tend to be presumed as the natural order of things in law. Everyone either is or should be an autonomous, free, rational, and self-governing individual according to the neoliberal construction of contemporary citizenship. In public health, this vision of human subjectivity manifests itself as the rational person who avoids perils to health because she seeks naturally to maximize her own longevity and well-being while avoiding risk. In HIV, the admonition to treat everyone as if he were HIV-positive is meant to appeal to the presumably HIV-negative individual to act rationally by employing a condom in order to protect himself from possible HIV transmission. Each individual acting according to this precept constitutes herself as a component of a larger social marketplace where self-interested behavior adds up to a larger common good: all are protected; viral transmission is blocked;

and the health of the collectivity advances without having to invoke communitarianism or altruism. It must be noted that in many ways this collective construction of individual subjectivity has worked insofar as it came to constitute an ethic of an era, was embodied and inhabited by people in everyday interactions, and reproduced and reinforced leading discourses in ways that presumably benefited public policy as a whole.

Nevertheless, like similar constructions of responsibility by state, biomedical, and social service actors in other sectors, these precepts run up against up a number of difficulties. Human subjectivity and conduct are never quite contained by dominant systems and their discourses. Indeed, everyday life often presents competing and inconsistent emotions and rationalities that make the execution of a singular ethic hard to realize even with the best of intentions. Neoliberal governance, as well, may bring with it hidden contradictions, silences, and pretenses that induce inconsistencies and semiotic snares that undermine its ostensible objectives. The limits of this vision of how people do act, or are supposed to act, become particularly evident in two realms: the criminal justice system and social science investigation of risky behavior.

It should first be noted that examination of the largest database of HIV-positive people in Canada, the Ontario HIV Treatment Network Cohort Study, shows that large proportions of people living with HIV are not sexually active or have a single long-term partner and, furthermore, that among those who are sexually active with different partners, safe sex continues to be widespread. In addition, in an era of effective treatment, at least among those on medication, large numbers—typically 80 to 90 percent—are achieving undetectable viral load, meaning that the likelihood of being infectious is much diminished. A sizeable portion of HIV transmission, then, appears to be occurring from people who do not even know that they are infected or who do know but have not been treated with antiretroviral medication. Nevertheless, many jurisdictions in North America have been quick to pass laws and prosecute HIV-positive people for either transmitting HIV (presumably through intent or neglect) or simply for not disclosing their HIV status regardless of potential for transmission. Examination of the demographic profile of those caught up in the criminal justice system shows again how frequently people with the predetermined moral status of the already suspect are more likely to be prosecuted and convicted (Mykhalovskiy and Betteridge 2012).

The court-mandated requirement for disclosure of HIV status flows from a particular model of human behavior which holds that (a) HIV-positive people can and should assume the responsibility of warning others of the potential for infection, and (b) prospective partners, once informed of that potential, will act appropriately to avoid infection. Closer examination of this legal, contractual model of sexual interaction reveals a problematic underside to rationalist presumptions. First, there is no clear evidence that disclosure of HIV status does reduce HIV transmission if only because consistent condom use does not require disclosure to happen and indeed, disclosure may in fact often be a conversational gambit acting as an invitation to unprotected sex (Marks and Crepaz 2001). The demand to disclose essentially requires HIV-positive people to place themselves in a situation to be rejected or stigmatized (Galletly and Dickson-Gomez 2009), and disclosure proves to be particularly difficult for people (often women) in a relationship of dependency (Siegel, Lekas, and Schrimshaw 2005) or those who feel disadvantaged by age, attractiveness, or ethnocultural background (Adam et al. 2005). In the words of some of the participants in our study (Adam, Elliott, et al. 2014, 44) of the effects of criminalization on people living with HIV,

> So you come here [as an immigrant], you are in a marital relationship or somebody is promising to marry you and he's your legal status and they infect you. Then you fear calling the police because this person is your breadwinner and he's almost like your everything. I went out with a guy who was HIV negative. I let him know my status but when we broke up, he started telling me how he's going to go to the police and tell the police. (Heterosexual, female, thirties)

> It's more of a moral issue on the other person and I don't think the media has the right to put that person's name or picture and flash it all over the news. Ten years ago when I lived in BC, I had a partner and he knew, and things went sour in the friendship and he got angry and he threatened to have me charged for not telling him that I was HIV-positive which was not true (Gay, male, forties)

Criminalization may in fact discourage people from disclosing as they may decide that it is better to let sleeping dogs lie rather than risk being placed in a position of vulnerability by a potentially vindictive partner (Adam, Elliott, et al. 2008; Galletly and Dickson-Gomez 2009). "Disclosure is an undertaking fraught with emotional pitfalls complicated by personal histories of having misread cues or having felt deceived leading up to their own seroconversion, then having to negotiate a stigmatized status with new people" (Adam, Elliott, et al. 2014). Far from the clear contractual interaction envisioned as the actions of autonomous subjects, the messiness of conflicting demands and emotions creates situations of indirect or situational management of disclosure that conventional legal precepts prove to be ill equipped to comprehend. From our study of the effects of criminalization of people living with HIV, we conclude, "Perhaps paradoxically, the elevation of disclosure as a strategy of HIV prevention by the courts and media coverage shifts perceptions and negotiations of HIV management in ways that may actually undermine effective HIV prevention by making disclosure feel more risky for HIV-positive people when it becomes an act subject to legal scrutiny. As well it may create a generalized expectation that HIV-positive people will always disclose, and therefore condom use is unnecessary because non-disclosure comes to signify HIV-negative status" (Adam, Corriveau, et al. 2014).

A now-voluminous research literature on unprotected sex also reveals the limits of the paradigm of the individually responsible sexual citizen that is institutionalized in health and law. Prevention of HIV has long meant the use of condoms in sexual encounters as condoms remain the primary most effective and affordable method of placing a barrier against HIV transmission. A wide range of epidemiological studies has demonstrated that condoms continue to be employed by most gay men most of the time. Condoms in practice, however, are associated with some well-known drawbacks: they are often experienced as interfering with sexual pleasure, and men with erectile difficulties in particular have a strong incentive to avoid them (Rhodes and Cusick 2002; Richters, Hendry, and Kippax 2003). They also run counter to a symbolic component in the communication of intimacy by preventing insemination (Mansergh et al. 2002; Whittier, St. Lawrence, and Seeley 2005). Condoms are not entirely fail-safe (Smith et al. 2015). The ostensibly straightforward use of condoms as a rational health strategy can also become caught up in a semiotic undertow. Unprotected sexual practices may come to be read as a sign of the special trust that partners in a couple have for each other (Flowers et al. 1997), thereby inhibiting partners from adopting condom use lest it be read as an accusation of infidelity. But apart from the semiotics of condoms themselves, a growing research literature on syndemics throws the presumptions that underlie the rational actor into relief.

Since the early days of HIV research, a cumulating evidentiary base in psychology and sociology has pointed to a series of measurable factors that predict greater frequency of unprotected sex (Mustanski et al. 2011). At first, childhood sexual abuse and adult domestic violence showed strong statistical associations with subsequent risk, then further investigation showed the effect of a larger context of childhood trauma, such as homophobic and racist bullying, on risk practices (Arreola et al. 2008; Dorais and Lajeunesse 2004; Mizuno et al. 2012). Personal disruption, depression, and social isolation emerged as another array of factors that repeatedly showed predictive value in quantitative and clinical investigation (Koblin, Husnik, et al. 2006; Koblin, Torian, et al. 2006). Psychotherapeutic accounts of gay men caught up in waves of dying friends and lovers spoke eloquently to the existential anxieties and experiential dimensions of the statistical findings (Odets 1995; Shernoff 2006). Drug and alcohol use proved as well to be factors consistently associated with lower rates of condom use (Kurtz 2005; Ostrow et al. 2009; Reback, Larkins, and Shoptaw 2004). Ron Stall and colleagues (2003; Stall, Friedman, and Catania 2007) dubbed these findings a syndemic of co-occurring epidemics, pointing out these conditions interacted with each other. Individuals most affected by these factors have elevated rates of risky behavior and seroconversion; multiple factors have a cumulative effect (Ferlatte et al. 2014; Halkitis et al. 2013; Herrick et al. 2014; Mimiaga et al. 2015). This pattern has now been reconfirmed in many places, pointing to a nexus of structural conditions and developmental processes, later reinforced through social networks and microcultures, where vulnerability to infection and onward transmission is greatly heightened (Adam, Elliott, et al. 2008; Adam, Husbands, et al. 2008; Egan et al. 2011; Kurtz 2005). In these circumstances, appealing repeatedly to the responsible individual proves ineffective and following up with punitive measures simply exacerbates the precipitating factors that underlie the problem.

Ironies and Contradictions of Responsibilization

Beyond the limits of the responsibilization paradigm are the less visible actions of governance happening in three spheres: the growth of a moral rhetoric unanchored from the public good, inconsistent efforts of governments to both reinforce and sometimes mop up the aftereffects of responsibilization policy, and the actions of corporations favoring market solutions at the highest possible cost to the people most affected by HIV. None of these consequences is particularly unique to HIV; similar issues come up in other arenas of neoliberal governance. Like those other arenas, neoliberal governance results in limited and chronically inadequate solutions for social challenges such as transmissible life-threatening diseases. Where individualized responsibility breaks down is in the presumption or expectation that people will act as consistent calculators of risk. It is a paradigm that makes no allowance for depression, drug use, personal turmoil, or sense of personal agency in situations of (sometimes subtle) social pressure. Ultimately it can lead to situations of a buyer beware ethic where everyone is presumed to be left to their own devices. Those who do not successfully navigate the marketplace of risk then have little recourse but to locate themselves as failures in the neoliberal game plan (Adam 2005; Rangel and Adam 2014).

Yet there are solutions on both the biomedical and social-psychological fronts that the state and corporate sectors are slow to implement. Over time, most governments in the Global North and South have sought to make treatment available to people with HIV. Those on consistent daily medication have a very good prognosis, but even in advanced industrial nations only a minority of HIV-infected people appear to be attaining this level of care (Gardner et al. 2011). In addition, health surveys show that large numbers of LGBT people are not known to their health care providers to be LGBT, often for fear of the treatment they will receive at the hands of these providers (Ayala et al. 2014; Dulai et al. 2011). Health care delivery does not meet a standard sufficient to identify and treat sexual health issues in order that rates of infection be brought down to levels common in the surrounding population (Institute of Medicine 2011).

Research shows that there are tools beyond the condom, for example, once-a-day (or potentially less) dosing with anti-HIV medications that can also prevent infection. Access to these medications remains highly restricted. Throughout the history of HIV treatment, drug research, largely financed by public money, has produced treatments that have, in turn, been marketed under patent by pharmaceutical corporations with astronomical markups that have severely limited access. Protracted struggles into the early 2000s, particularly in South Africa, resulted in the legal manufacture of cheaper generic antiretroviral treatments for the Global South. Today in the Global North, the drug that can be used as a preexposure prophylaxis against HIV infection is marketed at a cost of approximately $10,000 per person per year (though it can be manufactured for less than $100 per year), making it accessible to only the best insured in the richest countries. Targeted short-term interventions and therapeutic services to address syndemic issues could also make a significant difference in ongoing HIV transmission, but apart from a very few bright spots in the health care arena, such as LGBT-dedicated health services in a few major U.S. cities, these services do not reach those in need of them. The result of these structural barriers is rates of new HIV infection in the United States that run 76.5 times higher among African American gay men than in the general population (where the current rate is 15.3 cases per 10,000 people), 9.3 times higher among white gay men, 3.7 times higher among African Americans, and 1.3 times higher among Latinos (Centers for Disease Control and Prevention 2015).

Conclusion

In many ways, the history of HIV is not so much unique as an exemplary case study in the codification of human conduct as (ir)responsible. Striking at some of the most deeply emotional questions of human existence—sex and death—HIV brought forth both long-standing moral discourses rooted in religion and modern visions of responsible individualism. Discourses of responsibility in HIV, then, have drawn on traditional moral binaries that have predesignated who is to be held responsible in HIV transmission. While most evident in the early days of the epidemic, particularly the 1980s, these binaries form a substrate of signification that has not gone away. The normalization of HIV through medical and legal language in more recent decades has displaced much of the earlier moral rhetoric, at least in the public sphere. This language follows the usual contours of neoliberal responsibilization in advanced industrial societies, creating a configuration of responsibility that mandates condom use by individuals. Indeed, the emergence of HIV in the neoliberal era may, in turn, have contributed to the instantiation of a responsible sexual subject that refigured and redisciplined the sexual for the late twentieth and early twenty-first centuries. This configuration has its own partialities and blind spots deflecting attention from the responsibilities of corporate and state actors that could ameliorate the conditions that lead to heightened vulnerability and transmission.

NOTES

1. See http://ryanwhite.com/Ryans_Story.html.

NINE. Responsibilities of the Third Age and the
Intimate Politics of Sociality in Poland

JESSICA ROBBINS-RUSZKOWSKI

Competing Responsibilities in the
Context of Aging Populations

As life spans lengthen, more people than ever before are experiencing old age; in conjunction with falling birth rates, particular forms of (trans)national, regional, familial, and existential anxieties result. Often defined by the twin phenomena of retirement and debility, anxieties about old age are underpinned by contested moral ideologies about claiming and enacting responsibility for the lives of the oldest generations. Some contestations about responsibility in old age arise from the centrality of labor to the structuring of society; increasing numbers of retirees challenge social welfare systems as more people receive funds than contribute, leading to questions of who should financially support older people after they cease to earn wages. Other dilemmas stem from the experience of illness; of course, while illness is not limited to old age, it can be especially common during this phase of the life course. Illness and debility in old age raise the questions of who should provide care for older people, affecting social ties at scales both intimate and broad. Still other tensions arise from existential concerns that become prominent at the end of life.

In contemporary neoliberal contexts, in which ideal forms of moral person-hood fundamentally intertwine productivity, labor, and health, experiences of old age (retirement, debility, illness) can thus limit possibilities for moral personhood in late life. Achieving a good old age becomes possible for some, while others struggle for dignity, respect, and humanity in their last decades.

In contemporary Poland, such anxieties are part of sociocultural and political-economic transformations that have occurred since 1989. Notions of responsibility for old age involve complex historical reckonings in which the legacy of the socialist past looms large. Against the specter of a collectivist rationale, the logic of individual responsibility is popular not just as a means to solve financial problems, but as a moral imperative that is part of a broader East-West imaginary (Verdery 1996; Wolff 1994). That is, transformations in political economy have also brought about transformations in moral imaginations and social relations (Beidelman 1993).

At once economic, political, social, and moral, these contestations crosscut scales of practice and discourse, and are shot through with competing forms and notions of responsibility (Trnka and Trundle 2014; introduction, this volume). Specifying the variation in kinds of responsibility is necessary lest the dominant political-economic and moral logic of neoliberalism infiltrate our own analytic framework. It is equally necessary to show how certain forms coexist in the same institutions, types of social relations, and particular in-teractive contexts.

In this chapter, I aim to explore the mutual imbrication of several forms of responsibility by examining a historically particular phase of late life that has come to be known as the third age. I do this by analyzing one of its hall-mark institutions, the University of the Third Age (UTA)—specifically, the UTA in Wrocław, Poland—in the context of attempts to build civil society in eastern Europe.[1] I frame this ethnographic case within a discussion of de-mographic and political-economic transformations as Poland moved from state socialism to market democracy. Demographic concerns about shifting forms of responsibility between the state and its oldest citizens actually pre-date the political-economic shifts of 1989, which continue to structure the moral imagination of people in Poland and, as such, continue to matter as a category of practice (Robbins-Ruszkowski 2014).

In order to signify their acceptance of a modern citizenship, older Poles are encouraged to enact a form of self-care that appears to be a classic form of neoliberal responsibilization, but also resonates with older forms of self-care that predate postsocialist neoliberalization. In other words, discussions of civil society and the third age cannot fully explain the forms of responsibility and sociality at this institution. Moreover, the very practices through which older Poles cultivate a neoliberal citizenship also provide the means to create new social relations with age mates. This sociality and mutual responsibility takes on a particularly Polish form, constituted by the intersection of practices related to Catholicism, traditional gender roles, and the Polish nation itself. This romantic national framework shapes the spatiotemporal contours of a moral world in which older Poles can create new social relations. However, the particular forms of activity that occur within the UTA have certain class histories and require able-bodiedness, thus serving to exclude those who are unable to meet these standards.

By placing the third age and UTAS in historical political-economic context, and analyzing the goals and practices of one UTA in Poland, this chapter elucidates the intimate politics of sociality that must be considered in examinations of contemporary forms of responsibility. Running throughout the chapter are theoretical concerns for the forms of personhood that are assumed, fostered, or foreclosed, and for the kinds of (dis)connections that are created across scales of time and place. I suggest that what is known in Poland as *aktywność* (activity, activeness) constitutes a local idiom of care, morality, and sociality, and that understanding its complexities can advance our theorization of contemporary forms of responsibility by working across scales.

The Third Age: Responsibility amid Changing Demography and Political Economy

Demographically, that there exists a phase of life that can be called the third age (Laslett 1996) (or a segment of the population that can be called "the young-old" [Neugarten 1974]) is a relatively recent phenomenon, dating to the last several decades of the twentieth century and resulting from complex political, economic, social, and health factors (Omran 1971). The third age appears alongside political-economic transformations commonly referred to as development, such that people in the industrialized West were the first to begin living longer on this population-wide scale. In its classic formulation, the third age is meant to represent the time in the life course in which one has retired from formal employment, does not have care obligations, and is still healthy. Supposed to be an overwhelmingly positive phase of life in which one can focus on self-achievement and activity, the third age is explicitly opposed to the "dependence and decrepitude" of the ensuing "fourth age"

(Laslett 1996, 192). Related to discursive constructions of aging as successful, healthy, and productive, the third age presumes a desire for an individualist, autonomous ideal of personhood (Lamb 2014).

This way of thinking about the period of life between the ages of approximately fifty-five and seventy-five (Neugarten 1974) aligns with current neoliberal political-economic, sociocultural, and moral formations, in which persons are made responsible for forms of care formerly in the domain of the state. With its focus on independence, productivity, and health, the third age is an exemplar of neoliberal responsibilization and its shifting moralities and political economies (Greenberg and Muehlebach 2007; Muehlebach 2012; Rose 2006; Shamir 2008). This reperiodization of the life course is central to what Andrea Muehlebach has called the "modernist welfare chronotope" (2012, 149), in which neoliberal responsibilization is undertaken not only for the good of the individual, but for society as a whole.

Globally, UTAS are perhaps the best-known practical instantiations of the third age. Although models vary in terms of both institutional form and content, all UTAS share a focus on making old age a positive time in the life course through education.[2] Underlying this goal is the assumption that, without significant individual, social, and institutional effort, old age would be a largely negative experience.

In Poland, the first UTAS were established in the 1970s, roughly the same time that academic and policy concerns grew about Poland's changing demographic structure (e.g., Piotrowski 1973). As public health improved in the decades following World War II, people began to live longer. Because maintaining full employment of the population was central to socialist ideology, the socialist state encouraged early retirement. These policies, along with the large numbers of older people laid off after 1989, mean that Poland has a large population of retirees relative to its overall population size (Calasanti and Zajicek 1997). Currently, the retirement age is sixty-five for men and sixty for women; however, this will be raised to sixty-seven for both men and women over a period of years.

Postsocialist decentralization and privatization negatively affected the oldest generations in particular and health care in general. Rising prices and shifting pension indexing combined to result in higher expenses and less income, in real costs, for people living on pensions (Calasanti and Zajicek 1997; Synak 1992, 91). Surveys have found that only one-quarter of Polish pensioners can afford the medicines they need (Watson 2010; see also Ostrowska 2001, 2010; Watson 2006a, 2006b). For people who grew up in a system in which the state's responsibilities to its citizens included visits to the doctor, medicines, education, and child care—that is, the current oldest generations in Poland—the erosion of such guaranteed provisions and the dramatically increased costs associated with these services are a moral affront.[3]

It is in this context of a retracting welfare state that UTAS in Poland have become increasingly popular. There are currently over four hundred, over half of which began since 2004, although they have existed in Poland since 1976. Found in both cities and smaller towns, Polish UTAS vary in organizational structure, funding, and course offerings (Towarzystwo Inicjatyw Twórczych "ę" 2012). Older Poles experience discrimination in both public and private spheres, stemming in part from the association of older people with the past, discredited world order (Mucha and Krzyżowski 2010; Robbins-Ruszkowski 2013; Synak 1992); however, UTAS help some older people to overcome negative stereotypes and marginalization (Robbins-Ruszkowski 2013).

The UTA in Wrocław, a city of over 600,000 in southwestern Poland, was founded in 1976. Over 750 people currently attend the UTA, which is affiliated with the Institute of Pedagogy at the University of Wrocław, and has a permanent space in the basement of that building. Open to all people over age sixty at a nominal annual cost, most słuchacze (attendees) are women of middle to upper socioeconomic status. The institution offers a wide range of lecture series, seminars, classes, and workshops on a variety of topics, such as physics, languages, computers, dance, and sailing. Through lectures and published materials, the UTA encourages attendees to make aging a positive, active, and creative time through learning new disciplines and skills, and forming new friendships. Closer examination of this institution's funding, discourse, and practice will demonstrate connections between the overlapping forms of responsibility present there.

Building Civil Society in Eastern Europe by Funding the Third Age

In addition to introducing democracy and free-market capitalism, the transition in eastern Europe was supposed to transform social relations by introducing civil society, which the region was thought by many scholars and policy makers to lack.[4] In eastern Europe after 1989, those who promoted civil society have intended this term to refer to the realm of human interaction that is (supposedly) separate from either the state or the market, and therefore (supposedly) separate from politics or economics (e.g., Morawski 1992). Underpinning this desire for independence from the state is a view of socialism as entirely dominated by the state. In this imagined eastern Europe, all sociality is connected to the state; therefore, leaving socialism behind should also mean creating new kinds of social relations. Crucially, these new social relations should be nonkin social relations. As part of developing a modernist state in which politics was separate from kin ties and other "corrupting" influences, those tasked with "building civil society" aimed to promote nonkin social relations (Sampson 1996). Anxieties about irresponsible social relations that could impede the free flow of capital or constrain individual freedom pervade discussions of civil society.

The UTA in Wrocław is an example of civil society–building missions in eastern Europe. Although it has received funding from different sources throughout its almost forty-year history, among its current sources of financial and practical support are the University of Wrocław, the city of Wrocław, and the Polish-American Freedom Foundation, which was created after the collapse of state socialism in eastern Europe to build civil society and transform social relations. Specifically, the Polish-American Freedom Foundation was created in 2001 with half the profits ($120 million USD) from the Polish-American Enterprise Fund, which was funded by USAID. Established as part of the Support for East European Democracy Act of 1989, which gave formal economic and political support to states of the former Soviet bloc, the Polish-American Enterprise Fund was the most profitable of the nineteen enterprise funds funded by USAID.[5] According to its mission statement, "the Polish-American Freedom Foundation seeks to advance democracy, civil society, economic development and equal opportunity in Poland and, ultimately, in other Central and Eastern European countries" (Polish-American Freedom Foundation 2000). Established in 2005, the program focusing on UTAS has disbursed over $3 million USD, making it a significant driver in the recent growth of these institutions.

Funding from the Polish-American Freedom Foundation only partially explains the recent popularity of UTAS in Poland. Other key factors include Poland joining the European Union in 2004 and the growing cultural and practical significance of the West and its attendant forms of living. However, this funding makes evident that contemporary Polish UTAS are directly linked to American policies that were instrumental in shaping the transition from communism and socialism to democracy and capitalism. As part of westward-aspiring civil society, then, what are the forms of responsibility that are imagined, fostered, and practiced at UTAS? In the next sections, I demonstrate how certain aspects of the UTAS promote forms of responsibility that align with the goals of civil society builders; however, some forms of sociality exceed such neoliberal responsibilization.

Caring for the Self in the Third Age

In Poland, where the state's obligations to its citizens have been transformed and ultimately reduced during the lives of the oldest generations, various foundations, educational nonprofit organizations, and associations have arisen to train older people in techniques of self-care in order to take some of these obligations on themselves. Often included in such programming is the idea that self-care will also lead to self-transformation. Sometimes this self-transformation is explicitly framed in terms of Poland's political-economic changes. This can be quite explicit, as when Walentyna Wnuk, a former director of the UTA, spoke about her desire to create Euroseniorzy, or Euroseniors, which was accomplished through organizing trips to Brussels and Strasbourg for attendees (Robbins-Ruszkowski 2013, 163). As Wnuk described this trip, the former director linked the openness of European Union economies and societies to the habits and practices of older people, who should leave behind closed ways of living that they learned during socialist times. For Wnuk, transformations in political economy require transformations in persons.

The desire for self-care and neoliberalized responsibility was stated most explicitly by the director of a nongovernmental organization for older adults, whom I met through a colleague at the UTA in Wrocław. @ktywny Senior (@ctive Senior) has tried to cultivate responsibility in older residents of the city through a varied range of programming, including preventive health behaviors, computer training, learning how to use automatic banking machines, and communication classes. The director, Marek Ferenc, described @ktywny Senior as promoting "a responsible lifestyle" (*odpowiedzialny styl życia*), in contrast to "the negative consequences of an irresponsible lifestyle" (*negatywne konsekwencje życia nieodpowiedzialnego*) (Robbins-Ruszkowski 2015, 274–75). According to Ferenc, because older people expect their health to be managed by doctors, especially through prescribing pills, they need to be taught how to take care of their own health:

> These people are convinced—that is, there is this habit with us, that when, that you yourself are not responsible for your health, that only the doctor is responsible. This is a mistaken attitude, isn't it? Because I myself am responsible for my health. It's not the result of one day. It's my behavior throughout my whole life . . . hygiene . . . food, exercise . . . lots and lots and lots of factors, right?
> And it's . . . there is this belief among us, that if I'm sick, I will go to the doctor, the doctor will give me a golden pill . . . [laughter] you

know. . . . I'm joking, you know? All this is to say that this attitude that people have . . . doctor, doctor, doctor. One, another, the third, the fifth. Tests. One, another. Yeah and these tests . . . what results from these tests? Nothing.[6]

Instead of viewing health as something provided for them by doctors in the form of pills, older people should view health as the effect of a cumulative lifelong process of enacting certain behaviors, according to Ferenc. This goal of physical health was connected to other goals of @ktywny Senior, such as teaching computer skills, communication skills, and volunteering—all of which he saw as necessary because of the large number of people who were forced to take early retirement after 1989, and therefore did not experience the transformations in labor that occurred in the 1990s that would have properly inculcated them with neoliberal sensibilities (cf. Dunn 2004). These changes have led to older people feeling "unnecessary" (*niepotrzebni*); they can become needed—and responsible—through practicing preventive health behaviors, learning computer skills, and volunteering.[7]

Other times, connections to the political economy are less explicit, but still evident in the form and content of activities of the UTA, as evident in one lecture on how to cook healthily with various forms of fats. This was offered as part of the every-other-week lecture series Our Health in Our Hands (*Nasze zdrowie w naszych rękach*). The lecturer, a nutrition specialist, spent much of the forty-five-minute lecture dispensing advice on shopping for olive oil: which shops to seek out and which to avoid, the best times of the week and year to make purchases, how to distinguish the truly healthful kinds and brands from the fakes. Teaching older people about food was especially important, I was told by university-age students and health workers, because older people have particularly bad eating habits and do not understand the importance of different kinds of cooking fats. They must learn to take care of themselves by preparing healthy food and becoming the right kind of consumers.[8]

At the UTA, care of the self during aging is necessary not only because of the changing political economy, but also because of the phase of life itself. According to its former director, "late adulthood is the most individualized phase of life" due to the cumulative effect of differing life histories (Wnuk 2005, 16). According to this logic, each older adult is the person best equipped to know himself or herself, which can be done through evaluating one's own "attitude" (*postawa*) toward oneself and toward life (Wnuk 2005, 16). One can be "active" (*aktywne*) or "passive" (*pasywne*) about the bodily and social changes that occur in late life; however, cultivating an "adaptive capacity" (*zdolność adaptacyjna*) will best help one to "constructively react to the changes and problems that life brings" (Wnuk 2005, 17).[9] By so doing, older people can "become masters of one's selves," in the words of Deepak Chopra, as quoted by Wnuk (2005, 15). She explicitly connects being *aktywny*, and practicing *aktywność*, or activeness, with flexibility and self-management. The goals of the UTA thus align not only with much gerontological research but also with the "flexible citizenship" desired by neoliberal forms of governance (Ong 2003).

These goals of becoming responsible for oneself are also taken up by the *słuchacze* (attendees). Indeed, being *aktywny* is an unquestioned moral good for *słuchacze*. In interviews, many *słuchacze* shared with me their newfound athletic interests and talents: swimming, sailing, Nordic walking, aerobics classes. Some participated in several groups, going to swimming and exercise classes four times per week. Physical activities and other UTA course offerings came to dominate the lives of many women with whom I spoke. The UTA became a structuring force in their lives, sometimes taking priority over kinship obligations.

In personal reflections published in the *Kurier UTW: Nieregularnik Uniwersytetu Trzecieo Wieku* (UTA Courier: The Nonperiodical of the University of the Third Age), *słuchacze* report learning self-responsibilizing behaviors that they feel are transformative. For example, one attendee describes a summer of taking various physical exercise classes as helping her to improve her mood (Gasperowicz 2004), while another writes of learning how engaging in physical exercise "allows for lowering costs of health care and social care, and increasing the abilities to work of people of advanced ages" (Warmuz 2004, 22).[10] In learning to exercise, attendees at the UTAs see themselves as contributing to the broader polity; they take on the goal of refashioning their lives to meet the economic needs of the neoliberal state.

However, histories of the UTA suggest a more complex interpretation than that which focuses solely on neoliberal responsibilization. Indeed, improving the physical health of *słuchacze* has been a focus of UTAS since their beginnings in the 1970s. Additionally, the socialist state encouraged its subjects to be healthy; having a healthy body was necessary to contribute to building the socialist state. This historical perspective suggests that contemporary neoliberal practices of caring for the self through exercise and other healthy behaviors overlap with older forms of self-care.

Creating Intimate Sociality in the Third Age

In addition to improving the health of older persons so that they will make fewer demands on the state, these exercise and nutrition classes also offer opportunities for older Poles to make new friends and acquaintances. That is, the same practices through which older persons transform themselves are also the means through which they create new social ties. In fact, much of the discourse of the UTA is about the creation and quality of new social relations. This institutional focus on sociality predates the civil society–building projects of the postsocialist years and thus cannot be fully explained through such a lens.

Like the forms of self-care described above, the social aspects of the UTA have been central throughout its history. As stated in official documents effective from the 1970s through the 1990s, "The University is a social organization, directing engagement in the sphere of culture, education, and preservation of health of people in the older age, independent of their formal level of education" (Woźnicka 1997, 1; Bilewicz 2001, 15).[11] In this vision, the social is imagined as encompassing domains of "culture, education, and preservation of health"; this is a more expansive purpose than reducing the state's health care costs. In this text, the UTA claims responsibility for promoting sociality among older people. Activities at the UTA are imagined by its leaders as complementing each other, evident in an analysis of activities of the first słuchacze in the late 1970s: "The meetings that occurred here above all served to strengthen individual values and sympathies with interpersonal contacts and a feeling of joy in life. They were also a useful form of group therapy. Participants in these groups started to help each other to solve personal problems, related to, for instance, problems with apartments, doing the shopping, and jointly planned holiday trips or sanatorium visits" (Bilewicz 2001, 9–10).[12]

In these descriptions, "individual values" are intertwined with "interpersonal contacts." "Personal problems" become shared. Moreover, motivations for joining the UTA have long been explicitly social. Intake interviews done in the early years of the UTA (then referred to as Studium Trzeciego Wieku, STW, or Study Center of the Third Age) emphasized the importance of social relations and, in particular, of forming new friendships: "Among the reasons given for signing up for the STW were health and intellectual needs, but also emotional. They expected that in this institution they would find relief from problems, that it could lessen their uncertainty and fear about loneliness and death, anxiety, sadness, helplessness, and being lost. Participation in classes helped students in forming new friendships and lessened feelings of loneliness/isolation. Additionally participation improved and developed their psychophysical health through rehabilitation, sports, and rational recreation" (Bilewicz 2001, 11).[13]

Here, the UTA can be seen as an institution that addresses the bodily, intellectual, emotional, and social needs of the older person. The activities of the UTA provide a social means through which to ameliorate older Poles' shared bodily, mental, and emotional problems: namely, loneliness, sadness, and "helplessness" (*bezradność*).

More recently, this desire for social connection is also evident in both institutional discourse and practice. *Kuriery* are filled with reports on the meetings of embroidery groups and tourist groups, schedules of choir concerts and cabaret performances, and descriptions of holiday celebrations; the key feature of these descriptions is the evident pleasure in the celebration itself. In many interviews, women expressed *radość* (joy) at the newfound *koleżeństwo* (collegiality, friendship, camaraderie) that they found at the UTA. Anna, a seventy-four-year-old retired forestry worker, described meeting "many nice people" (*dużo sympatycznych ludzi*) with whom she developed friendships that extended beyond the bounds of the UTA. Women from her English class gathered at her *działka* (allotment garden) to socialize. Dominika, a sixty-three-year-old who had worked in banking, said that she had "lacked contact with people" (*brakowało mi kontaktu z ludźmi*), despite participating in exercise classes organized through her housing development. These comments expressing a desire for new social relations are highly representative of the słuchacze with whom I spoke. Even the few that did not make new friends at the UTA recognized that the UTA's role as a social connector was paramount.

However, this phenomenon begs the question of how such problems have come to exist in the first place. Why do older people feel a sense of loneliness, helplessness (bezradność) and being lost (*zagubienie*)? Why are older people in such need of relief (*ulga*)? How do new friendships satisfy this need, and whose responsibility is it to satisfy these older adults' emotional needs? What has happened to existing friendships such that new ones must be formed? Why are friendships with neighbors less satisfying than with other retirees learning English? In short, how has old age become an experience defined by social isolation, and how do activities of the UTA remedy (and how are they understood to remedy) such isolation?

The beginnings of an answer can be found in three important demographic characteristics of słuchacze, both past and present. First, many słuchacze do not have spouses. In the late 1970s, 68 percent of słuchacze reported being unmarried—never married, divorced, or widowed (Bilewicz 2001, 11). In 2004,

63 percent reported being unmarried (Wnuk 2004, 3). Of the słuchacze I met, over half were widowed. In Poland, marital pairs are the normative ideal and structure many aspects of social life; this norm, combined with the fact of change brought about by the death of a spouse, can result in significant isolation for people without spouses.

Second, many contemporary słuchacze live a significant distance from children or grandchildren. Or, if children or grandchildren are local, the grandchildren are old enough that their grandparents, the słuchacze, are not involved in daily care. Following Poland's joining the European Union in 2004, over one million Poles left the country to seek work elsewhere (indeed, a primary motivation for some słuchacze to learn English or computer skills is to communicate with kin abroad). Grandparents play an enormous role in the care of grandchildren (more than once, I heard people refer to the institution of the *babcia*, or grandmother, as the *skarb* [treasure] of the Polish nation, in reference to the child care that they provide, making it possible for both parents to work outside the home). Having grandchildren who live far away thus means a lack of a highly culturally valued (and time-consuming) kinship obligation. Indeed, throughout my years of fieldwork at UTAS, I never met a słuchacz who was at that time the primary caregiver for a young (under six) grandchild, although many had done so before. In this context where such kinship responsibilities structure moral expectations for activity, the lack of such an everyday kin role can lead to feelings of being unneeded and unappreciated.

Finally, słuchacze are overwhelmingly women. In the 1970s, over 75 percent of słuchacze were women (Bilewicz 2001, 12). In 2012, the national percentage was over 80 percent (Towarzystwo Inicjatyw Twórczych "ę" 2012). Among those I met, over 90 percent were women. This gender disparity can partially be explained through life expectancy, morbidity, and mortality rates, as Polish women tend to live longer and healthier lives than Polish men. However, this statistical explanation alone cannot explain the dramatically higher prevalence of women at the UTAS. If this were a sufficient explanation, we would expect to see an increase in the number of men at the UTAS as these epidemiological figures changed over time; however, in recent decades, the difference in life expectancy for men and women has decreased, as men have started living longer too. Rather, as expressed in motivations for joining the UTA in the 1970s and more recently, older women's experiences of loneliness and isolation can be seen as evidence of the stripping away of their meaningful forms of social life. That is, because Poland continues to be a place in which women are expected to carry out the work of maintaining social relations, a proper old age for Polish women thus centers on their responsibility to care for the family. Without the presence of spouses, children, and grandchildren, many older Polish women thus seek out other forms of social engagement.

Underlying these gendered demographic explanations are histories of labor and ideals of sociality. Although not all słuchacze at the UTA were retired, most were. People told me that, in addition to a lack of kin, they also lacked the collegial friendships of their former workplaces. Although some people still met up with friends from their working days, many did not; it was rare that these contacts occurred more than a few times a year. The church has historically and continues to provide opportunities for sociality, and especially feminine sociality; however, as I explain later in this chapter, church-based sociality is not comparable to that of the UTA. That women cope with the isolation of retirement by seeking new friendships reveals a gendered dimension to sociality in Poland. Women are described as being more aktywne than men, who are frequently described as pasywne in old age. Women are thought to be responsible for and interested in maintaining social ties, or, in the words of both men and women research participants, "the world of people" (świat ludzi). Men, however, are thought to be more interested in hobbies like fishing, hiking, and tinkering (majsterkowanie)—in short, the world of things (świat rzeczy). In retirement, older men are more likely to engage in these practices than to seek out new friendships through social organizations like UTAs. Lacking both family and work colleagues, older Polish women appreciate the UTA for its network of similarly isolated peers, most of whom are also eager to form new social ties, including attendant practices of obligation and responsibility.

However, why are these friendships created at the UTA different in kind from the other friendships of Dominika, the woman who felt she lacked contact with people? Although she did not then have grandparental responsibilities and her spousal obligations were quite minimal, she regularly participated in activities in her neighborhood. However, she found these neighborly friendships insufficient. Rather, Dominika emphasized the possibility afforded by the UTA of choosing her own friends. With neighbors, she said, "One cannot really choose." She described the same sentiments in her work life as well; that is, she also could not choose her coworkers. In socialist Poland, work structured social relations across many spheres of life (e.g., apartment buildings were often filled with workers from the same state enterprise, and vacations were often organized and allocated through places of employment). For people of Dominika's age, many of the people who had filled her social world were people about whom she had no choice. Moreover, social relations during state socialism can be remembered as being especially instrumental, as the shortage economy required people to negotiate and barter for goods and favors.[14] Other women at the UTA and elsewhere described experiences of maintaining friendships with persons whom they found unpleasant, but from whom they needed something; these relations were motivated by histories of exchange and the potential for future transactional needs. Because this form of social responsibility was understood to be linked to the socialist state, it could not be experienced as moral in the same way that kin responsibilities were. Of course, this is not meant to suggest that exchange-based friendships are actually opposed to more affinity-based friendships; however, these idealized binary forms continue to structure expectations and understandings of friendships.

It is thus in contrast to her lifetime of experiences during state socialism that Dominika expressed joy at creating friendships motivated by shared personal interests. At the UTA, Dominika said, one can avoid certain persons if one wishes by simply saying "hello" and moving on. There, she has found she can focus on others who share her interests in certain activities (e.g., learning English, physical exercise, reading). These friendships based on shared interests constitute a new form of social relation for Dominika and others, yet also allow for a continuation of her gendered moral personhood as a socially engaged and active woman. Although these relations begin from shared interests in certain activities, they expand in scope to include more transactional forms of relations (e.g., providing references for and connections to medical specialists, caring for each other's gardens when one is away) that reintroduce obligations and responsibilities. Yet the origin of these friendships continues to shape people's understandings of them as distinct from other kinds of social relations. Over time, these friendships create a community of women who take responsibility for ensuring each other's continued existence as social persons. It is to the possibilities and limits of such intimate sociality that I now turn.

Reproducing the Nation in the Third Age

At the UTA, the conscious creation of the third age allows older people a discursive structure in which they can care for themselves and others. These friendships are recognizably Polish; that is, key features of Polish identity writ large are evident in the form and content of sociality at the UTA. Specifically, the Polish nation, Catholic religion, and traditional gender roles figure prominently.[15] Such national dimensions structure a shared framework within which słuchacze can create social relations, practice aktywność and become responsible for themselves and others.

This framework is established in the space and temporality of the UTA itself. On the wall of the UTA's main classroom hangs a picture displaying an iconic image of the University of Wrocław by the Odra River with the words "UTA: our little fatherland" (UTW: naszą małą ojczyzną). Over the door of the room hangs a wooden cross, a common feature in many public institutions in Poland (despite official separation of church and state). The structure of the institution's calendar aligns with that of the University of Wrocław, following the governmental and religious holidays as observed and dictated by the Polish state. Programming at the UTA reflects these calendrical moments through celebrations of holidays like Christmas and Children's Day. At Christmastime, the UTA organizes gatherings featuring common holiday (Wigilia) dishes, singing of carols (kolędy), and sharing of Christmas Eve communion wafers (opłatki) (e.g., Krautforst 2000). On Children's Day, UTA outreach groups visit local schoolchildren. Important moments in the life cycle of the UTA such as the beginning or end of the academic year often feature regional church and government leaders (e.g., bishops, mayors) who highlight the common interests of their group and the UTA.

It is not only at specially defined ritual moments, however, that programming at the UTA features national and Catholic elements. The UTA choir regularly performs patriotic Polish songs from the late nineteenth and early twentieth centuries. These songs are well known by older Poles and are a common feature of activities for older people in diverse contexts. Older Poles also sing these songs during more informal social gatherings. The historical Polish nation is also invoked through the structure of the UTA itself. One of the subgroups within the UTA is the club for "admirers of the kresy" (Klub miłośników kresów). Kresy is the term for Poland's former eastern borderlands that are now part of Ukraine, Belarus, and Lithuania. Many people and cultural institutions from the kresy moved to Wrocław as Poland's borders moved west after World War II. The kresy thus hold special significance for many people in Wrocław as their ancestral home and the site of a lost ideal of Polish high culture. Indeed, many słuchacze were themselves born in the kresy. As described in the first issue of the Kurier, "the eastern borderlands were the bulwark of Polishness and culture" (kresy wschodnie były ostoją polskości i kultury) (Krautforst 2000). Cabaret groups performed songs from the kresy, events during which many in the audience were singing along and had tears in their eyes. The invocations of this lost world constitute the means through which słuchacze create new social relations.

The poetry of the słuchacze makes a fruitful context for understanding the nature of the intimate sociality that is forged at the UTA. The topics of poems frequently contain patriotic expressions of love for Wrocław or Poland itself; for Mary, Jesus, or Pope John Paul II; and for the natural world (most commonly, seasons and flowers). The poems' tones tend to be melancholy, nostalgic, wistful, or reverent, especially regarding topics of nation, religion, and nature. In the 2004 issue of the *Kurier*, there are poems about Polish Independence Day, Our Lady of Sorrows (Maryja Licheńska, an important Polish shrine to the Virgin Mary), the lonely but redemptive suffering of illness, and rhyming couplets that reproduce stereotypical male and female gender roles. The 2001 issue features a few playful lines of verse from the "boys" (*chłopaki*) of the UTA to the "ladies" (*panie*) on the occasion of International Women's Day (March 8). In this verse, women are represented as creating a warm and pleasant atmosphere at the UTA, just as they do at home, through their "care" (*troska*). Such feminine care for the home is at the center of a romantic, nationalist, Catholic Polishness (Graff 2009; Porter-Szücs 2011). These creative products suggest a particularly Polish form of sociality that holds together various scales of experience (bodily, religious, national) and upon which other forms can be overlaid. Practices of responsibility that occur through the UTA are thus suffused with Polishness.

Religion forms a central part of the UTA's discourse and practice, and the women who attend (like most older Poles) tend to identify as Catholic; many słuchacze spoke of being involved in their local parishes and attending services regularly. However, it is crucial to note that they view the UTA as a different form of sociality than the church. In fact, several women remarked that the UTA is superior to other forms of social engagement for older adults such as parish clubs or neighborhood senior clubs, which are petty, gossipy, and small in focus. In contrast, they see the UTA as an opportunity for a sociality that is based not on religion or neighborhood, but rather on bettering one's self through education. This move toward a sociality that is not exclusively religious or local should be interpreted within long-standing forms of class distinction. For instance, the popularity of foreign-language classes resonates with the centuries-long practice of the landowning Polish class speaking French and German (Jakubowska 2012, 184–85). Given the continuity through the socialist era of the Polish nobility's symbolic power in the realm of culture (Jakubowska 2012), słuchacze who learn foreign languages and perform in cabarets can be understood as cultivating a particular kind of old age that resonates with elements of the socialist and presocialist past, even as it takes on contemporary meanings. In other words, even as these women are creating friendships that feel new to them, they are also reproducing deeper histories of class aspirations and labor structures that carry new political significance in the context of Poland's membership in the European Union.

In the context of a civil society–building organization such as the UTA, attempts by słuchacze to seek out social relations beyond the church could be interpreted as striving for a civic, rather than ethnic, national identity, in which civic maps onto the West and ethnic onto the East.[16] However, słuchacze do participate in and aspire to both religious and nonreligious forms of social life, demonstrating the inadequacy of these labels as categories of practice (Zubrzycki 2001, 2002). Although Catholicism remains central to the forms of sociality in which the słuchacze engage at the UTA, it coexists amid other practices that are not explicitly religious. The national framework within which this sociality occurs is a religious one, to be sure, but it is also shaped by histories of class distinction and labor structures.

Both material privilege and class aspirations allow some older Polish women to escape or limit kin obligations and engage in practices of self-transformation that are increasingly valued in Polish society. It is their earlier lives spent laboring in certain occupations that provide adequate pensions for such hobbies, but, perhaps more importantly, it is their class aspiration that encourages them to privilege nonkin over kin relations, and to seek out new relations beyond parishes and neighborhoods. In this way women's experiences in old age bear the traces of their own labor and kin histories. Thus although these women are taking on responsibility for themselves in ways that seem to be neoliberal, they are doing so within a context of shared personal and national histories in which other forms of responsibility continue to matter.

Aktywność: Local Idioms of Responsibility, Care, and Sociality

The end of state socialism brought about different kinds of responsibilities between the state and its citizens, between generations, and between persons. The neoliberal desire for civil society in eastern Europe mobilizes local desires for citizens to create a certain form of responsibility to each other. Older Polish women seek out UTAS to overcome the loneliness and isolation that can come from a decrease in work and kin obligations by creating new friendships. This desire for social relations suggests that seeking aktywność actually indicates a desire for sociality itself.

Friendships formed at the UTA are discursively structured by romantic ideals of the Polish nation. In this context, explicitly opposed to the socialist past, people seek out friends with whom they share interests, rather than from whom they seek a particular transactional need; this framework persists even as such friendships take on transactional elements. This motivation for friendship, and the activities through which these friendships are created and maintained, tend to appeal to older Poles of higher classes or who have such class aspirations. Socialist and presocialist histories and nineteenth-century class divisions and aspirations continue to matter in contemporary Poland.

However, possibilities for sociality and responsibility are threatened by illness and disability, and by economic marginality. In the publications of the UTA and in my years of research there, illness is strikingly absent, appearing only as something to prevent through proper use of the right kinds of cooking fats, or in whispers or poems. Yet these experiences often occur when ties of responsibility and obligation are most fully engaged. How do discourses of responsibility and sociality apply to experiences of old age that fall outside the normative ideal of aktywność? What happens when being sick strips people of the capacity for aktywność? Do new forms of responsibility and care emerge? Research among older Poles experiencing various forms of debility (e.g., paralysis following a stroke, postoperative rehabilitation, Alzheimer's disease) suggests that although concerns of aktywność fall away, people sustain moral personhood through practices of sociality that similarly draw on personal histories, presocialist and socialist pasts, and ideals of the Polish nation (Robbins 2013). In both third- and fourth-age contexts, similarities in forms of responsibility and care emerge. In order to more completely understand the competing responsibilities of contemporary life, we must think across the analytic scale as well as seek out ethnographic diversity. Such comparative research and analysis is necessary in order to understand more fully the points of convergence and divergence in existing and emergent multiple forms of responsibility.

ACKNOWLEDGMENTS

Many thanks to editors Susanna Trnka and Catherine Trundle, and two anonymous reviewers, for their insightful critical commentaries on this chapter. This chapter also benefited from careful and generous readings by Elana Buch, Laura Heinemann, Julia Kowalski, Aaron Seaman, and Kristin Yarris. Support for this research and writing was provided by the Wenner-Gren Foundation (Dissertation Fieldwork Grant #7736), the National Science Foundation (DDIG #0819259), IREX (International Research and Exchanges Board, with funds provided by the U.S. Department of State through the Title VIII program), the Woodrow Wilson International Center for Scholars (U.S. Department of State, Title VIII), Elderhostel/Road Scholar, several units at the University of Michigan (Center for Russian, East European, and Eurasian Studies; Department of Anthropology; Institute for Research on Women and Gender; and Rackham Graduate School), and Wayne State University. None of these organizations is responsible for the views expressed herein. As always, my greatest thanks are reserved for the research participants who so kindly shared their stories and experiences with me.

NOTES

1. This chapter draws on almost two years of ethnographic fieldwork in Wrocław and Poznań, Poland, conducted between 2006 and 2014. The longest fieldwork period was eighteen months between 2008 and 2010. Besides UTAS, sites of research included other social groups for older people and several medical care institutions.

2. Developed by the French scholar Pierre Vellas at the University of Toulouse in 1973, the institution was replicated elsewhere within a few years in Europe and Canada, and flourished in Britain in the 1980s. By 2012, they were found in sixty countries worldwide (Formosa 2014, 2–7).

3. Age and generation have come to the fore as particularly salient markers of attitudes toward contemporary postsocialist transformations (e.g., Caldwell 2007; Dunn 2004; Haukanes and Trnka 2013; Parsons 2014; Pozniak 2013, 2014; Thelen 2003; however, see Haukanes 2013 and Ringel 2013 for contrasting cases).

4. See Buchowski (1996) and Hann (1996) for a discussion of whether civil society was actually absent in state socialist societies.

5. The other half of the profits was returned to the U.S. government.

6. "Ci ludzie są przekonani, czyli u nas taki jest zwyczaj, że jak, za zdrowie nie jesteś sama odpowiedzialna, tylko lekarz jest odpowiedzialny. To jest błędny podejścia, prawda? Bo za zdrowia jestem ja odpowiedzialny, sam. Potem nie jest wydarzeń jednego dnia, tylko to jest moje postępowanie przez cały życie . . . higiena życia . . . ja . . . Jedzenia, sportu . . . wielu wielu wielu czynniku, prawda? . . . I to . . . U nas jest taki przekonany, żeby jestem chory, pójdę do lekarzy, lekarz mi da złotą tabletkę. daja. . . . wiesz. Przekazam. Żartuję, nie? Przez to powiedzieć że taki postawienie ludzi—lekarz, lekarz, lekarz. Jeden, drugi, trzeci, piąty. Badanie. Jedne, drugie. No badanie . . . co z tego wynika z tego badania? Nic." (Marek Ferenc, interview by Robbins, September 4, 2009).

7. See Parsons (2014) for an ethnographic investigation of the need to be needed among Russians following the end of the Soviet Union.

8. This sort of consumer education aligns with the ethnographic record from across the former socialist bloc where consumer choice was a new phenomenon and trust was something that had to be created anew (e.g., Mandel and Humphrey 2002); however, this lecture occurred almost twenty years after the end of state socialism.

9. "Trzeba konstruktywnie reagować na zmiany, problemy, jakie przynosi życie. . . . Starać się o wysoki poziom zdolności adaptacyjnych, akceptując zmiany w życiu" (Wnuk 2005, 17).

10. "Pozwala na zmniejszenie kosztów opieki zdrowotnej i opieki społecznej, zwiększenie zdolności do pracy osób w podeszłym wieku" (Warmuz 2004, 22).

11. "Uniwersytet jest organizacją społeczną, prowadzącą działalność w dziedzinie kultury, oświaty i ochrony zdrowia obejmującą osoby w starszym wieku niezależnie od ich formalnego poziomu wykształcenia" (Woźnicka 1997, 1, in Bilewicz 2001, 15).

12. "Odbywające się tu spotkania służyły przede wszystkim wzmocnieniu indywidualnych wartości i wrażliwości w kontaktach międzyludzkich oraz poczucia radości życia. Okazały się one też bardzo korzystną formą terapii grupowej. Uczestnicy zajęć zaczęli okazywać sobie wzajemną pomoc w rozwiązywaniu osobistych problemów, związanych na przykład ze sprawami mieszkaniowymi, dokonywaniem zakupów, wspólnym planowaniem wyjazdów na wczasy czy do sanatorium" (Bilewicz 2001, 9–10).

13. "Wśród powodów zgłaszania się do STW wymieniali oni zarówno potrzeby zdrowotne i poznawcze, jak też emocjonalne. Oczekiwali, że w tej instytucji znajdą ulgę w trapiących ich kłopotach, że zmniejszy się ich niepewność, lęk przed samotnością czy śmiercią, niepokój, smutek, bezradność i zagubienie. Udział w zajęciach pomagał studentom w nawiązaniu nowych przyjaźni oraz zmniejszał poczucie osamotnienia. Nadto poprawiał i rozwijał sprawność psychofizyczną poprzez rehabilitację, sport i racjonalny wypoczynek" (Bilewicz 2001, 11).

14. For example, see Dunn (2004) for a discussion of getting things done *po znajomości*, or "through acquaintances," in Poland, and Ledeneva (1998) for a discussion of *blat* in Russia.

15. See Graff (2009), Porter (2000), Porter-Szücs (2011), and Zubrzycki (2006) for discussions of the historical, religious, and gendered dimensions of Polish national identity.

16. See Kohn (1944) for a classic explication of this dichotomy.

TEN. Genetic Bystanders: *Familial Responsibility and the State's Accountability to Veterans of Nuclear Tests*

CATHERINE TRUNDLE

This chapter focuses on claims of political accountability and accusations of blame and harm made by veterans of British nuclear bomb tests, and attends to emergent modes of genetic relationality and responsibility. In doing so I reveal how new genetic technologies and the visions of personhood and interrelationality they constitute intersect with claims of debility, risk, and entitlement. As Julie Livingston (2005, 3) argues, "in instances of debility . . . the question of our responsibilities toward one another becomes more overt. Safety nets and moral economies are tested. Key relationships undergo both public and private scrutiny."[1] How test veterans understand gendered kin roles, military modes of citizenship, and state responsibility all become visible through these claim-making processes.

Theoretically, this chapter aims to challenge the concept of responsibilization more generally, and genetic responsibilization more specifically, in order to account for biopolitical claims of dependency, blame, helplessness, and culpability, and to show responsibility's intimate and complex relationship with practices of irresponsibilization. Ethnographically, the analysis pivots around a brief interaction between a radiobiologist and a veteran who participated in British nuclear bomb tests in the Pacific in the 1950s. The narrative tracks backward from this interaction to recent developments within experimental science that are reconfiguring the biological role of the gene, and trace forward to the subsequent translation of this scientific knowledge by nuclear test veterans who contextualize it within the frames of their own grievances toward the state, bodily experience, and family ties.

The relational gene that emerged in their encounter was both potent and potentially dangerous, and, most importantly, on the move. Genes that are seen to cross boundaries and borders have always been unsettling, prompting both fear and hope in popular culture. Whether in engineered life escaping the confines of the lab, the blurring of species within genetic engineering (Van Dijck 1998), or stem cell therapy, mobile genes have the potential to upset basic cultural notions of personhood, kinship, intimacy, and obligations between citizens and the state. This chapter thus juxtaposes the specificities of intimate genetic ties within one family with the potential for such scientific knowledge to transform wider social and political life.

Section I: Theoretical and Historical Contexts

Responsibilization and Irresponsibilization

Building on Foucault's (1991) notion of governmentality, scholars have developed the concept of responsibilization to capture the processes by which power becomes entangled with practices of self-actualization, self-care, empowerment, and prudence. As Alan Hunt (2003, 187) characterizes it, "Responsibilization refers to a form of governing that discursively imposes specific responsibilities on individuals relating to their own conduct or that of another for whom they are presented as being responsible. Much responsibilization is entirely conventional: parents for their children, employers for the work of their employees. But the techniques lend itself to expansion. Increasingly, patients are deemed responsible for the management of their recovery from illness, expected to adopt right activities. Pregnant women are responsibilized for the well-being of their fetuses, expected to abstain from an expanding range of 'risky' behavior."

While responsibilization has been present in other historical periods (associated with particular social roles, such as those expected of a mother, a priest, or a male breadwinner), scholars argue that its current manifestation and association with neoliberalism is distinct for its emphasis on a more individualized mode of responsibility (Hunt 2003, 189) that expects "individuals to take on board a greater responsibility for their own conduct and their care of the self in responding to risks" (184). Practices and rhetorics of responsibilization are thus associated with the state's active work to divest some of the risks and responsibilities previously assumed by government (dealt with through welfare, health care, education, or policing, for example) onto newly empowered and active individuals, groups, or communities. According to Lemke (2001, 201), "The neo-liberal forms of government feature not only direct intervention by means of empowered and specialized state apparatuses, but also characteristically develop indirect techniques for leading and controlling individuals without at the same time being responsible for them. The strategy of rendering individual subjects 'responsible' (and also collectives, such as families, associations, etc.) entails shifting the responsibility for social risks such as illness, unemployment, poverty, etc., and for life in society into the domain for which the individual is responsible and transforming it into a problem of 'self-care.'"

In this vein, in the last decade, with the rise of genetic research, techniques, and products, scholars have identified a new vital politics through which people are becoming somatically responsibilized. This literature emphasizes the processes by which genetic risk is embodied and negotiated in ways that are far from passive, and which engender "enterprising, self-actualizing, responsible personhood. . . . The patient is to become skilled, prudent and active, an ally of the doctor, a proto-professional—and to take their own share of the responsibility for getting themselves better. Patients at genetic risk and their families are not passive elements in the practice of cure" (Novas and Rose 2000, 488–89).

> Genetic risk does not imply resignation in the face of an implacable biological destiny: it induces new and active relations to oneself and one's future. In particular, it generates new forms of "genetic responsibility," locating actually and potentially affected individuals within new communities of obligation and identification. Far from generating fatalism, the rewriting of personhood at a genetic level and its visualization through a "molecular optic" transforms the relations between patient and expert in unexpected ways, and is linked to the development of novel "life strategies," involving practices of choice, enterprise, self-actualization and prudence in relation to one's genetic make-up. (Novas and Rose 2000, 485)

Such life strategies are evident in myriad examples, from the rise of personalized genetic testing to prophylactic measures to avoid the somatic consequences of dangerous genes. But how does the telos of responsibilization shift when people do not respond to their genetic risk with an active ethos of enterprising empowerment? This chapter seeks to examine genetic vulnerabilities that do not engender choices but a sense of victimhood, innocence, and injustice, where risks in the future are not the main concern, but instead irreversible harm done in the past that governs demands for others to be held responsible in the present.

Despite an emphasis on the activation of the self within responsibilization literature, scholars do point out that genetic illnesses are by their very nature intersubjective and relational, drawing into view familial pasts and futures, and decisions regarding marriage and reproduction, career choices, and financial planning (Novas and Rose 2000, 487), which "are made in a web of entanglements involving actual and potential kin, employers, partners and children" (Rose 2001, 19). Moreover, scholars show how a range of biosocial groups have formed around notions of genetic risk in order to organize for public support, rights to health care, and which engage in the development of new biomedical research, treatments, and technologies (Rabinow 1996; Rose 2001). As such groups show, demands for more autonomy and control often parallel claims for care and dependence.

It is not only the place of dependencies that needs to be foregrounded here, but a fine-tuning of the diverse range of genetic relationalities that are envisaged and constituted, particularly along gendered lines. Steinberg (1996) argues that it is women and women's bodies that are socially held responsible for carrying genetic risk and defect, and that they are the actors who grapple with the responsibility of transmitting their own and their partner's genetic material to children. Correspondingly, Nina Hallowell shows how British women with a genetic risk of breast cancer enact their choices and responsibility toward genetic testing and genetic knowledge in ways that "maintain their identity as selves-in-relation—as carers, mothers, sisters, daughters" (1999, 613), and ultimately as selflessly, sacrificially concerned with the well-being of kin. Such studies thus assume that it is centrally women who must morally grapple with the relational consequences and care work of abnormal genes. In this chapter, however, I show how men can also be held to account, or hold themselves to account for familial forms of genetic risk and harm, as both fathers and husbands.

In tracing actors' engagements with the relational gene, this chapter engages with the notion of irresponsibilization, to explore how assertions of responsibility get rejected or recast. In relation to contemporary techniques of risk, Alan Hunt proposes the concept of irresponsibilization to account for "those responses to risk in which individuals refuse to accept responsibility for tackling risks resulting from their own choices and instead transfer responsibility and blame onto others" (2003, 184). The concept of irresponsibilization offers us ways in which to think about how refusing to accept responsibility can be a moral act that does not reject the idea of responsibility per se, but relocates it and implicates others in the well-being of the self.

The concept of irresponsibilization as currently framed has its limits, however. As Hunt articulates it, responsibility is owned or rejected in a fairly clear-cut fashion by adversaries, and done so with active, willful agency. Yet as this chapter shows, responsibility is a far more unstable force: it can move more fluidly and obliquely back and forth between actors and groups, can be claimed at certain moments and rejected in others, can retreat or be sidelined but does not disappear, can be unintentionally lost rather than actively rejected, and can be uneasily shared or transformed over time.

Moreover, the word *irresponsible* implies a lack or a refusal, a rejection of something one ought to possess. Using this word as Hunt suggests requires going against the grain of our linguistic sensibility. Yet I argue this unfamiliar, repurposed usage is productive precisely because it works to rupture the link we implicitly make between a lack or rejection of responsibility, and morally suspect modes of personhood.

The notion of irresponsibilization has been used in relation to genetics. Biebricher (2011) argues that, contrary to an emphasis on the proactive patient, individuals can take genetic information about themselves to be fatalistically determining, relieving them of some of the effortful burdens and choices involved in somatic self-making. In relation to, for example, obesity, where people struggle to lose weight and can be given a genetic explanation for their condition, "genetic irresponsibilization might therefore be said to provide a welcome and less psychologically devastating way to deal with the experience of failure. It might subsequently make it easier to respond to failure in a more productive way and it might also help mitigate the potentially paralyzing effects of anticipating and fearing failure" (Biebricher 2011, 477). With the promise of irresponsibilization, however, comes potential costs, Biebricher (2011, 475) argues, particularly in the form of increased social stigmatization or social othering, which some studies show parallels the somatization and molecularization of illness etiologies. While this is a useful exploration of the burdens of responsibility and the double-edged nature of genetic fatalism, it explains the rejection of responsibility in individual and psychological rather than political terms. What if responsibility is rejected not only to avoid guilt or psychic harm but also to hold someone else to account, to redraw the lines of responsibility out of the self and family to larger entities such as the state? How do responsibilities transform as they shift back and forth between an individual, his family, and the state? And how might we understand genetic irresponsibilization in a case when it involves assertions of a social contract, biological citizenship, or sacrifices that must be repaid?

Operation Grapple

Reflecting on these questions, this chapter charts understandings of the gene by nuclear test veterans. I have conducted research among British and New Zealand nuclear test veterans since 2009 in both the United Kingdom and New Zealand, and have carried out life history interviews; participant observation in test veteran groups, events, and gatherings; observation at their legal cases against the Ministry of Defence (MoD) in the High and Supreme courts in London; and archival research. Most of my interlocutors were veterans of the army, navy, or air force aged in their seventies and eighties who, in their late teens or early twenties, were sent to serve at Christmas Island.[2] Now part of the Republic of Kiribati, in the 1950s Christmas Island was under British jurisdiction. Following World War II, the United States' ascent to global hegemon status was facilitated in part by its world-leading nuclear capabilities and nuclear physics research. Seeking geopolitical parity, the British government hoped to demonstrate its military might and ensure future scientific collaboration with the United States by developing its own hydrogen bomb. Following a series of smaller tests off the coast and in the outback of Australia, Britain shifted its nuclear bomb program to the Pacific where, between 1957 and 1958, it detonated nine atmospheric nuclear bombs, many in the megaton range. Around 28,000 British armed forces personnel and five hundred New Zealand naval personnel were deployed to the testing sites to prepare the sites and execute and record the bomb tests.

Decades later, often in the 1980s, many nuclear test veterans began to suspect that their illnesses were caused by exposure to low-level radiation (fallout). Suffering from a broad range of ailments and diseases such as cancers, stomach and digestive problems, skin conditions, and muscular complaints, they have struggled to receive political or medical confirmation that their illnesses are linked to service at Christmas Island. Many men applied for military disability pensions, and many were turned down. Instead of vesting blame in the invisible working of radionuclides, the state asserts that any higher rates of illness are more likely to be the result of individualized lifestyle choices such as diet, smoking, and exercise. In the face of medical, legal, and bureaucratic doubt and denial, test veterans formed groups and associations to seek justice and publicize their claims. Within this context, test veterans have sought to commission their own scientific research and develop their own fluency in radiobiology. In the mid-2000s the New Zealand Nuclear Test Veterans Association commissioned a cytogenetic study, which concluded that a sample of fifty nuclear test veterans had three times more chromosomal translocations (aberrations) than a control sample. With the positive proof that this offered, test veterans turned increasingly to the promise of genetics in their quest to find evidence for somatic debility. The case study that follows charts one example of the process by which genetic knowledge transforms test veterans' understandings of their bodies and their relationships, and the responsibilities that their damaged gene engendered.

Section II: An Ethnographic Case

Translating Knowledge into Responsibility

In exploring types of genetic relationality, it is crucial to stay cognizant of the transforming nature of this scientific field, which itself has undergone significant shifts in recent decades that emphasize these new modes of interconnection, with both human and nonhuman domains coming into relational view. Margaret Lock (2012) argues that earlier forms of genetic reductionism and exceptionalism have given way to new models of genomics that assume both complexity and flexibility (see also Harvey 2009; Kerr 2000). New fields like epigenetics and nutrigenomics have shifted genetics to a systems approach that traces how genes interact with wider cellular, social, and physical environments (Groves 2013; Harvey 2009, 122). The new genomics "deals not with probability but with uncertainty," possibility, and subjective potentiality (Harvey 2009, 127; see also Lemke 2004). We have also witnessed what Heather Widdows (2009) refers to as the "communal turn in genetic ethics," as scholars grapple with familial responsibilities to disclose, know, or act upon genetic information for the well-being of kin. The gene has thus become somatically influential and morally relational in novel ways that engender new forms of responsibility.[3]

Such transformations are evident in the work of radiobiologist professor Carmel Mothersill of McMaster University, who studies irradiated fish. Until recently, scientific research has focused on the fertility and fecundity of irradiated animals, investigating, for example, samples of fish living downstream from nuclear plants. Studies have advanced since the advent of effective cell culture techniques and the emergence of in vitro techniques for studying DNA.[4] Experimenting on fish cell cultures, Mothersill has been studying "bystander effects." Her work shows how an irradiated cell sends signals to an unirradiated cell, a process that induces a genomic response in the unirradiated cell similar to that in the irradiated cell. This, Mothersill explains, challenges our knowledge about radiation dose-response mechanisms, the cellular effects of very low-level radiation, and even, potentially, treatments for cancer. She elaborates, "There could be implications where hot particles (minute dust or sand particles, containing a radioisotopic metal for example, such as is common in fallout) have lodged in the gut or gill of the animal. The local point source could cause bystander effects in other parts of the animal" (Mothersill and Seymour 2009, 913).

Mothersill's research also demonstrates that these bystander effects go beyond signaling between the cells of one organism to that of a population. Her studies show how the cells of irradiated fish can communicate signals through water to the cells of unirradiated fish, causing the unirradiated fish to show cellular, genetic change similar to that of the irradiated fish. These signals are secreted into water and are present for at least six hours. Mothersill's research also tentatively shows how this type of cellular signaling can also occur between species.

Studies of signaling between organisms are not new. Some research suggests that plants, for example, can signal to nearby and distinct plant species that pests are present, and some planktonic crustaceans, when eaten by fish, send warning signals to nearby crustaceans that cause them to develop protective spiny shells (Mothersill and Seymour 2009, 914). Indeed, in many animals, secreted chemicals such as pheromones, allomones, and synomones are used by organisms to attract, repel, or protect against other organisms. As Mothersill points out, "Signaling between individuals [organisms] is well known as a protective mechanism alerting members of the same species to the presence of predators . . . or enabling social controls, habit identification etc., at the population level" (Mothersill and Seymour 2009, 915). However, what is new in bystander effect research is the application of these questions and insights to the cellular level, with the implication that these already-documented and proven chemical signaling processes might in fact be higher-order, later-stage processes driven by cellular signaling shifts. By isolating and tracking bystander effects in animals, this proves that the signals at play are not operating through "neural or behavioral pathways" (915) but cellular communications. Fundamentally, and radically, this research suggests that animals, including potentially humans, can intersubjectively affect each other at the cellular, genetic level through signaling mechanisms.

Mothersill explains cellular bystander effects in relation to evolutionary tendencies that are adaptive but not always protective in today's world. Bystander effects can induce a type of immunization in which, on exposure to the signals of an irradiated organism, proteins are produced in unirradiated animals to prepare them for and protect them against future exposure, and that these chemical changes endure long after the initial exposure. Furthermore, genomic instability can also be produced in the affected unirradiated cells, which can include, for example "DNA double strand breaks . . . mutations, chromosomal aberrations, [or] growth decay" (Mothersill et al. 2009, 3335). This too can be understood as an adaptive response to environmental changes and threats. As she explains, "Genomic instability is thought by some to be a mechanism allowing for higher than normal mutation frequencies to be tolerated. Thus we may be looking at some sort of evolution-enabling mechanism which allows the genome to become unstable so that directed changes sensitive to environmental conditions can happen and be selected for" (Mothersill and Seymour 2009, 916). However, this toleration of genetic mutation is not switched off when a temporary stressor is no longer present, and can thus become maladaptive in today's Anthropocene, saturated as it is with multichemical stressors.[5]

While studies so far demonstrate that the bystander effect produces both harmful and protective qualities in affected cells, Mothersill believes that further research is needed to determine whether the bystander effect is, overall, a positive or negative evolutionary factor in human health. This research is thus still in an early phase with questions still unanswered, such as how these results in fish translate to human biology, and indeed how these findings are relevant to radiation risk assessments (Mothersill et al. 2009). Mothersill's research demonstrates the explorative, inbuilt, and emerging uncertainty that marks the field of genomics research.

I first met Carmel Mothersill in Manchester in 2010 at a conference titled "Low Level Radiation and Health." The one-day event was small scale, attracting around fifty people. It was held in a Quaker meeting house, a modest, badly heated community hall tucked inconspicuously back from a central city street. It was as far from a lavish, industry-funded, crisp-suited science conference as was humanly possible. Many in the audience were antinuclear campaigners, dressed in colorful, casual clothing. Yet the scientists presenting were all established academics tenured at respected universities, or senior officials within government radiation protection agencies.[6] Despite their professional standing, these scientists' approach to radiation risk existed outside of the official standards of bureaucratic, governmental institutions that manage radiation risk. This fact, as well as their distance from the nuclear industry, was palpable in the hall's worn retro furnishings, the modest sandwiches, and the cheap, stackable plastic chairs. Yet that the scientists' theories were not yet institutionally legitimated at the level of industry or politics did not place them on the fringes of science. The field of genetic research is a largely contested, rapidly moving science, and as Atkinson, Glasner, and Lock (2009, 4) point out, social scientists "may have significantly overestimated the degree of shared understanding that exists between different scientists working in this field" of genetics.

Calmly spoken and using clear, simple terminology, Mothersill outlined her research on the bystander effect in trout. Listening in the audience was Pete, a British test veteran who had attended to find out more about the genetic effects of radiation exposure. In his late seventies, and as an organizer, leader, and representative of test veterans, he liked to keep up to date with developments in genetic research, especially after the promising results of the New Zealand cytogenetic research that many test veterans were now citing. Pete listened pensively to Mothersill's talk. During question time he thanked her, and asked, "If an irradiated cell can affect a nonirradiated cell, then can husbands with irradiated cells affect their wives? A lot of veterans and their wives have MS." She replied cautiously. This was currently unknown, she explained, but it wasn't impossible. Pete wondered whether the exchange of sexual fluids might be the means by which these signals were being transmitted. Mothersill explained that more research needed to be done to determine the effects and mechanisms in humans. Despite her tentative reasoning, Pete found her argument compelling. Afterward he said to me, "I had a colleague at the bomb testing site . . . big fella, lovely wife. She died of multiple sclerosis. My wife has multiple sclerosis. There's a chap, over in [the next town]. His wife had multiple sclerosis. And of course they all seem to me to be connected. And it was only when they were talking about the aberrated cells affecting the nonaberrated cells, it made sense."

Pete talked of aberrated cells affecting nonaberrated cells, without any of the qualifications of uncertainty that Mothersill had carefully wrapped around the cell in her talk. Facts were extracted and simplified, but also recontextualized and reinscribed with meaning. As Cambrosio (2009, 466) makes clear, "In order to be mobilized, facts have to be reconfigured to adapt to or reformat local processes. In short, researchers examining knowledge production have come to the conclusion that the trajectories of scientific objects can be characterized by an essential tension between abstraction from and connection to specific arrangements." In linking knowledge to experience, Pete forged a link between damaged cells and illness (stripping out the information about the possible positive effects of bystander mechanisms), and added a new fact, imagining semen as a human conduit for the process.

A week following the conference, I met with Pete at his house. Pete explained that soon after he joined the air force, at the age of twenty-three, he was sent to Christmas Island in the Pacific. He worked in the transport squadron, loading and unloading planes. He witnessed six nuclear bomb tests during a year on the island, more than most British servicemen, who saw on average one or two tests. Throughout the interview Pete kept referring to his semen as "causing" his family's health problems. As he adopted an increasingly molecularized vision of his body, Mothersill's theory had by this time assumed causal solidity for Pete.

The bystander effects model provides a new framework through which we might think through the ways in which culture and nature, biology and sociality are tightly intertwined. Rabinow's (1996) concept of biosociality offers similar ontological openings, by revealing how the conceptual underpinnings of sociobiology have been and can be inverted. If sociobiology aimed to show how our evolutionary biology drives cultural and social patterns, then biosociality demonstrates how culture can now shape and intervene in nature, in novel, fundamentally molecular ways (through such practices as new reproductive technologies or genetically modified organisms) that render life artificial. Rose also argues that "the new human vital order has become so thoroughly imbued with artifice that even the natural has to be produced by a labour on the self—natural food, natural childbirth and the like. Even choosing not to intervene in living processes becomes a kind of intervention" (2001, 19). In this way, as Marilyn Strathern (1992) puts it, we are well and truly "after nature." Rabinow saw biosociality as resulting from new biotechnological intervention, as ultimately driven by human agency and culture. By contrast, a theory of bystander effects, with its scientific optic of the fleshy, internal body, posits that nature itself (as genetic processes) is by organic design always socially and intersubjectively configured, even before humans devise the technological capacities to intervene at the molecular level—although they do need emergent technology to recognize and see this reality (Mol 2003).[7]

This raises two questions: How do the twin processes by which the molecular is socialized and naturalized shape ideas of genetic responsibility? What, from an anthropological perspective, are the consequences of this reconfiguration of the body as genetically leaky and socially permeable, and how does it extend discussions of responsibilization? Below I outline three domains in which responsibility is and could be recalibrated: kinship, gender, and biological citizenship. The following discussion is thus both ethnographically present and futuristically explorative, in that it charts what conceptual transformations have occurred for test veterans such as Pete, and those which the logic of genetic bystander theory could lead us toward, and how indeed this scientific concept is good to think with in interrogating anthropological categories and assumptions.

Section III: Competing Responsibilities

Familial Responsibility

The bystander effect, as understood by test veterans, challenges core distinctions in our models of kinship between vertical and lateral relations, and temporal and spatial relatedness. It de-emphasizes reproduction, conception, birth, and heredity as the blueprint of life and the central or only hallmarks of biological kinship, and challenges the idea that "DNA binds a person's past and future into a single . . . narrative," which acts as the primary way in which we are biologically related (Finkler 2000, 10). In his influential description of American kinship models, Schneider (1968) describes an important Western distinction between kin by nature and kin by law, and while subsequent work on kinship has critiqued or reworked this model, it is a useful binary to work with and against here.[8] As he argues, relatives by nature are those that are forged through shared substance (biogenetic material) that is inextinguishable and unchanging, fixed at conception and birth. Relatives by law (largely though marriage), by contrast, are those that are reversible and severable, underpinned by choice rather than biogenetic substances.

Yet anthropologists have shown that such distinctions are not made in all cultural contexts. The Hua of Papua New Guinea, for example, do not distinguish so tightly between affines and blood relatives, and people are made relatives slowly over time through cohabitation, by sharing the bodily vital essence of *nu*. A new wife who moves to her husband's village will thus gradually shift from being a stranger to being kin as the nu of her husband's kin infiltrates her body through exposure to bodily substances—semen, food cooked by relatives' hands, sweat, even shadows that fall on her body (Meigs 1988). Weismantel (1995) and Carsten (1995) also demonstrate the ways that groups conceive of relatedness as a process that is forged through sharing food, emotions, and substances. Theories of intersubjective cellular communication, should they gain mainstream scientific ground, will lend scientific weight to such processual ontologies.

For Pete, new ideas of affinal kinship (as biologically rendered) were expressed when talking about his wife's ill health. "It upsets me, to think . . . she has become like me, because of me." Pointing out how Pete claimed a type of genetic transference to his wife ("like me") is not to suggest that marriage kin are being conflated with blood-based kin here (with all of the resulting anxieties about incest that would go with this in Euro-American models of kinship), but that affinal kin categories can now be reworked to included degrees of biological relatedness that are processual and spatially cast, rather than fixed through reproduction.[9] Bystander theory thus suggests new ways in which to anthropologically link intimacy and cohabitation with blood and biology. It also reveals fresh conceptual avenues through which kinship and intimacy can become medicalized (Finkler 2000; Webster 2009). The by-stander effect is potentially troubling for kin relations. It problematizes prox-imity, intimacy, and familial connection as new causal components of illness. In this sense, the bystander effect could lead to new ways in which we learn to manage "risky relations" (Featherstone et al. 2006). The bystander effect thus encourages a wider, somewhat troubling, level of cellular responsibility within families or domestic spaces, in which bodies can become sources of pollution and contagion in novel ways across the life span.

Masculine Responsibility

Genetic bystander effects also rework gendered ideas of the body and its social roles. It is significant that Pete focused on his semen as a conduit of harm. Semen is a powerfully symbolic substance and commonly acts as a signifier of masculinity, representing virility, potency, and physical strength, and can also embody men's abilities to protect their families, be responsible, and create life (Pomales 2013).[10] In an example that offers many parallels to nuclear test veterans, in terms of militarism and contested latent illnesses, Suzie Kilshaw (2009) shows how UK veterans who claimed to suffer from Gulf War Syndrome held themselves responsible for infecting and contami-nating their wives and causing their ill health. They reported that their semen caused their wives to have a burning sensation during sex, and sometimes they believed that, merely through bodies being in spatial proximity, they had mysteriously caused their wives to develop symptoms similar to theirs, particularly chronic fatigue. Kilshaw's participants also saw their semen as carrying within it damaged genes, which were responsible for their children's birth defects. The men associated an ideal military masculinity with strength, and their ability to protect their families from harm, an act that their con-taminating blood and semen prevented them from achieving. The normal iconography of blood and semen as associated with life and vigor are here reversed, to signify danger and illness, and contaminated semen becomes a symbol for lost masculinity. Bodies are vulnerable and permeable, "allowing agents from the outside to pass into the body, but they are also porous and allow substances to leak out of the body" (Kilshaw 2009, 83).

As Pete's interview revealed, nuclear test veterans often felt a similar sense of guilt and blame for being unable to protect their kin from harm, and believed that their own bodies were the cause of their family's ongoing and emerging suffering. Some test veterans recounted how, once they left the armed forces, their ill health had affected their ability to hold down a good job and provide sufficiently for their families, which often meant that their wives sought or increased their hours of employment. When some of their wives also became sick, their test veteran husbands psychologically struggled with not being able, or being able only in a limited way, to step into the responsible provider and protector role when called to do so.

Responsibilities are, however, complexly engendered and multiple in the context of genetic knowledge. Genetic bystander theory offers test veterans diverse frameworks through which to affectively make sense of their gendered duties to kin. Scholars have shown that while theories of genetic causation can create feelings of responsibility for passing on genes, they can also offer people a way to minimize feelings of guilt and blame (e.g., Nelkin 1996, 545), by demonstrating that illness is not located in the realm of mind, lifestyle, and personal effort. In this vein, the idea of the bystander effect offers an illness model rooted in the realms of biology and hard science that does not rely upon soft psychological factors that include lifestyle choices or intersubjective behavioral patterns that are stress inducing and deleterious to health (Raspberry and Skinner 2007). Individuals commonly expect and are expected to exert effortful control over such domains of action and thus hold themselves more individually responsible for their manifestation. Pete explained, "The worst thing was—you don't know—I was carrying this . . . aberrated genetics, and even if I'd known, there wasn't much I could have done." A biological model of illness ultimately created a knowledge framework in which it was possible to evoke modes of irresponsibilization by tracing blame and causation back to the historical events and political actors of nuclear testing that caused chromosomes to mutate in the first place, drawing the state into the realm of genetic responsibility and culpability, a topic that I now address.

Biopolitical Responsibility

As is demonstrated above in negotiating familial and gendered responsibility, test veterans experienced feeling left alone with the responsibility to deal with their damaged bodies within intimate spheres. Here, genetic responsibility in family settings meant coping with emotions of guilt and blame for being the conduit of harm, for being unable to fulfill expected responsibilities to others. This section complicates this picture. It demonstrates how participants also traced primary and underlying responsibility for their damaged genes back to the state. Responsibilities, then, are often multilayered and sometimes nested, and some are seen as more fundamental and causative than others. In this instance, primary responsibility ultimately signified state culpability.

Rendering the state responsible involved first contrastively demonstrating the innocence of test veterans. Pete explained that, as young, naive men with a military ethos of unquestioning obedience, they had been unaware of the dangers posed by nuclear bomb experiments and had trusted the assurances given by their superiors as to the safety of the tests. "When I was coming up to twenty-three [years old], within two months of getting married I was [told] by the air force that I was going to Christmas Island. At the time we didn't realize this was part of the [nuclear] experiment. Because we were all youngsters, and we didn't know." Once stationed on the island, he explained that they continued to know very little about the tests. "They didn't actually call them bombs — they just called them devices. They weren't referred to as bombs." Normally, he explained, when working in the hangars loading and unloading the supply planes, "You [could] see everything that was going on." However, when it came to the planes used to drop the bombs, secrecy shrouded procedures. "So when they actually loaded the aircraft up, they went behind screens. . . . There was a hangar here. They pushed the aircraft in, [and] the screens were put up, so you couldn't see anything. You couldn't see what the bomb looked like." When I asked test veterans about their knowledge of the somatic effects of radiation at the time of the tests, they also described themselves using the idiom of ignorance. Pete explained, "You trusted what you were told. . . . [The officers and scientists told us] it wasn't harmful. I didn't even really understand what a gene did back then or how it all worked with radiation."[11]

In my interviews and casual conversations with test veterans, and also in their engagements with the media, test veterans understood responsibility qua culpability as based on knowledgeable action. These narratives worked to justify and explain test veterans' willing participation in the testing program. As actors intricately involved in the execution of experiments that they claimed have harmed them, these narratives emphasized the low-ranked, passive nature of their service roles, and their innocence in the face of bodily harm done to them. These assertions implicated and responsibilized the state as the architect, enactor, and overseer of a dangerous techno-military experiment and de-emphasized their own agency.

An emphasis on culpability reveals the different motivations that drive people to engage with biomedical knowledge. Scholars of biological citizenship claim that new "economies of hope" are vital to the contemporary bioscientific realm, as biosocial groups envisage potential cures and affectively invest in hopes for future improvement and biotechnic innovation (Rose 2006). According to Brekke and Sirnes (2011, 347), these theories postulate that "hope becomes a life-inducing and vitalizing force, opening new avenues of civic participation and engagement." Yet Brekke and Sirnes's own research on stem cell activism in the United States shows that within the "new discourse of hope . . . the driving force is not so much future possibilities as present despair" (2011, 349; see also Lock 2012, 146) in which their interlocutors sought public recognition for the debilities that their incurable diseases caused them. Actors also engage with biosciences in order to explain why illness has occurred, to locate a social source of suffering, and, as for test veterans, to strengthen a morally loaded sense of blame and answerability for those who have caused their bodily suffering (Trundle 2011). Little optimism was expressed by Pete and his fellow test veterans in their engagements with new scientific models. Pete asserted to me that he understood his and his wife's genetic damage as permanent: "If a cell is aberrated, then it stays aberrated."[12] He thus engaged with the bystander effects model not in order to find health, but to chronicle current suffering in his family, and to broaden the state's culpability and blame to a wider range of victims. If there was hope, it was for the expression of political guilt, acknowledgment, and recognition. It was political, rather than biological, wrongs that could be righted.

In the process of seeking recognition, test veterans felt that the burden of responsibility for proving the state's fault fell unfairly on them. In discussing his engagement with war disability pension officials and MoD bureaucrats, which often took the impersonal form of letters and e-mails, Pete explained, "You can't get it [your pension claim] past them, and they should bring themselves down [from their offices] and say [what they think], 'There's no evidence to support this claim. It is up to the appellant to prove that they've been affected.'" Pete continued, "But how could I prove, how could I prove that my semen has affected my wife, and my daughter? How am I supposed to do that? Fifty years I've been at it. So what they're doing is putting the onus back on the appellant . . . the victim." Test veterans did not want to become active drivers of the quest for genetic information, but have thus far been unable to responsibilize the state into the proactive, protective roles that they desired it to fulfill, and which they saw as fundamental to the social contract of military citizenship. Here the sacrifices of service were seen as one side of an explicit bargain (often referred to in the United Kingdom as the military covenant). On the other side, test veterans believed that the MoD and state should demonstrate a preemptive, caring, and generous attitude toward protecting and providing for veterans' health care needs and concerns (Trundle 2012).

The states' trenchant resistance to such claims is perhaps understandable, given that the science remains contested and partial, and because being responsibilized for certain genetic bystander effects in the population would significantly shift the types of claims that the state could face. Genetic bystander theory has the potential to link the social, environmental, and political determinants of health to much wider communities and kin networks—secondarily affected bodies—and broaden the responsibilities of the state or corporations to multiple leaky bodies, de-emphasizing individual effort and empowerment, and recasting the biopolitical categories of victimhood and blame and the stakes of financial accountability in the process. This point was not lost on Pete. "But, when you think, if, for instance, what's going to happen? Say we decided the question I asked was brought to the fore. Then suddenly they [the MoD] have got to pay for every single person who could have been contaminated or have been aberrated! . . . And that's why they don't want to own up to it . . . that's the reason it won't be admitted, Catherine, because it's ad infinitum. . . . Now like, if as Carmel said . . . if it can affect the women, then how many others are there like that?"

Concluding Thoughts

How do claims of genetic dependency, vulnerability, state culpability, blame, and despair square with theories of genetic responsibilization? While practices of empowerment and self-actualization offer a useful center to this concept, as this chapter and indeed this book show, they do not capture the interlinking calls to responsibility made by modern subjects. And while practices of self-empowerment and actualization are important values within late liberal and neoliberal settings, they are not the only modes of responsibility at play. The flip side of individual prudence is a collective's culpability for the risk it poses to others, and the counter to the proactive enterprising and hopeful somatic self is the self that believes it has been irrevocably biologically damaged with little option for recourse but to demand recognition and recompense. In this chapter I have sought to show how a range of different but interlinked responsibilities are evoked, and how, in the relational ties of dependence between servicemen and their kin, and servicemen and the state, these are also inevitably tied to modes of irresponsibilization. (Ir)responsibility emerges as an unstable force that shifts between actors and is renegotiated and sometimes fought over, lost, and won based on the degrees of power each has in the encounter. Veterans like Pete assume and wrestle with responsibility in certain intimate and gendered moments of family life, while in other more politicized and collective spheres (veteran gatherings, radiation conferences) responsibility is vociferously rejected. Finally, taking the lead from new theories within radiobiology regarding the emergent relational gene, I argue that these competing (ir)responsibilities that link the cultural and the corporeal need to be included in our discussions of responsibility not only because they have been previously sidelined, but because they are potentially becoming more scientifically, socially, and politically prescient. Responsibility is not simply the product of ideological, ethical, or political projects, but also reflects the basic demands that our bodies make on relational and political life.

NOTES

1. In conversation with disability studies, Livingston uses the concept of debility to link a wider set of experiences: chronic illness, aging, and disability, "the impairment, lack, or loss of certain bodily abilities" (2005, 113) in which one must learn to live with decreased bodily capacity.

2. I also interviewed lawyers, medical researchers, veteran advocates, widows of test veterans, and the children and grandchildren of deceased test veterans.

3. Anthropological approaches to genetics have also paralleled this transformation in the last decade, shifting away from earlier attempts to refute genetic determinism (e.g., Finkler 2000) or demote the gene (Lock 2012) to engaging with the complexity and uncertainty that is emerging within postgenomic science. Yet at the same time that social and natural sciences have reconfigured the gene, scholars have noted that in popular culture and the media "genomic fetishism" (Rajan 2006) still persists, and media accounts tend to display the now-familiar ontological hallmarks of biological reductionism and oversimplification (Webster 2009, 488). Correspondingly, economic institutions and interests that have been built around the potent gene still commonly treat the gene as prophetic (Groves 2013). The gene has thus become more indeterminate and more overwrought at the same time.

4. A key advantage of in vitro research is the simplification that it allows, as the specific effects, signals, and mechanisms of one biological component can be isolated and mapped outside of the complex biological system with which they interact. This strength also represents a disadvantage to the method, as "cell cultures lack the complexity of functional organs and thus do not truly represent the effects that toxins exert on organ or organism functionality" (O'Dowd et al. 2009, 464). Such research, therefore, necessarily demonstrates a pragmatic reductionist approach. Yet this pragmatic reductionism is distinct from the ontological reductionism in popular or

commercial imaginings of the gene. As the philosopher of science Hub Zwart argues, pragmatic reductionism "does not contain grand ontological claims about nature as such, but basically says that, although the real world is no doubt tremendously complex, it will be difficult if not impossible to do justice to this complexity in the context of laboratory research. In order to understand a particular phenomenon, the relationship between a limited number of determining factors will be studied. Not because scientists believe that this is all, or that everything is determined by (or can be explained on the basis of) a limited set of mono-causal relationships, but simply because the number of factors that can be meaningfully studied in a laboratory is limited. Once the relationship between these factors has been established, researchers will try to extrapolate their research findings to the real world, in the expectation that, out there, things will prove much more complicated. In other words, reductionism is a methodological requirement. It is basically a (highly successful, but from a philosophical perspective rather problematic) research strategy" (2007, 193).

5. Mothersill explains that this biological capacity for cellular change is potentially more significant and deleterious to health in the modern age. Recent human-made chemicals, toxins, and activities produce many of the "acute and transitory stressors" that we now face, which "compromise a surveillance system which evolved over billions of years" (Mothersill and Seymour 2009, 916).

6. Their presence reflected a shifting relationship between science and its publics based on the principles of engagement and accountability, with many scientists now expected to educate, inform, and listen to stakeholders and affected members of the public (Porter et al. 2013).

7. In his theorization of biosociality, Rabinow predicted that people would draw together in social networks based on chromosomal abnormality, a prediction that, at the time, seemed somewhat farfetched, but which has proven incisive. In this theorization, people are the agents drawing together and creating networks based on biology. But theories of bystander effects propose that it can also be the chromosomes themselves that are coming together, quite literally, with social outcomes that follow. This thus has the potential to create new types of biosocial networks based on a much more intimate, quotidian sense of sharing genes than Rabinow envisaged between fellow disease sufferers or gene carriers on a local, national, or global scale.

8. See, for example, Galvin (2001).

9. Indeed, this demonstrates that while we think of incest as based on cultural rules about biological connectedness, it is in fact only certain processes of biological connectedness that can be traced through reproductive, vertical lineage routes, which underpin incest rules, and that other types of biological relatedness could fall outside of and not trouble this social prohibition. It also opens up what genetic relatedness means in terms of the types of cells being passed on or affected, for example, germ cells (that contain the genetic material for reproduction) versus somatic cells (nonreproductive cells).

10. For example, in Pomales's (2013) study of men's decisions surrounding vasectomies in Costa Rica, vasectomies represented both a threat to and an enactment of masculinity. This prophylactic measure could threaten the men's sense of masculinity

when their gender identity was tied to potent sexual virility. Simultaneously, however, the men also understood the procedure positively in terms of their ability and desire to protect and provide for their existing families, by preventing them from fathering more children than they could afford to financially support.

11. By the 1950s, radiobiology and nuclear science had determined the deleterious health effects of both high-level and low-level radiation, although the causative relationship between different low exposure levels and types and their exact biological effects were (and continue to be) debated.

12. According to biology, this is true for many types of cell mutations. However, it is important to note that not all cell mutations and translocations are harmful to human health, and DNA repair mechanisms do revert some mutations back to a normal or benign cell state.

4-Traders. 2014. "ArcelorMittal: Ostrava Invests in Environmental and Production Improvements." February 21. http://www.4-traders.com/ARCELORMITTAL-6333 /news/ARCELORMITTAL-Ostrava-invests-in-environmental-and-production -improvements-17983230/.

Aaron, Kiikpoye K. 2012. "New Corporate Social Responsibility Models for Oil Companies in Nigeria's Delta Region: What Challenges for Susstainability?" *Progress in Development Studies* 12 (4): 259–73.

Abdullah, Ibrahim. 1992. "Profit versus Social Reproduction: Labor Protests in the Sierra Leonean Iron-Ore Mines, 1933–38." *African Studies Review* 35:13–41.

Abdullah, Ibrahim, ed. 2004. *Between Democracy and Terror: The Sierra Leone Civil War*. Dakar: CODESRIA.

Adam, Barry D. 1989. "The State, Public Policy and AIDS Discourse." *Contemporary Crises* 13:1–14.

Adam, Barry D. 2005. "Constructing the Neoliberal Sexual Actor: Responsibility and Care of the Self in the Discourse of Barebackers." *Culture, Health and Sexuality* 7 (4): 333–46.

Adam, Barry D. 2006. "Infectious Behaviour." *Social Theory and Health* 4:168–79.

Adam, Barry D., Patrice Corriveau, Richard Elliott, Jason Globerman, Ken English, and Sean Rourke. 2014. "HIV Disclosure as Practice and Public Policy." *Critical Public Health* 25 (4): 386–97.

Adam, Barry D., Richard Elliott, Patrice Corriveau, and Ken English. 2014. "Impacts of Criminalization on the Everyday Lives of People Living with HIV in Canada." *Sexuality Research and Social Policy* 11:39–49.

Adam, Barry D., Richard Elliott, Winston Husbands, James Murray, and John Maxwell. 2008. "Effects of the Criminalization of HIV Transmission in Cuerrier on Men Reporting Unprotected Sex with Men." *Canadian Journal of Law and Society* 23 (1–2): 137–53.

Adam, Barry D., Winston Husbands, James Murray, and John Maxwell. 2005. "AIDS Optimism, Condom Fatigue, or Self Esteem?" *Journal of Sex Research* 42 (3): 238–48.

Adam, Barry D., Winston Husbands, James Murray, and John Maxwell. 2008. "Silence, Assent, and HIV Risk." *Culture, Health and Sexuality* 10 (8): 759–72.

Altman, Dennis. 1986. *AIDS in the Mind of America*. Garden City, NY: Doubleday.

Amnesty International. 1999. "Sierra Leone: A Peace Agreement but No Justice." July 8. Accessed December 11, 2014. http://www.amnesty.org/en/library/info/AFR51/007/1999/en.

Amsler, Mark, and Cris Shore. 2015. "Responsibilisation and Leadership in the Neoliberal University: A New Zealand Perspective." *Discourse: Studies in the Cultural Politics of Education.* doi:10.1080/01596306.2015.1104857.

Anders, Gerhard. 2014. "Transitional Justice, States of Emergency, and Business as Usual in Sierra Leone." *Development and Change* 45:524–42.

APNZ. 2012. "Kate Wilkinson Resigns as Labour Minister." *New Zealand Herald*, November 5. Accessed September 6, 2014. http://www.nzherald.co.nz/business/news/article.cfm?c_id=3&objectid=10845309.

Apori-Nkansah, Lydia. 2008. "Transitional Justice in Postconflict Contexts: The Case of Sierra Leone's Dual Accountability Mechanisms." PhD diss., Walden University.

Appel, Hannah C. 2012. "Walls and White Elephants: Oil Extraction, Responsibility, and Infrastructural Violence in Equatorial Guinea." *Ethnography* 13 (4): 439–65. Accessed March 9, 2014. http://eth.sagepub.com/content/13/4/439.

ArcelorMittal Ostrava. 2008. "2008 Corporate Responsibility Report." Accessed March 14, 2014. http://www.arcelormittal.com/ostrava/pdf/report_Mittal_en.pdf.

Arendt, Hannah. 1998. *The Human Condition.* Chicago: University of Chicago Press.

Arreola, Sonya, Torsten Neilands, Lance Pollack, Jay Paul, and Joseph Catania. 2008. "Childhood Sexual Experiences and Adult Health Sequelae among Gay and Bisexual Men." *Journal of Sex Research* 45 (3): 246–52.

Arsenijević, Damir. 2011a. "Gendering the Bone: The Politics of Memory in Bosnia and Herzegovina." *Journal for Cultural Research* 15 (2): 193–205.

Arsenijević, Damir. 2011b. "Mobilising Unbribable Life: The Politics of Contemporary Poetry in Bosnia and Herzegovina." In *Towards a New Literary Humanism*, edited by Andy Mousley, 166–80. London: Palgrave Macmillan.

Arthur, Paige. 2009. "How 'Transitions' Reshaped Human Rights: A Conceptual History of Transitional Justice." *Human Rights Quarterly* 31:321–67.

Article 19 and Forum of Conscience. 2000. "Moments of Truth in Sierra Leone: Contextualizing the Truth and Reconciliation Commission." August. Accessed December 11, 2014. http://www.article19.org/data/files/pdfs/publications/sierra-leone-moments-of-truth.pdf.

Asad, Talal. 2003. *Formations of the Secular: Christianity, Islam, Modernity.* Stanford, CA: Stanford University Press.

Atkinson, Paul, Peter Glasner, and Margaret Lock. 2009. "Genetics and Society: Perspectives from the Twenty-First Century." In *Handbook of Genetics and Society: Mapping the New Genomic Era*, edited by Paul Atkinson, Peter Glasner, and Margaret Lock, 1–15. London: Routledge.

Auld, Graeme, Steven Bernstein, and Benjamin Cashore. 2008. "The New Corporate Social Responsibility." *Annual Review of Environment and Resources* 33:413–35.

Ayala, George, Keletso Makofane, Glenn-Milo Santos, Sonya Arreola, Pato Hebert, Matthew Thomann, Patrick Wilson, Jack Beck, and Do Tri. 2014. "HIV

Treatment Cascades That Leak." *AIDS and Clinical Research* 5 (8). doi: 10.4172 /2155-6113.1000331.

Babidge, Sally. 2013. "'Socios': The Contested Morality of 'Partnerships' in Indigenous Community-Mining Company Relations, Northern Chile." *Journal of Latin American and Caribbean Anthropology* 18 (2): 274–93.

Bacon, Nicola, and Nina Mguni. 2010. "Taking the Temperature of Local Communities: The Wellbeing and Resilience Measure—WARM." Young Foundation, November. http://youngfoundation.org/publications/taking-the-temperature-of-local-communities-the-wellbeing-and-resilience-measure-warm/.

Baker, Tom. 2002. "Risk, Insurance, and the Social Construction of Responsibility." In *Embracing Risk: The Changing Culture of Insurance and Responsibility*, edited by Tom Baker and Jonathan Simon, 33–51. Chicago: University of Chicago Press.

Barad, Karen. 2007. *Meeting the Universe Halfway: Quantum Physics and the Entanglement of Matter and Meaning*. Durham, NC: Duke University Press.

Barlow, Karen. 2014. "Scott Morrison Seeks Migration Act Changes to Overhaul Processing of Asylum Seeker Claims." *ABC News Online*, June 25. Accessed September 6, 2014. http://www.abc.net.au/news/2014-06-25/morrison-pushes-for-asylum-seeker-processing-overhaul/5549388.

Barnes, Barry. 2000. *Understanding Agency: Social Theory and Responsible Action*. London: Sage.

Baroch, Pavel. 2014. "Miliardy nestačily, smog na Ostravsku loni opět zhoustl." *Aktuálně*, January 21. Accessed March 9, 2014. http://zpravy.aktualne.cz/domaci /miliardy-nestacily-smog-na-ostravsku-loni-opet-zhoustl/r~12844d04828811e 39d22002590604f2e/.

Baur, Dorothea, and Hans Peter Schmitz. 2012. "Corporations and NGOs: When Accountability Leads to Co-optation." *Journal of Business Ethics* 106 (1): 9–21.

Bayer, Kurt. 2012. "Charges Dropped against Ex-Pike River Boss Peter Whittall." *New Zealand Herald*, December 12. Accessed September 6, 2014. http://www.nzherald .co.nz/nz/news/article.cfm?c_id=1&objectid=11171336.

BBC News. 2012. "Raigmore Hospital Cleanliness 'Poor.'" August 8. Accessed August 14, 2014. http://www.bbc.co.uk/news/uk-scotland-highlands-islands-19179894.

Beck, Ulrich. 1992. *Risk Society: Towards a New Modernity*. Thousand Oaks, CA: Sage.

Beidelman, T. O. 1993. *Moral Imagination in Kaguru Modes of Thought*. Washington, DC: Smithsonian Institution Press.

Benard, Bonnie. 1991. "Fostering Resiliency in Kids: Protective Factors in the Family, School, and Community." Washington, DC: Department of Education.

Benard, Bonnie. 2002. "From Risk to Resiliency: What Schools Can Do." Portland, OR: Western Center for Drug-Free Schools and Communities.

Benard, Bonnie. 2004. *Resiliency: What We Have Learned*. San Francisco: WestEd.

Bennett, Jane. 2010. *Vibrant Matter: A Political Ecology of Things*. Durham, NC: Duke University Press.

Benson, Peter, and Stuart Kirsch. 2010. "Capitalism and the Politics of Resignation." *Current Anthropology* 51 (4): 459–86.

Beveridge, William Henry. 1942. *Social Insurance and Allied Services: Report by Sir William Beveridge.* London: His Majesty's Stationery Office.

Biebricher, Thomas. 2011. "(Ir-)responsibilization, Genetics and Neuroscience." *European Journal of Social Theory* 14:469–88.

Biehl, João, and Adriana Petryna. 2011. "Bodies of Rights and Therapeutic Markets." *Social Research* 78 (2): 359–86.

Bilewicz, Aleksandra. 2001. *Uniwersytet Trzeciego Wieku we Wrocławiu w latach 1976–2001. Część 1.* [University of the Third Age in Wrocław in the years 1976–2001, part 1]. Wrocław: TINTA.

Blair, Tony. 1996. "Battle for Britain." *Guardian* 29:2.

Blowfield, Michael, and Jedrzej George Frynas. 2005. "Setting New Agendas: Critical Perspectives on Corporate Social Responsibility in the Developing World." *International Affairs* 81 (3): 499–513.

Boin, Arjen, and Allan McConnell. 2007. "Preparing for Critical Infrastructure Breakdowns: The Limits of Crisis Management and the Need for Resilience." *Journal of Contingencies and Crisis Management* 15 (1): 50–59.

Bond, David. 2013. "Governing Disaster: The Political Life of the Environment during the BP Oil Spill." *Cultural Anthropology* 28 (4): 694–715.

Bosher, Lee, Andrew Dainty, Patricia Carrillo, and Jacqueline Glass. 2007. "Built-In Resilience to Disasters: A Pre-emptive Approach." *Engineering, Construction and Architectural Management* 14 (5): 434–46.

Boston, Johnathan, John Martin, June Pallot, and Pat Walsh. 1996. *Public Management: The New Zealand Model.* Auckland: Oxford University Press.

Bottrell, Dorothy. 2013. "Responsibilised Resilience? Reworking Neoliberal Social Policy Texts." *M/C Journal* 16 (5).

Bourdieu, Pierre. 1972. *Outline of a Theory of Practice.* Translated by Richard Nice. Cambridge: Cambridge University Press.

Brekke, Ole Andreas, and Thorvald Sirnes. 2011. "Biosociality, Biological Citizenship and the New Regimes of Hope and Despair: Interpreting 'Portraits of Hope' and the 'Mehmet Case.'" *New Genetics and Society* 30 (4): 347–74.

Brodwin, Paul. 2013. *Everyday Ethics: Voices from the Front Line of Community Psychiatry.* Berkeley: University of California Press.

Brooks, Robert B., and Sam Goldstein. 2004. *The Power of Resilience: Achieving Balance, Confidence, and Personal Strength in Your Life.* Chicago: McGraw-Hill.

Brown, Alexander. 2009. *Personal Responsibility: Why It Matters.* London: Bloomsbury.

Brown, Phil, Rachel Morello-Fosch, and Stephen Zavestoski, eds. 2011. *Contested Illnesses.* Berkeley: University of California Press.

Brown, Wendy. 2001. *Politics out of History.* Princeton, NJ: Princeton University Press.

Bruneau, Michael. 2006. "Enhancing the Resilience of Communities against Extreme Events from an Earthquake Engineering Perspective." *Journal of Security Education* 1 (4): 159–67.

Bruneau, William, and Donald C. Savage. 2002. *Counting Out the Scholars: How Performance Indicators Undermine Universities and Colleges.* Toronto: Lorimer.

Bryant, Rebecca. 2006. "Betrayals of the Past." *Postcolonial Studies* 9 (3): 311–24.

Bryant, Rebecca. 2010. *The Past in Pieces: Belonging in the New Cyprus*. Philadelphia: University of Pennsylvania Press.

Buchowski, Michał. 1996. "The Shifting Meanings of Civil and Civic Society in Poland." In *Civil Society: Challenging Western Models*, edited by Chris Hann and Elizabeth Dunn, 79–98. New York: Routledge.

Calasanti, Toni M., and Anna M. Zajicek. 1997. "Gender, the State, and Constructing the Old as Dependent: Lessons from the Economic Transition in Poland." *Gerontologist* 37 (4): 452–61.

Caldwell, Melissa L. 2007. "Elder Care in the New Russia: The Changing Face of Compassionate Social Security." *Focaal*, no. 50: 66–80.

Cambrosio, Alberto. 2009. "Introduction." In *Handbook of Genetics and Society: Mapping the New Genomic Era*, edited by Paul Atkinson, Peter Glasner, and Margaret Lock, 465–68. London: Routledge.

Campbell, Bonnie. 2012. "Corporate Social Responsibility and Development in Africa: Redefining the Roles and Responsibilities of Public and Private Actors in the Mining Sector." *Resources Policy* 37 (2): 138–43.

Carrithers, Michael. 1985. "An Alternative Social History of the Self." In *The Category of the Person: Anthropology, Philosophy, History*, edited by Michael Carrithers, Steven Collins, and Steven Lukes, 234–56. Cambridge: Cambridge University Press.

Carsten, Janet. 1995. "The Substance of Kinship and the Heat of the Hearth: Feeding, Personhood and Relatedness among Malays in Pulau Langkawi." *American Ethnologist* 22 (2): 223–41.

Centers for Disease Control and Prevention. 2015. "HIV in the United States: At a Glance." Accessed January 28, 2015. http://www.cdc.gov/hiv/statistics/basics /ataglance.html.

Chandler, David. 2012. "Resilience and Human Security: The Post-interventionist Paradigm." *Security Dialogue* 43 (3): 213–29.

Chandler, David. 2014. "Beyond Neoliberalism: Resilience, the New Art of Governing Complexity." *Resilience* 2 (1): 47–63.

Čisté Nebe. 2016. "Poběž s maskou za Čisté nebe." July 18. Accessed July 20, 2016. http://www.cistenebe.cz/.

Clarke, John. 2005. "New Labour's Citizens: Activated, Empowered, Responsibilized, Abandoned?" *Critical Social Policy* 25 (4): 447–63.

Clarke, Kamari. 2010. "Rethinking Africa through Its Exclusions: The Politics of Naming Criminal Responsibility." *Anthropological Quarterly* 83 (3): 625–51.

Clarke, Kamari Maxine. 2009. *Fictions of Justice: The International Criminal Court and the Challenge of Legal Pluralism in Sub-Saharan Africa*. Cambridge: Cambridge University Press.

Clarke, Kamari Maxine. 2011. "The Rule of Law through Its Economies of Appearances: The Making of the African Warlord." *Indiana Journal of Global Legal Studies* 18 (1): 7–40.

Coaffee, Jon. 2010. "Protecting Vulnerable Cities: The UK's Resilience Response to Defending Everyday Urban Infrastructure." *International Affairs* 86 (4): 939–54.

Comaroff, John L., and Jean Comaroff. 2006. "Law and Disorder in the Postcolony: An Introduction." In *Law and Disorder in the Postcolony*, edited by Jean Comaroff and John L. Comaroff, 1–56. Chicago: University of Chicago Press.

Comfort, L. K. 2010. *Designing Resilience.* Pittsburgh: University of Pittsburgh Press.

Constantinou, Marios. 2006. "Reasons of State and the Constitutional Logic of Quasi-stateness: The Post-colonial Contradictions of Cyprus's Integration in the European Confederation." *Postcolonial Studies* 9 (3): 295–310.

Cornum, Rhonda, Michael D. Matthews, and Martin E. P. Seligman. 2011. "Comprehensive Soldier Fitness: Building Resilience in a Challenging Institutional Context." *American Psychologist* 66 (1): 4.

Coulter, Chris. 2009. *Bush Wives and Girl Soldiers: Women's Lives through War and Peace in Sierra Leone.* Ithaca, NY: Cornell University Press.

Coumans, Catherine. 2011. "Occupying Spaces Created by Conflict." *Current Anthropology* 52 (s3).

Crane, Andrew, Guido Palazzo, Laura J. Spence, and Dirk Matten. 2014. "Contesting the Value of 'Creating Shared Value.'" *California Management Review* 56 (2): 130–53.

Crittenden, Patricia M. 1985. "Maltreated Infants: Vulnerability and Resilience." *Journal of Child Psychology and Psychiatry* 26 (1): 85–96.

Croope, Silvana V., and Sue McNeil. 2011. "Improving Resilience of Critical Infrastructure Systems Postdisaster." *Transportation Research Record: Journal of the Transportation Research Board* 2234 (1): 3–13.

Crossland, Zoe. 2000. "Buried Lives: Forensic Archaeology and the Disappeared in Argentina." *Archaeological Dialogues* 7 (2): 146–59.

Crossland, Zoe. 2002. "Violent Spaces: Conflict over the Reappearance of Argentina's Disappeared." In *Matériel Culture: The Archaeology of Twentieth-Century Conflict*, edited by John Schofield, William Gray Johnson, and Colleen M. Beck, 115–31. London: Routledge.

Crouch, Colin. 2006. "Modelling the Firm in Its Market and Organizational Environment: Methodologies for Studying Corporate Social Responsibility." *Organization Studies* 27 (10): 1533–51.

Crouch, Colin. 2011. *The Strange Non-death of New-Liberalism.* Cambridge: Polity.

Czech Hydrometeorological Institute. 2014. *Graphic Yearbook 2013.* Accessed July 20, 2016. http://portal.chmi.cz/files/portal/docs/uoco/isko/grafroc/13groc/gr13e/Obsah_GB.html

"Czech Republic: 'Rescue Plan for Ostrava.'" 2013. *Mladá Fronta Dnes*, September 13.

D'Antonio, Salvatore, Luigi Romano, Abdelmajid Khelil, and Neeraj Suri. 2009. "Increasing Security and Protection through Infrastructure Resilience: The INSPIRE Project." In *Critical Information Infrastructures Security*, vol. 5508, edited by R. Setola and S. Geretshuber, 109–18. Berlin: Springer.

Davies, William. 2014. "Neoliberalism: A Bibliographic Review." *Theory, Culture and Society*, March 7. http://theoryculturesociety.org/william-davies-a-bibliographic-review-of-neoliberalism/.

Davis, Colin. 1996. *Levinas: An Introduction.* Cambridge: Polity.

Davis, Diane. 2012. "Urban Resilience in Situations of Chronic Violence." MIT Center for International Studies, May. Accessed May 5, 2012. http://web.mit.edu/cis/urban resiliencereport2012.pdf.

Davis, Elizabeth Anne. Forthcoming. *The Good of Knowing: War, Time, and Transparency in Cyprus*. Durham, NC: Duke University Press.

Davis, Mark. 2002. "HIV Prevention Rationalities and Serostatus in the Risk Narratives of Gay Men." *Sexualities* 5 (3): 281–99.

Davis, R., and D. M. Franks. 2014. "Costs of Company-Community Conflict in the Extractive Sector." Corporate Social Responsibility Initiative Report, John F. Kennedy School of Government, Harvard University, Cambridge, MA. Accessed February 16, 2015. https://www.hks.harvard.edu/m-rcbg/CSRI/research/Costs%20of%20Conflict_Davis%20%20Franks.pdf.

Dean, Mitchell. 1999. *Governmentality: Power and Rule in Modern Society*. London: Sage.

De Beers. 2011. "Creating Shared Value." Accessed February 16, 2015. http://www.debeersgroup.com/content/dam/de-beers/corporate/documents/Archive%20Reports/RTS10_Economics_June_2011.PDF.

Demetriou, Olga, and Ayla Gürel. 2008. "Human Rights, Civil Society and Conflict in Cyprus: Exploring the Relationships." Case Study Report WP3. SHUR: Human Rights in Conflicts: The Role of Civil Society. Programme of the European Commission.

Department of Social Security. 1998. *New Ambitions for Our Country: A New Contract for Welfare*. Command Paper 3805. London: The Stationary Office.

Doane, Deborah. 2005. "Beyond Corporate Social Responsibility: Minnows, Mammoths and Markets." *Futures* 37 (2–3): 215–29.

Doherty, Andrew, John Dora, and Colin Newsome. 2012. "Enhancing Resilience in Britain's Railway Infrastructure." *Proceedings of the Institution of Civil Engineers, Civil Engineering* 165 (6): 20–26.

Dorais, Michel, and Simon Lajeunesse. 2004. *Dead Boys Can't Dance*. Montreal: McGill-Queen's University Press.

Dorfman, Ariel. 2006. "The Missing and Photograph: The Uses and Misuses of Globalization." In *Spontaneous Shrines and the Public Memorialization of Death*, edited by Jack Santino, 255–60. New York: Palgrave Macmillan.

Dostál, Miroslav, Anna Pastorková, Stepan Rychlik, Eva Rychlíková, Vlasta Švecová, Eva Schallerová, and Radim J. Šrám. 2013. "Comparison of Child Morbidity in Regions of Ostrava, Czech Republic, with Different Degrees of Pollution: A Retrospective Cohort Study." *Environmental Health* 12 (74): 1–11.

Dostál, Miroslav, Anna Pastorková, Vlasta Švecová, and Radim J. Šrám. 2013. "Studie zdravotního stavu dětí v Ostravě 2001–2009" [The follow-up of children's health in Ostrava 2001–2009]. *Alergie* 1: 16–28.

Douglas, Mary. 1980. *Evans-Pritchard*. Brighton, UK: Harvester.

Dreyfus, Hubert L., and Paul Rabinow. 1983. "On the Genealogy of Ethics: An Overview of Work in Progress." In *Michel Foucault: Beyond Structuralism and Hermeneutics*, 2nd ed., 340–72. Chicago: University of Chicago Press.

Drury, John, Chris Cocking, and Steve Reicher. 2009. "The Nature of Collective Resilience: Survivor Reactions to the 2005 London Bombings." *International Journal of Mass Emergencies and Disasters* 27 (1): 66–95.

Dulai, Joshun, David Le, Olivier Ferlatte, Rick Marchand, and Terry Trussler. 2011. "Sex Now across Canada." Vancouver: Community Based Research Centre.

Dunn, Elizabeth. 2004. *Privatizing Poland: Baby Food, Big Business, and the Remaking of Labor.* Ithaca, NY: Cornell University Press.

Egan, James, Victoria Frye, Steven Kurtz, Carl Latkin, Minxing Chen, Karin Tobin, Cui Yang, and Beryl Koblin. 2011. "Migration, Neighborhoods, and Networks." *AIDS and Behavior* 15: S35–S50.

Elford, Jonathan. 1987. "Moral and Social Aspects of AIDS." *Social Science and Medicine* 24 (6): 543–49.

Elias, Norbert. 1978. *The History of Manners: The Civilizing Process,* vol. 1. New York: Pantheon.

Epstein, Steven. 1996. *Impure Science: AIDS, Activism, and the Politics of Knowledge.* Berkeley: University of California Press.

Fagan, Adam. 2004. *Environment and Democracy in the Czech Republic.* Cheltenham, UK: Edward Elgar.

Fassin, Didier. 2013. "Children as Victims." In *People Come First,* edited by João Biehl and Adriana Petryna, 109–32. Princeton, NJ: Princeton University Press.

Fassin, Didier. 2014. "The Immunity of Humanitarianism." In *Moral Anthropology: A Critical Reader,* edited by Didier Fassin and Samuel Lézé, 328–37. London: Routledge.

Featherstone, Katie, Paul Atkinson, Aditya Bharadwaj, and Angus Clarke. 2006. *Risky Relations: Family, Kinship and the New Genetics.* Oxford: Berg.

Ferguson, James. 2006. *Global Shadows: Africa in the Neoliberal World Order.* Durham, NC: Duke University Press.

Ferlatte, Olivier, Travis Hottes, Terry Trussler, and Rick Marchand. 2014. "Evidence of a Syndemic among Young Canadian Gay and Bisexual Men." *AIDS and Behavior* 18:1256–63.

Ferme, Mariane C. 2001. *The Underneath of Things: Violence, History, and the Everyday in Sierra Leone.* Berkeley: University of California Press.

Ferrándiz, Francisco. 2006. "The Return of Civil War Ghosts: The Ethnography of Exhumations in Contemporary Spain." *Anthropology Today* 22 (3): 7–12.

Ferrándiz, Francisco, and Alejandro Baer. 2008. "Digital Memory: The Visual Recording of Mass Grace Exhumations in Contemporary Spain." *Forum: Qualitative Social Research* 9 (3), article 45.

Fine, Susan B. 1991. "Resilience and Human Adaptability: Who Rises above Adversity?" *American Journal of Occupational Therapy* 45 (6): 493–503.

Finkler, Kaja. 2000. *Experiencing the New Genetics: Family and Kinship on the Medical Frontier.* Philadelphia: University of Pennsylvania Press.

Finnström, Sverker. 2008. *Living with Bad Surroundings: War, History, and Everyday Moments in Northern Uganda.* Durham, NC: Duke University Press.

Fischer, John Martin. 2006. *My Way: Essays on Moral Responsibility.* Oxford: Oxford University Press.

Fleming, Peter, and M. T. Jones. 2013. *The End of Corporate Social Responsibility: Crisis and Critique*. London: Sage.

Flemr, Jan. 2011. "Smoke from Czech Steel Hub Is Harming Kids." Yahoo! News, December 1. Accessed March 9, 2014. https://ph.news.yahoo.com/no-breath-relief-kids-dirty-czech-steel-hub-071154914.html.

Flowers, Paul, Jonathan Smith, Paschal Sheeran, and Nigel Beail. 1997. "Health and Romance." *British Journal of Health Psychology* 2:73–86.

Floyd, Caren. 1996. "Achieving Despite the Odds: A Study of Resilience among a Group of African American High School Seniors." *Journal of Negro Education* 65 (2): 181–89.

Flynn, Stephen. 2004. *America the Vulnerable: How Our Government Is Failing to Protect Us from Terrorism*. New York: HarperCollins.

Flynn, Stephen E. 2008. "America the Resilient: Defying Terrorism and Mitigating Natural Disasters." *Foreign Affairs* 87:2.

Formosa, Marvin. 2014. "Four Decades of Universities of the Third Age: Past, Present, Future." *Ageing and Society* 34 (1): 1–25.

Fornah, Aminatta. 2003. *The Devil That Danced on the Water: A Daughter's Quest*. New York: Atlantic Monthly Press.

Foucault, Michel. 1977. *Discipline and Punish: The Birth of the Prison*. London: Penguin.

Foucault, Michel. 1988. *The History of Sexuality*, vol. 3: *The Care of the Self*. New York: Knopf Doubleday.

Foucault, Michel. 1991. "Governmentality." In *The Foucault Effect: Studies in Governmentality*, edited by Graham Burchell, Colin Gordon, and Peter Miller, 87–104. Chicago: University of Chicago Press.

Foucault, Michel. 1997. *Ethics: Subjectivity and Truth*. Edited by Paul Rabinow. Translated by Robert Hurley et al. New York: New Press.

Frynas, Jędrzej George. 2009. "Corporate Social Responsibility in the Oil and Gas Sector." *Journal of World Energy Law and Business* 2 (3): 178–95.

Frynas, Jedrzej George. 2012. "Corporate Social Responsibility or Government Regulation? Evidence on Oil Spill Prevention." *Ecology and Society* 17 (4): 1–14.

Galletly, C. L., and J. Dickson-Gomez. 2009. "HIV Seropositive Status Disclosure to Prospective Sex Partners and Criminal Laws That Require It." *International Journal of STD and AIDS* 20:613–18.

Galvin, Kathey-Lee. 2001. "Schneider Revisited: Sharing and Ratification in the Construction of Kinship." In *New Directions in Anthropological Kinship*, edited by Linda Stone, 109–24. Lanham, MD: Rowman and Littlefield.

Gandsman, Ari. 2009. "'Do You Know Who You Are?': Radical Existential Doubt and Scientific Certainty in the Search for the Kidnapped Children of the Disappeared in Argentina." *Ethos* 37 (4): 441–65.

Ganti, Tejaswini. 2014. "Neoliberalism." *Annual Review of Anthropology* 43:89–104.

Gardner, Edward, Margaret McLees, John Steiner, Carlos del Rio, and William Burman. 2011. "The Spectrum of Engagement in HIV Care and Its Relevance to Test-and-Treat Strategies for Prevention of HIV Infection." *Clinical Infectious Diseases* 52 (6): 793–800.

Gardner, Katy, Zahir Ahmed, Fatema Bashir, and Masud Rana. 2012. "Elusive Partnerships: Gas Extraction and CSR in Bangladesh." *Resources Policy* 37 (2): 168–74.

Garmezy, Norman, and Ann S. Masten. 1986. "Stress, Competence, and Resilience: Common Frontiers for Therapist and Psychopathologist." *Behavior Therapy* 17 (5): 500–521.

Gasperowicz, Teresa. 2004. "Wakacje Z Gimnastyka" [School vacation with exercise class]. *Kurier UTW* 9:18.

Gilberthorpe, Emma, and Glenn Banks. 2012. "Development on Whose Terms? CSR Discourse and Social Realities in Papua New Guinea's Extractive Industries Sector." *Resources Policy* 37 (2): 185–93.

Gilligan, Carol. 1982. *In a Different Voice.* Cambridge, MA: Harvard University Press.

Gluckman, Max, ed. 1972. *The Allocation of Responsibility.* Manchester, UK: Manchester University Press.

Godelier, Maurice. 1999. *The Enigma of the Gift.* Translated by Nora Scott. Chicago: University of Chicago Press.

Goldstein, Daniel M. 2012. "Decolonising 'Actually Existing Neoliberalism.'" *Social Anthropology* 20: 304–9.

Gond, Jean-Pascal, Nahee Kang, and Jeremy Moon. 2011. "The Government of Self-Regulation: On the Comparative Dynamics of Corporate Social Responsibility." *Economy and Society* 40 (4): 640–71.

Gordon, Avery F. 1997. *Ghostly Matters: Haunting and the Sociological Imagination.* Minneapolis: University of Minnesota Press.

Graff, Agnieszka. 2009. "Gender, Sexuality, and Nation—Here and Now: Reflections on the Gendered and Sexualized Aspects of Contemporary Polish Nationalism." In *Intimate Citizenships: Gender, Sexualities, Politics*, edited by Elżbieta Oleksy, 133–46. New York: Routledge.

Greco, Monica. 1993. "Psychosomatic Subjects and the 'Duty to Be Well': Personal Agency Within." *Economy and Society* 22 (3): 357–72.

Greenberg, Jessica, and Andrea Muehlebach. 2007. "The Old World and Its New Economy: Notes on the 'Third Age' in Western Europe Today." In *Generations and Globalization: Youth, Age, and Family in the New World Economy*, edited by Jennifer Cole and Deborah Durham, 190–213. Bloomington: Indiana University Press.

Groves, Christopher. 2013. "Road Maps and Revelations: On the Somatic Ethics of Genetic Susceptibility." *New Genetics and Society* 32 (3): 264–84.

Grubbs, Larry. 2010. *Secular Missionaries: Americans and African Development in the 1960s.* Amherst: University of Massachusetts Press.

Gusfield, Joseph. 1963. *Symbolic Crusade.* Urbana: University of Illinois Press.

Habermas, Jürgen. 1987a. *The Theory of Communicative Action*, vol. 1. Boston: Beacon.

Habermas, Jürgen. 1987b. *The Theory of Communicative Action*, vol. 2. Boston: Beacon.

Hage, Ghassan. 2003. *Against Paranoid Nationalism: Searching for Hope in a Shrinking Society.* Sydney: Pluto.

Hage, Ghassan, and Robyn Eckersley, eds. 2012. *Responsibility.* Melbourne: Melbourne University Press.

Halkitis, Perry, Robert Moeller, Daniel Siconolfi, Erik Storholm, Todd Solomon, and Kristen Bub. 2013. "Measurement Model Exploring a Syndemic in Emerging Adult Gay and Bisexual Men." *AIDS and Behavior* 17:662–73.

Hallowell, Nina. 1999. "Doing the Right Thing: Genetic Risk and Responsibility." *Sociology of Health and Illness* 21 (5): 597–621.

Hann, Chris. 1996. "Introduction: Civil Society and Political Anthropology." In *Civil Society: Challenging Western Models*, edited by Chris Hann and Elizabeth Dunn, 1–24. New York: Routledge.

Hann, Chris, and Elizabeth Dunn, eds. 1996. *Civil Society: Challenging Western Models*. New York: Routledge.

Harm Reduction International. 2014. "What Is Harm Reduction?" Accessed March 3, 2014. http://www.hri.global/what-is-harm-reduction.

Harper, Janice. 2004. "Breathless in Houston." *Medical Anthropology* 23 (4): 295–326.

Harvey, Alison. 2009. "From Genetic Risk to Post-genomic Uncertainties: Nutrigenomics and the Birth of the Genetic Entrepreneur." *New Genetics and Society* 28 (2): 119–37.

Haukanes, Haldis. 2013. "Precarious Lives? Narratives of Hope, Loss, and 'Normality' across Two Generations of Czechs." *Focaal* 66:47–57.

Haukanes, Haldis, and Susanna Trnka. 2013. "Memory, Imagination and Belonging across Generations: Perspectives from Postsocialist Europe and Beyond." *Focaal* 66:3–13.

Hayner, Priscilla. 2007. "Negotiating Peace in Sierra Leone: Confronting the Justice Challenge." December. Geneva: Humanitarian Dialogue Report, Center for Humanitarian Dialogue, and New York: International Center for Transitional Justice. Accessed December 11, 2014. http://www.hdcentre.org/uploads/tx_news /90NegotiatingpeaceinSierraLeone-ConfrontingtheJusticechallenge.pdf.

Hayward, Janine. 1997. "The Principles of the Treaty of Waitangi." In *National Overview*, vol. 2, edited by A. Ward, 475–94. Wellington: GP.

Hazan, Pierre. 2010. "Transitional Justice after September 11: A New Rapport with Evil." In *Localizing Transitional Justice*, edited by Rosalind Shaw and Lars Waldorf, with Pierre Hazan, 49–65. Stanford, CA: Stanford University Press.

Heitlinger, Alena, and Susanna Trnka. 1998. *Young Women of Prague*. London: Macmillan.

Held, Virginia. 1993. *Feminist Morality: Transforming Culture, Society, and Politics*. Chicago: University of Chicago Press.

Held, Virginia. 2006. *Ethics of Care*. Oxford: Oxford University Press.

Herrick, Amy, Ron Stall, James Egan, Sheree Schrager, and Michele Kipke. 2014. "Pathways towards Risk." *Journal of Urban Health* 91 (5): 969–82.

Hilgers, Mathieu. 2012. "The Historicity of the Neoliberal State." *Social Anthropology* 20:80–94.

Hill, Jane H., and Judith T. Irvine, eds. 1993. *Responsibility and Evidence in Oral Discourse*. New York: Cambridge University Press.

Hilson, Gavin. 2012. "Corporate Social Responsibility in the Extractive Industries: Experiences from Developing Countries." *Resources Policy* 37 (2): 131–37.

Ho, Karen. 2009. *Liquidated: An Ethnography of Wall Street*. Durham, NC: Duke University Press.

Hobbes, Thomas. [1651] 1963. *Leviathan*. Edited by John Plamenatz. Cleveland, OH: Meridian.

Hoekelman, R. A. 1991. "A Pediatrician's View: Remedies to Enhance Resilience." *Pediatric Annals* 20 (9): 455–56.

Hoffman, Daniel. 2011. *The War Machines: Young Men and Violence in Sierra Leone and Liberia*. Durham, NC: Duke University Press.

Holling, Crawford S. 1973. "Resilience and Stability of Ecological Systems." *Annual Review of Ecology and Systematics* 4:1–23.

Holy, Ladislav. 1996. *The Little Czech and the Great Czech Nation*. Cambridge: Cambridge University Press.

Howard, Donna E. 1996. "Searching for Resilience among African-American Youth Exposed to Community Violence: Theoretical Issues." *Journal of Adolescent Health* 18 (4): 254–62.

Hunt, Alan. 2003. "Risk and Moralization in Everyday Life." In *Risk and Morality*, edited by Richard Victor Ericson and Aaron Doyle, 165–92. Toronto: University of Toronto Press.

Hunter, Ian. 1994. *Rethinking the School: Subjectivity, Bureaucracy, Criticism*. St. Leonards, NSW: Allen and Unwin.

Hyatt, Susan. 1997. "Poverty in a 'Post-welfare' Landscape: Tenant Management Policies, Self-Governance and the Democratization of Knowledge in Great Britain." In *Anthropology of Policy: Critical Perspectives on Governance and Power*, edited by Cris Shore and Susan Wright. London: Routledge.

Hynes, William, and Stephen M. Purcell. 2012. "Security for Critical Infrastructure and Urban Areas: A Holistic Approach to Urban Safety, Security and Resilience." In *Future Security*, edited by Nils Aschenbruck, Peter Martini, Michael Meier, and Jens Tölle, 165–75. Berlin: Springer.

IIED. 2002. "Breaking New Ground: The Report of the Mining, Minerals and Sustainable Development Project," 16–30. London: International Institute for Environment and Development and World Business Council for Sustainable Development. Accessed November 11, 2014. http://www.iied.org/mmsd/mmsd_pdfs/finalreport_01.pdf.

Ijagbemi, E. A. 1968. "A History of the Temne in the Nineteenth Century." PhD diss., Department of History, University of Edinburgh.

Ingold, Tim. 2000. *The Perception of the Environment: Essays in Livelihood, Dwelling and Skill*. London: Routledge.

Institute of Medicine. 2011. *The Health of Lesbian, Gay, Bisexual, and Transgender People*. Washington, DC: National Academies Press.

Jakubowska, Longina. 2012. *Patrons of History: Nobility, Capital and Political Transitions in Poland*. Burlington, VT: Ashgate.

Jalloh, Charles Chernor. 2014. *The Sierra Leone Special Court and Its Legacy: The Impact for Africa and International Criminal Law*. Cambridge: Cambridge University Press.

Jessop, Bob. 2013. "Putting Neoliberalism in Its Time and Place: A Response to the Debate." *Social Anthropology* 21:65–74.

Jones, Karen, and Kevin Williamson. 1979. "The Birth of the Schoolroom: A Study of the Transformation in the Discursive Conditions of English Popular Education in the 1st-Half of the 19th-Century." *Ideology and Consciousness* 6:59–110.

Joseph, Jonathan. 2013. "Resilience as Embedded Neoliberalism: A Governmentality Approach." *Resilience* 1 (1): 38–52.

Keat, Russell, and Nicholas Abercrombie. 1991. *Enterprise Culture*. London: Routledge.

Keen, David. 2005. *Conflict and Collusion in Sierra Leone*. Oxford: James Currey.

Kelsall, Tim. 2005. "Truth, Lies, Ritual: Preliminary Reflections on the Truth and Reconciliation Commission." *Sierra Leone Human Rights Quarterly* 27:361–91.

Kelsall, Tim. 2013. *Culture under Cross-Examination: International Justice and the Special Court for Sierra Leone*. Cambridge: Cambridge University Press.

Kelsey, Jane. 1995a. *Economic Fundamentalism*. London: Pluto.

Kelsey, Jane. 1995b. *The New Zealand Experiment: A World Model for Structural Adjustment?* Auckland: Auckland University Press.

Kelty, Chris M. 2008. "Responsibility: McKeon and Ricoeur." Anthropology of the Contemporary Research Collaboratory. ARC Working Paper no. 12.

Kemp, Deanna, and John R. Owen. 2013. "Community Relations and Mining: Core to Business but Not 'Core Business.'" *Resources Policy* 38 (4): 523–31.

Kerr, Anne. 2000. "(Re)constructing Genetic Disease: The Clinical Continuum between Cystic Fibrosis and Male Infertility." *Social Studies of Science* 30 (6): 846–94.

Kertzer, David. 1987. *Ritual Politics and Power*. New Haven, CT: Yale University Press.

Key, John. 2012. "4. Pike River Mine Disaster—Royal Commission Report and Health and Safety in Mining Industry." Parliamentary Debates (Hansard), New Zealand Parliament, November 6, vol. 685, 6264. Accessed September 9, 2014. http://www .parliament.nz/en-nz/pb/business/qoa/50HansQ_20121106_00000004/4-pike -river-mine-disaster—royal-commission-report-and.

Kilburn, Michael, and Miroslav Vaněk. 2004. "The Ecological Roots of a Democracy Movement." In *Human Rights Dialogue*. Carnegie Council for Ethics in International Affairs. Accessed March 9, 2014. https://www.carnegiecouncil.org /publications/archive/dialogue/2_11/section_1/4443.html/:pf_printable.

Kilshaw, Suzie. 2009. *Impotent Warriors: Gulf War Syndrome, Vulnerability and Masculinity*. Oxford: Berghahn.

Kingfisher, Catherine, and Jeff Maskovsky. 2008. "Introduction: The Limits of Neoliberalism." *Critique of Anthropology* 28:115–26.

Kirsch, Stuart. 2006. *Reverse Anthropology: Indigenous Analysis of Social and Environmental Relations in New Guinea*. Palo Alto, CA: Stanford University Press.

Kirsch, Stuart. 2010a. "Sustainability and the BP Oil Spill." *Dialectical Anthropology* 34 (3): 295–300.

Kirsch, Stuart. 2010b. "Sustainable Mining." *Dialectical Anthropology* 34 (1): 87–93.

Kirsch, Stuart. 2014. *Mining Capitalism: Dialectical Relations between Corporations and Their Critics*. Berkeley: University of California Press.

Kirtsoglou, Elizabeth. 2010. "Rhetoric and the Workings of Power: The Social Contract in Crisis." *Social Analysis* 54 (1): 1–14.

Kleinman, Arthur. 2006. *What Really Matters: Living a Moral Life amidst Uncertainty and Danger.* Oxford: Oxford University Press.

Knight, Marc, and Alpasian Özerdem. 2004. "Guns, Camps and Cash: Disarmament, Demobilization and Reinsertion of Former Combatants in Transitions from War to Peace." *Journal of Peace Research* 41:499–516.

Koblin, Beryl, Marla Husnik, Grant Colfax, Yijian Huang, Maria Madison, Kenneth Mayer, Patrick Barresi, Thomas Coates, Margaret Chesney, and Susan Buchbinder. 2006. "Risk Factors for HIV Infection among Men Who Have Sex with Men." *AIDS* 20:731–39.

Koblin, B., L. Torian, G. Xu, V. Guilin, H. Makki, D. MacKellar, and L. Valleroy. 2006. "Violence and HIV-Related Risk among Young Men Who Have Sex with Men." *AIDS Care* 18 (8): 961–67.

Kohn, Hans. 1944. *The Idea of Nationalism: A Study in Its Origins and Background.* New York: Macmillan.

Kovras, Iosif. 2008. "Unearthing the Truth: The Politics of Exhumations in Cyprus and Spain." *History and Anthropology* 19 (4): 371–90.

Krautforst, Nina. 2000. "Lubię Poniedziałki [I like Mondays]." *Kurier UTW: Nieregularnik Uniwersytetu Trzeciego Wieku* 1:3.

Kurtz, Steven. 2005. "Social Context, Sexual Practices, and Risks for HIV Transmission among Men Who Have Sex with Men." *Sexuality and Culture* 9 (4): 3–28.

Kyriakou, Nikolas. 2011. "Enforced Disappearances in Cyprus: Problems and Prospects of the Case Law of the European Court of Human Rights." *European Human Rights Law Review* (2): 190–99.

Kyriakou, Nikolas. 2012a. "An Affront to the Conscience of Humanity: Enforced Disappearance in International Human Rights Law." LD thesis, European University Institute.

Kyriakou, Nikolas. 2012b. "The International Convention for the Protection of All Persons from Enforced Disappearance and Its Contributions to International Human Rights Law, with Specific Reference to Extraordinary Rendition." *Melbourne Journal of International Law* 13:1–38.

Laidlaw, James. 2010. "Agency and Responsibility: Perhaps You Can Have Too Much of a Good Thing." In *Ordinary Ethics: Anthropology, Language, and Action*, edited by Michael Lambek, 143–64. New York: Fordham University Press.

Laidlaw, James. 2014. *The Subject of Virtue: An Anthropology of Ethics and Freedom.* Cambridge: Cambridge University Press.

Lamb, Sarah. 2014. "Permanent Personhood or Meaningful Decline? Toward a Critical Anthropology of Successful Aging." *Journal of Aging Studies* 29:41–52.

Lambek, Michael, ed. 2010a. *Ordinary Ethics: Anthropology, Language, and Action.* New York: Fordham University Press.

Lambek, Michael. 2010b. "Toward an Ethics of the Act." In *Ordinary Ethics: Anthropology, Language, and Action*, edited by Michael Lambek, 39–63. New York: Fordham University Press.

Larner, Wendy. 2000. "Post-welfare Governance: Towards a Code of Social and Family Responsibility." *Social Politics*, summer: 244–65.

Larner, Wendy, and Richard Le Heron. 2005. "Neoliberalising Spaces and Subjectivities: Reinventing New Zealand Universities." *Organization* 12 (6): 843–62.

Laslett, Peter. 1996. *A Fresh Map of Life: The Emergence of the Third Age*. London: Macmillan.

Ledeneva, Alena. 1998. *Russia's Economy of Favors: Blat, Networking, and Informal Exchange*. Cambridge: Cambridge University Press.

Lemke, Thomas. 2001. "'The Birth of Bio-politics': Michel Foucault's Lecture at the Collège de France on Neo-liberal Governmentality." *Economy and Society* 30 (2): 190–207.

Lemke, Thomas. 2004. "Disposition and Determinism: Genetic Diagnostics in Risk Society." *Sociological Review* 52 (4): 550–66.

Lentzos, Filippa. 2006. "Rationality, Risk and Response: A Research Agenda for Biosecurity." *Biosocieties* 1 (4): 453–64.

Lentzos, Filippa, and Nikolas Rose. 2009. "Governing Insecurity: Contingency Planning, Protection, Resilience." *Economy and Society* 38 (2): 230–54.

Levinas, Emmanuel. 1990. *Time and the Other*. Translated by R. Cohen. Pittsburgh: Duquesne University Press.

Li, Fabiana. 2015. *Unearthing Conflict: Corporate Mining, Activism and Expertise in Peru*. Durham, NC: Duke University Press.

Livesey, Sharon M., and Kate Kearins. 2002. "Transparent and Caring Corporations? A Study of Sustainability Reports by the Body Shop and Royal Dutch/Shell." *Organization and Environment* 15 (3): 233–58.

Livingston, Julie. 2005. *Debility and the Moral Imagination in Botswana*. Bloomington: Indiana University Press.

Lock, Margaret. 2012. "From Genetics to Post Genomics and the Discovery of the New Social Body." In *Medical Anthropology at the Interstices: Histories, Activisms and Futures*, edited by Marcia Inhorn and Emily Wentzell, 129–60. Durham, NC: Duke University Press.

Locke, John. [1699] 1967. *Two Treatises of Government*. Edited by P. Laslett. Cambridge: Cambridge University Press.

Loraux, Nicole. 2002. *The Divided City: On Memory and Forgetting in Ancient Athens*. Translated by Corinne Pache, with Jeff Fort. New York: Zone.

Luning, Sabine. 2012. "Corporate Social Responsibility (CSR) for Exploration: Consultants, Companies and Communities in Processes of Engagements." *Resources Policy* 37 (2): 205–11.

Lupton, Deborah. 1999. *Risk*. London: Routledge.

Luthar, Suniya S. 1991. "Vulnerability and Resilience: A Study of High-Risk Adolescents." *Child Development* 62 (3): 600–616.

Macfie, Rebecca. 2014. *Tragedy at Pike River Mine: How and Why 29 Died*. Wellington: Awa Press.

Mandel, Ruth, and Caroline Humphrey, eds. 2002. *Markets and Moralities: Ethnographies of Postsocialism*. Oxford: Berg.

Mansergh, Gordon, Gary Marks, Grant Colfax, Robert Guzman, Melissa Rader, and Susan Buchbinder. 2002. "'Barebacking' in a Diverse Sample of Men Who Have Sex with Men." *AIDS* 16:653–59.

Manyena, Siambabala Bernard. 2006. "The Concept of Resilience Revisited." *Disasters* 30 (4): 434–50.

Marks, Gary, and Nicole Crepaz. 2001. "HIV-Positive Men's Sexual Practices in the Context of Self-Disclosure of HIV Status." *Journal of Acquired Immune Deficiency Syndromes* 27 (1): 79–85.

Marshall, Thomas Humphrey. 1950. *Citizenship and Social Class, and Other Essays*. Cambridge: Cambridge University Press.

Mattingly, Cheryl. 2014. *Moral Laboratories: Family Peril and the Struggle for a Good Life*. Berkeley: University of California Press.

Mayerfeld, Jamie. 2002. *Suffering and Moral Responsibility*. Oxford: Oxford University Press.

Mbembe, Achille. 2001. *On the Postcolony*. Berkeley: University of California Press.

McCarthy, Elise. 2007. "Land of Saints and Tigers: The Transformation of Responsibility in Ireland." *Journal of the Society for the Anthropology of Europe* 7:3–7.

McGee, Brant. 2009. "Community Referendum: Participatory Democracy and the Right to Free, Prior and Informed Consent to Development." *Berkeley Journal of International Law* 27:570.

McKeon, Richard. 1957. "The Development and Significance of the Concept of Responsibility." *Revue International de Philosophie* 1:3–32.

Meigs, Anna. 1988. *Food, Sex, and Pollution: A New Guinea Religion*. New Brunswick, NJ: Rutgers University Press.

Mendeloff, David. 2009. "Trauma and Vengeance: Assessing the Psychological and Emotional Effects of Post-conflict Justice." *Human Rights Quarterly* 31:592–62.

Mill, J. S. 1975. *Three Essays*. London: Oxford University Press.

Miller, Peter. 2001. "Governing by Numbers: Why Calculative Practices Matter." *Social Research* 68:379–96.

Miller, Peter, and Nikolas Rose. 1990. "Governing Economic Life." *Economy and Society* 19 (1): 1–31.

Miller, Peter, and Nikolas Rose. 2008. *Governing the Present: Administering Economic, Social and Personal Life*. Malden, MA: Polity.

Mimiaga, Matthew, Conall O'Cleirigh, Katie Biello, Angela Robertson, Steven Safren, Thomas Coates, Beryl Koblin, Margaret Chesney, Deborah Donnell, Ron Stall, and Kenneth Mayer. 2015. "The Effect of Psychosocial Syndemic Production on 4-Year HIV Incidence and Risk Behavior in a Large Cohort of Sexually Active Men Who Have Sex with Men." *Journal of Acquired Immune Deficiency Syndrome* 68 (3): 329–36.

Minow, Martha. 1998. *Between Vengeance and Forgiveness: Facing History after Genocide and Mass Violence*. Boston: Beacon.

Mizuno, Yuko, Craig Borkowf, Gregorio Millett, Trista Bingham, George Ayala, and Ann Stueve. 2012. "Homophobia and Racism Experienced by Latino Men Who Have Sex with Men in the United States." *AIDS and Behavior* 16:724–35.

Mol, Annemarie. 2003. *The Body Multiple: Ontology in Medical Practice*. Durham, NC: Duke University Press.

Mol, Annemarie. 2008. *The Logic of Care: Health and the Problem of Patient Choice*. London: Routledge.

Mollona, Massimiliano. 2009. *Made in Sheffield: An Ethnography of Industrial Work and Politics*. Oxford: Berghahn.

Morawski, Witold. 1992. "Economic Change and Civil Society in Poland." In *Democracy and Civil Society in Eastern Europe*, edited by Paul G. Lewis, 91–112. New York: St. Martin's.

Morris, Gerard. 2014. "How the Law Let Down the Pike River Miners and Their Families." *Australian Mining*, February 27.

Mothersill, C., and C. Seymour. 2009. "Communication of Ionizing Radiation Signals—A Tale of Two Fish." *International Journal of Radiation Biology* 85 (11): 909–19.

Mothersill, C., R. W. Smith, T. G. Hinton, K. Aizawa, and C. B. Seymour. 2009. "Communication of Radiation-Induced Signals in Vivo between DNA Repair Deficient and Proficient Medaka (*Oryzias latipes*)." *Environmental Science and Technology* 43 (9): 3335–42.

Mrazek, Patricia J., and David A. Mrazek. 1987. "Resilience in Child Maltreatment Victims: A Conceptual Exploration." *Child Abuse and Neglect* 11 (3): 357–66.

Mucha, Janusz, and Łukasz Krzyżowski. 2010. "Aging in Poland at the Dawn of the 21st Century." *Polish Sociological Review* 170 (2): 247–60.

Muehlebach, Andrea. 2012. *The Moral Neoliberal: Welfare and Citizenship in Italy*. Chicago: University of Chicago Press.

Muehlebach, Andrea Karin. 2007. "The Moral Neoliberal: Welfare State and Ethical Citizenship in Contemporary Italy." PhD diss., University of Chicago.

Mustanski, Brian, Michael Newcomb, Steve Du Bois, Steve Garcia, and Christian Grov. 2011. "HIV in Young Men Who Have Sex with Men." *Journal of Sex Research* 48 (2): 218–53.

Mykhalovskiy, Eric, and Glenn Betteridge. 2012. "Who? What? Where? When? And with What Consequences? An Analysis of Criminal Cases of HIV Non-disclosure in Canada." *Canadian Journal of Law and Society* 27 (1): 31–53.

Navaro-Yashin, Yael. 2012. *The Make-Believe Space: Affective Geographies in a Postwar Polity*. Durham, NC: Duke University Press.

Nelkin, Dorothy. 1996. "The Social Dynamics of Genetic Testing: The Case of Fragile-X." *Medical Anthropology Quarterly* 10 (4): 537–50.

Nelson, Diane M. 2009. *Reckoning: The Ends of War in Guatemala*. Durham, NC: Duke University Press.

Neugarten, Bernice L. 1974. "Age Groups in American Society and the Rise of the Young-Old." *Annals of the American Academy of Political and Social Science* 415 (1): 187–98.

Newmont. 2013. "Beyond the Mine." Accessed September 12, 2014. http://sustainability report.newmont.com/.

New Zealand Department of Social Welfare. 1998. *Towards a Code of Social and Fam-*

ily Responsibility. He Kaupapa Kawenga Whanau, Kawenga Hapori: Public Discussion Document. Wellington.

Neyland, Daniel. 2012. "Parasitic Accountability." *Organization* 19 (6): 845–63.

Nichols, Hans. 2005. "Truth Challenges Justice in Freetown." *Washington Times*, January 5. Accessed January 15, 2015. https://www.globalpolicy.org/component/content/article/163/29151.html.

Nietzsche, Friedrich. 1969. *On the Genealogy of Morals.* Translated by Walter Kaufmann and R. J. Hollingdale. New York: Random House.

Novas, Carlos, and Nikolas Rose. 2000. "Genetic Risk and the Birth of the Somatic Individual." *Economy and Society* 29 (4): 485–513.

Obama, Barack. 2009. Inaugural address. Washington, DC, January 20.

Odets, Walt. 1995. *In the Shadow of the Epidemic.* Durham, NC: Duke University Press.

O'Dowd, Colm, Carmel E. Mothersill, Michael T. Cairns, Brian Austin, Fiona M. Lyng, Brendan McClean, Anita Talbot, and James E. J. Murphy. 2009. "Gene Expression and Enzyme Activity of Mitochondrial Proteins in Irradiated Rainbow Trout (*Oncorhynchus mykiss,* Walbaum) Tissues in Vitro." *Radiation Research* 171 (4): 464–73.

Olaru, Bogdan, ed. 2008. *Autonomy, Responsibility, and Health Care: Critical Reflections.* Bucharest, Romania: Zeta.

O'Malley, Pat. 1996. "Risk and Responsibility." In *Foucault and Political Reason: Liberalism, Neo-liberalism and Rationalities of Government,* by Andrew Barry, Thomas Osborne and Nikolas Rose, 189–207. Chicago: University of Chicago Press.

O'Malley, Pat. 2010. "Resilient Subjects: Uncertainty, Warfare and Liberalism." *Economy and Society* 39 (4): 488–509.

Omran, Abdel R. 1971. "The Epidemiologic Transition: A Theory of the Epidemiology of Population Change." *Milbank Memorial Fund Quarterly* 49 (4): 509–38.

Ong, Aihwa. 1999. *Flexible Citizenship: The Cultural Logics of Transnationality.* Durham, NC: Duke University Press.

Ong, Aihwa. 2003. *Buddha Is Hiding: Refugees, Citizenship, the New America.* Berkeley: University of California Press.

Oomen, Barbara. 2005. "Donor-Driven Justice and Its Discontents: The Case of Rwanda." *Development and Change* 36:887–910.

Ostrava Město Kultury. 2013. "Vítkovice." Accessed November 14, 2014. http://www.ostrava2015.cz/web/structure/vitkovice-61.html?lang=en.

Ostrow, David, Michael Plankey, Christopher Cox, Li Xiuhong, Steven Shoptaw, Lis Jacobson, and Ronald Stall. 2009. "Specific Sex Drug Combinations Contribute to the Majority of Recent HIV Seroconversions among MSM in the Macs." *Journal of Acquired Immune Deficiency Syndromes* 51 (3): 349–55.

Ostrowska, Antonina. 2001. "In and out of Communism: The Macrosocial Context of Health in Poland." In *The Blackwell Companion to Medical Sociology,* edited by William C. Cockerham, 334–46. Malden, MA: Blackwell.

Ostrowska, Antonina. 2010. "Polish Women 50+: How Do We Age?" *Polish Sociological Review* 172 (4): 411–28.

Owen, John R., and Deanna Kemp. 2013. "Social Licence and Mining: A Critical Perspective." *Resources Policy* 38 (1): 29–35.

Paraschos, Andreas. 2012. "The Missing on the Altar of Money: Opacity in the Management of Millions, Secret Funds, Favors and Careerism Make the Scandal" [Στον βωμό των χρημάτων οι αγνοούμενοι—αδιαφάνεια στη διαχείριση εκατομμυρίων, μυστικά κονδύλια, ρουσφέτια και καριερισμοί συνθέτουν το σκάνδαλο]. *Kathimerini*, April 1.

Pargament, Kenneth I., and Patrick J. Sweeney. 2011. "Building Spiritual Fitness in the Army: An Innovative Approach to a Vital Aspect of Human Development." *American Psychologist* 66 (1): 58.

Parsons, Michelle A. 2014. *Dying Unneeded: The Cultural Context of the Russian Mortality Crisis.* Nashville: Vanderbilt University Press.

Patton, Cindy. 1990. *Inventing AIDS.* New York: Routledge.

Patton, Cindy. 1996. *Fatal Advice.* Durham, NC: Duke University Press.

Payne, Leigh A. 2008. *Unsettling Accounts: Neither Truth nor Reconciliation in Confessions of State Violence.* Durham, NC: Duke University Press.

Pearce, Neil. 2011. "Non-allergic Asthma." Paper presented at the ISAAC Twenty-Year Anniversary Symposium, University of Auckland, Auckland, New Zealand, January 27.

Peck, Jamie, and Nik Theodore. 2012. "Reanimating Neoliberalism: Process Geographies of Neoliberalization." *Social Anthropology* 20:177–85.

Peck, Jamie, and Adam Tickell. 2002. "Neoliberalizing Space." *Antipode* 34 (3): 380–404.

Peek, Bobby, Dana Sadykova, Darek Urbaniak, Jan Haverkamp, Jan Šrytr, Pippa Gallop, and Sunita Dubey. 2009. "ArcelorMittal: Going Nowhere Slowly, a Review of the Global Steel Giant's Environmental and Social Impacts in 2008–2009." Friends of the Earth Europe, CEE Bankwatch Network, and Global Action on ArcelorMittal, May. Accessed March 9, 2014. http://bankwatch.org/documents/ArcelorMittal_Going_Nowhere.pdf.

"Personal Responsibility Key on Wellington Bus Route." 2012. *New Zealand Herald,* July 23. Accessed July 23, 2014. http://www.nzherald.co.nz/nz/news/article.cfm?c_id=1&objectid=10821498.

Persson, Asha, and Christy Newman. 2008. "'Making Monsters.'" *Sociology of Health and Illness* 30 (4): 632–46.

Peters, Krijn. 2011. *War and the Crisis of Youth in Sierra Leone.* Cambridge: Cambridge University Press.

Peterson, Christopher, Nansook Park, and Carl A. Castro. 2011. "Assessment for the US Army Comprehensive Soldier Fitness Program: The Global Assessment Tool." *American Psychologist* 66 (1): 10.

Piotrowski, Jerzy. 1973. *Miejsce Człowieka Starego W Rodzinie I Społeczeństwie.* Warsaw: Państwowe Wydawnictwo Naukowe.

Pithart, Petr. 2002. "The Fourth Overseas Journey of Thomas Garrigue Masaryk." Petr Pithart [blog], September 21. Accessed November 3, 2014. http://www.pithart.cz/archiv_textu_detail.pp?id=169.

Plato. 1907. *The Apology and Crito.* Edited by Isaac Flagg. New York: American Book.

Pleva, Martin. 2008. "ArcelorMittal: Víme, že škodíme. Zlepšíme se." Deník.cz, October 19. Accessed October 5, 2012. http://www.denik.cz/ekonomika/arcelormittal _skoda_zlepseni20081018.html.

Polish-American Freedom Foundation. 2000. Annual Report. Accessed August 1, 2016. http://www.en.pafw.pl/publications/repository/pdf/PAFF_%20Annual _Report_2000.pdf.

Pomales, Tony O. 2013. "Men's Narratives of Vasectomy: Rearticulating Masculinity and Contraceptive Responsibility in San Jose, Costa Rica." *Medical Anthropology Quarterly* 27 (1): 23–42.

Porter, Brian. 2000. *When Nationalism Began to Hate: Imagining Modern Politics in 19th Century Poland.* New York: Oxford University Press.

Porter, James, Clare Williams, Steven Wainwright, and Alan Cribb. 2013. "On Being a (Modern) Scientist: Risks of Public Engagement in the UK Interspecies Embryo Debate." *New Genetics and Society* 31 (4): 408–23.

Porter, Michael E., and Mark R. Kramer. 2011. "Creating Shared Value." *Harvard Business Review* 89 (1/2): 62–77.

Porter-Szücs, Brian. 2011. *Faith and Fatherland: Catholicism, Modernity, and Poland.* New York: Oxford University Press.

Power, Michael. 1994. *The Audit Explosion.* London: Demos.

Power, Michael. 1997. *The Audit Society: Rituals of Verification.* Oxford: Oxford University Press.

Pozniak, Kinga. 2013. "Generations of Memory in the 'Modern Socialist Town' of Nowa Huta, Poland." *Focaal* 66:58–68.

Pozniak, Kinga. 2014. *Nowa Huta: Generations of Change in a Model Socialist Town.* Pittsburgh: University of Pittsburgh Press.

PRRC. 2012a. *Royal Commission on the Pike River Coal Mine Tragedy, Commission's Report,* vol. 1. Accessed September 6, 2014. http://pikeriver.royalcommission.govt .nz/Volume-One–Contents.

PRRC. 2012b. *Royal Commission on the Pike River Coal Mine Tragedy, Commission's Report,* vol. 2. Accessed September 6, 2014. http://pikeriver.royalcommission.govt .nz/Volume-Two–Contents.

Rabinow, Paul. 1996. *Essays on the Anthropology of Reason.* Princeton, NJ: Princeton University Press.

Rabinow, Paul, and Nikolas Rose. 2006. "Biopower Today." *BioSocieties* 1 (2): 195–217.

Radio New Zealand. 2014. "Harassment Tip List Off Target." August 13. Accessed January 15, 2014. http://www.radionz.co.nz/news/national/252048/harassment-tip -list-off-target.

Raffoul, François. 2010. *The Origins of Responsibility.* Bloomington: Indiana University Press.

Rajak, Dinah. 2011. *In Good Company: An Anatomy of Corporate Social Responsibility.* Palo Alto, CA: Stanford University Press.

Rajan, Kaushik S. 2006. *Biocapital: The Constitution of Postgenomic Life.* Durham, NC: Duke University Press.

Rak, Carl F., and Lewis E. Patterson. 1996. "Promoting Resilience in At-Risk Children." *Journal of Counseling and Development* 74 (4): 368–73.

Rancière, Jacques. 2010. *Dissensus: On Politics and Aesthetics.* London: Bloomsbury.

Rangel, J. Cristian, and Barry D. Adam. 2014. "Everyday Moral Reasoning in the Governmentality of HIV Risk." *Sociology of Health and Illness* 36 (1): 60–74.

Rashid, Ismail. 2000. "Paying the Price: The Sierra Leone Peace Process. Accord Sierra Leone: Lome Peace Negotiations." Conciliation Resources. Accessed December 11, 2014. http://www.c-r.org/accord-article/lom%C3%A9-peace.

Raspberry, Kelly, and Debra Skinner. 2007. "Experiencing the Genetic Body: Parents' Encounters with Paediatric Clinical Genetics." *Medical Anthropology* 26 (4): 355–91.

Rawls, John. 1971. *A Theory of Justice.* Oxford: Oxford University Press.

Reback, Cathy, Sherry Larkins, and Steven Shoptaw. 2004. "Changes in the Meaning of Sexual Risk Behaviors among Gay and Bisexual Male Methamphetamine Abusers before and after Drug Treatment." *AIDS and Behavior* 8 (1): 87–98.

Reid, Julian. 2012. "The Neoliberal Subject: Resilience and the Art of Living Dangerously." *Revista Pléyade* 10:143–65.

Reiser, Stanley J. 1985. "Responsibility for Personal Health: A Historical Perspective." *Journal of Medicine and Philosophy* 10:7–17.

Reivich, Karen, and Andrew Shatté. 2002. *The Resilience Factor: 7 Essential Skills for Overcoming Life's Inevitable Obstacles.* New York: Broadway.

Reno, William. 1995. *Corruption and State Politics in Sierra Leone.* Cambridge: Cambridge University Press.

Renshaw, Layla. 2011. *Exhuming Loss: Memory, Materiality and Mass Graves of the Spanish Civil War.* Walnut Creek, CA: Left Coast.

Rhodes, Tim, and Linda Cusick. 2002. "Accounting for Unprotected Sex." *Social Science and Medicine* 55:211–26.

Richards, Paul. 1996. *Fighting for the Rain Forest: War, Youth, and Resources in Sierra Leone.* London: Heinemann.

Richards, Paul. 2005. "War as Smoke and Mirrors: Sierra Leone 1991–2, 1994–5, 1995–6." *Anthropological Quarterly* 78:377–402.

Richards, Paul, Steven Archibald, Khadija Bah, and James Vincent. 2003. "Where Have All the Young People Gone? Transitioning Ex-Combatants towards Community Reconstruction after the War in Sierra Leone." Unpublished report submitted to the National Commission for Disarmament, Demobilization and Reintegration (NCDDR), Government of Sierra Leone. Accessed December 11, 2014. http://www.scribd.com/doc/23530737/Richards-et-al-2003-Where-have-all-the-youth-gone.

Richters, Juliet, Olympia Hendry, and Susan Kippax. 2003. "When Safe Sex Isn't Safe." *Culture, Health and Sexuality* 5 (1): 37–52.

Ringel, Felix. 2013. "Differences in Temporal Reasoning: Temporal Complexity and Generational Classes in an East German City." *Focaal* 66:25–35.

Robbins, Jessica C. 2013. "Understanding *Aktywność* in Ethnographic Contexts: Aging, Memory, and Personhood in Poland." *Forum Oświatowe* [Educational forum] 1 (48): 87–101.

Robbins, Joel. 2009. "Value, Structure, and the Range of Possibilities: A Response to Zigon." *Ethnos: Journal of Anthropology* 74 (2): 277–85.

Robbins-Ruszkowski, Jessica C. 2013. "Challenging Marginalization at the Universities of the Third Age in Poland." *Anthropology and Aging Quarterly* 34 (2): 157–69.

Robbins-Ruszkowski, Jessica C. 2014. "Thinking with 'Postsocialism' in an Ethnographic Study of Old Age in Poland." *Cargo: Journal for Social/Cultural Anthropology* 12 (1–2): 35–50.

Robbins-Ruszkowski, Jessica C. 2015. "'Active Aging' as Citizenship in Poland." In *Generations: Rethinking Age and Citizenship*, edited by Richard Marback, 270–86. Detroit: Wayne State University Press.

Rogers, Douglas. 2012. "The Materiality of the Corporation: Oil, Gas, and Corporate Social Technologies in the Remaking of a Russian Region." *American Ethnologist* 39 (2): 284–96.

Rolston, Jessica Smith. 2014. *Mining Coal and Undermining Gender: Rhythms of Work and Family in the American West.* New Brunswick, NJ: Rutgers University Press.

Rolston, Jessica Smith. 2015. "Turning Protesters into Monitors: Appraising Critical Collaboration in the Mining Industry." *Society and Natural Resources* 28 (2): 165–79.

Rose, Nikolas. 1989. *Governing the Soul: The Shaping of the Private Self.* London: Routledge.

Rose, Nikolas. 1996a. "Authority and the Genealogy of Subjectivity." In *Detraditionalization: Critical Reflections on Authority and Identity*, edited by Paul Heelas, Scott Lash, and Paul Morris, 294–327. Oxford: Blackwell.

Rose, Nikolas. 1996b. "The Death of the Social? Re-figuring the Territory of Government." *Economy and Society* 25 (3): 327–56.

Rose, Nikolas. 1996c. "Governing 'Advanced' Liberal Democracies." In *Foucault and Political Reason: Liberalism, Neo-liberalism and Rationalities of Government*, edited by Andrew Barry, Thomas Osborne, and Nikolas Rose, 144–62. Chicago: University of Chicago Press.

Rose, Nikolas. 1999a. "Inventiveness in Politics." *Economy and Society* 28 (3): 467–93.

Rose, Nikolas. 1999b. *Powers of Freedom: Reframing Political Thought.* Cambridge: Cambridge University Press.

Rose, Nikolas. 2001. "The Politics of Life Itself." *Theory, Culture and Society* 18:1–30.

Rose, Nikolas. 2006. *The Politics of Life Itself: Biomedicine, Power and Subjectivity in the Twenty-First Century.* Princeton, NJ: Princeton University Press.

Rose, Nikolas, and Peter Miller. 1992. "Political Power beyond the State: Problematics of Government." *British Journal of Sociology* 43 (2): 173–205.

Rotberg, Robert I., and Dennis Thompson, eds. 2000. *Truth v. Justice: The Morality of Truth Commissions.* Princeton, NJ: Princeton University Press.

Rousseau, Jean-Jacques. 1762. "The Social Contract or Principles of Political Right." Translated by G. D. H. Cole. Constitution Society. Accessed May 26, 2012. http://www.constitution.org/jjr/socon.htm.

Rutter, Michael. 1985. "Resilience in the Face of Adversity." *British Journal of Psychiatry* 147 (1): 598–611.

Sampson, Steven. 1996. "The Social Life of Projects: Importing Civil Society to

Albania." In *Civil Society: Challenging Western Models,* edited by Chris Hann and Elizabeth Dunn, 121–42. New York: Routledge.

Sanford, Victoria. 2004. *Buried Secrets: Truth and Human Rights in Guatemala.* New York: Palgrave Macmillan.

Sant Cassia, Paul. 2005. *Bodies of Evidence: Burial, Memory, and the Recovery of Missing Persons in Cyprus.* New York: Berghahn.

Schabas, William A. 2003. "The Relationship between Truth Commissions and International Courts: The Case of Sierra Leone." *Human Rights Quarterly* 25:1035–66.

Schabas, William. 2004a. "Conjoined Twins of Transitional Justice? The Sierra Leone Truth and Reconciliation Commission and the Special Court." *Journal of International Criminal Justice* 2:1082–99.

Schabas, William. 2004b. "A Synergistic Relationship: The Sierra Leone Truth and Reconciliation Commission and the Special Court for Sierra Leone." *Criminal Law Forum* 15:3–54.

Scheper-Hughes, Nancy. 2007. "Violence and the Politics of Remorse: Lessons from South Africa." In *Subjectivity: Ethnographic Investigations,* edited by João Biehl, Byron Good, and Arthur Kleinman, 179–234. Berkeley: University of California Press.

Schmidt, Vivian, and Mark Thatcher, eds. 2013. *Resilient Liberalism in Europe's Political Economy.* Cambridge: Cambridge University Press.

Schmidt, Vivian, and Mark Thatcher. 2014. "Given the Abject Failure of the Neoliberal Policy Offer, Why Has It Persisted as the Dominant Approach to Policymaking?" *LSE Blog,* September 6. http://blogs.lse.ac.uk/politicsandpolicy/why-are-neo -liberal-ideas-so-resilient/.

Schneider, David. 1968. *American Kinship: A Cultural Account.* Chicago: University of Chicago Press.

Scott, Geoff, Hamish Coates, and Michelle Anderson. 2008. *Learning Leaders in Times of Change: Academic Leadership Capabilities for Australian Higher Education.* Sydney: Australian Council for Education Research. http://research.acer.edu.au /higher_education.

Scott, James C. 1985. *Weapons of the Weak: Everyday Forms of Peasant Resistance.* New Haven, CT: Yale University Press.

Shamir, Ronen. 2008. "The Age of Responsibilization: On Market-Embedded Morality." *Economy and Society* 37 (1): 1–19.

Shared Value Initiative. 2014. *Extracting with Purpose: Creating Shared Value in the Oil and Gas and Mining Sectors' Companies and Communities.* http://sharedvalue.org /resources/report-extracting-purpose.

Shaw, Rosalind. 2002. *Memories of the Slave Trade: Ritual and the Historical Imagination in Sierra Leone.* Chicago: University of Chicago Press.

Shaw, Rosalind, and Lars Waldorf. 2010. "Introduction: Localizing Transitional Justice." In *Localizing Transitional Justice,* edited by Rosalind Shaw and Lars Waldorf, with Pierre Hazan, 4–26. Stanford, CA: Stanford University Press.

Shaw, Susan. 2005. "The Politics of Recognition in Culturally Appropriate Care." *Medical Anthropology Quarterly* 19 (3): 290–309.

Sherbourne, Cathy, and Sarah Gaillot. 2011. *Promoting Psychological Resilience in the US Military.* Santa Monica, CA: Rand.

Shernoff, Michael. 2006. *Without Condoms.* New York: Routledge.

Shever, Elana. 2010. "Engendering the Company: Corporate Personhood and the 'Face' of an Oil Company in Metropolitan Buenos Aires." *PoLAR: Political and Legal Anthropology Review* 33 (1): 26–46.

Shore, Cris. 2008. "Audit Culture and Illiberal Government." *Anthropological Theory* 8 (3): 278–99.

Shore, Cris, and Susanna Trnka. 2013. "Observing Anthropologists: Professional Knowledge, Practice and Lives." In *Up Close and Personal: On Peripheral Perspectives and the Production of Anthropological Knowledge*, edited by Cris Shore and Susanna Trnka, 1–33. Oxford: Berghahn.

Shore, Cris, and Susan Wright. 1997. "Policy: A New Field of Anthropology." In *The Anthropology of Policy: Critical Perspectives on Governance and Power*, 3–39. New York: Routledge.

Shore, Cris, and Susan Wright. 1999. "Audit Culture and Anthropology: Neo-liberalism in British Higher Education." *Journal of the Royal Anthropological Institute* 7 (4): 759–63.

Shore, Cris, and Susan Wright. 2000. "Coercive Accountability." In *Audit Cultures: Anthropological Studies in Accountability, Ethics and the Academy*, edited by Marilyn Strathern, 57–89. London: Routledge.

Shore, Cris, and Susan Wright. 2011. "Conceptualising Policy: Technologies of Governance and the Politics of Visibility." In *Policy Worlds: Anthropology and the Analysis of Contemporary Power*, edited by Cris Shore, Susan Wright, and Davide Però, 1–26. Oxford: Berghahn.

Shore, Cris, and Susan Wright. 2015. "Audit Culture Revisited: Rankings, Ratings and the Reassembling of Society." *Current Anthropology* 56 (3): 421–44.

Siebert, Al. 2005. *The Resiliency Advantage: Master Change, Thrive under Pressure, and Bounce Back from Setbacks.* San Francisco: Berrett-Koehler.

Siegel, Karolynn, Helen-Maria Lekas, and Eric Schrimshaw. 2005. "Serostatus Disclosure to Sexual Partners by HIV-Infected Women before and after the Advent of HAART." *Women and Health* 41 (4): 63–85.

Skýbová, Pavla. 2009. "Závěrečná zpráva o projektu. Nebe nad Ostravou." November 29. Ostrava: Vzduch.

Slack, Keith. 2012. "Mission Impossible? Adopting a CSR-Based Business Model for Extractive Industries in Developing Countries." *Resources Policy* 37 (2): 179–84.

Smart, Barry. 2003. *Economy, Culture and Society.* Buckingham, UK: Open University Press.

Smith, Dawn, Jeffrey Herbst, Xinjiang Zhang, and Charles Rose. 2015. "Condom Effectiveness for HIV Prevention by Consistency of Use among Men Who Have Sex with Men (MSM) in the U.S." *Journal of Acquired Immune Deficiency Syndrome.* doi:10.1097/QAI.0000000000000461.

Smith, Jessica, and Frederico Helfgott. 2010. "Flexibility or Exploitation? Corporate

Social Responsibility and the Perils of Universalization." *Anthropology Today* 26:20–23.

Southwick, Steven M., Meena Vythilingam, and Dennis S. Charney. 2005. "The Psychobiology of Depression and Resilience to Stress: Implications for Prevention and Treatment." *Annual Review of Clinical Psychology* 1:255–91.

Šrám, Radim, Blanka Binkova, Miroslav Dostal, Michaela Merkerova-Dostalova, Helena Libalova, Alena Milcova, Pavel Rossner Jr., Andrea Rossnerova, Jana Schmuczerova, Vlasta Svecova, Jan Topinka, and Hana Votavova. 2013. "Health Impact of Air Pollution to Children." *International Journal of Hygiene and Environmental Health* 216 (5): 533–40.

Stahn, Carsten. 2001. "Accommodating Individual Criminal Responsibility and National Reconciliation: The UN Truth Commission for East Timor." *American Journal of International Law* 95:952–66.

Stall, Ron, M. S. Friedman, and J. Catania. 2007. "Interacting Epidemics and Gay Men's Health." In *Unequal Opportunity*, edited by R. Wolitski, R. Stall, and R. Valdiserri. Oxford: Oxford University Press.

Stall, Ron, Thomas Mills, John Williamson, Trevor Hart, Greg Greenwood, Jay Paul, Lance Pollack, Diane Binson, Dennis Osmond, and Joseph Catania. 2003. "Association of Co-occurring Psychosocial Health Problems and Increased Vulnerability to HIV/AIDS among Urban Men Who Have Sex with Men." *American Journal of Public Health* 93 (6): 939–42.

Steinberg, Deborah Lynn. 1996. "Languages of Risk: Genetic Encryptions of the Female Body." *Women: A Cultural Review* 7 (3): 259–70.

Stevenson, Lisa. 2014. *Life beside Itself: Imagining Care in the Canadian Arctic.* Berkeley: University of California Press.

Strathern, Marilyn. 1992. *After Nature: English Kinship in the Late Twentieth Century.* Cambridge: Cambridge University Press.

Strathern, Marilyn, ed. 2000a. *Audit Cultures: Anthropological Studies in Accountability, Ethics and the Academy.* London: Routledge.

Strathern, Marilyn. 2000b. "Introduction: New Accountabilities." In *Audit Cultures: Anthropological Studies in Accountability, Ethics and the Academy*, edited by Marilyn Strathern, 1–18. London: Routledge.

Sudetic, Chuck. 2013. "Roma in Political Life: Czech Republic—Dependency and Political Development." Open Society Foundations, September 10. Accessed March 14, 2014. http://www.opensocietyfoundations.org/voices/roma-political-life-czech-republic-dependency-and-political-development.

Synak, Brunon. 1992. "From State to Local Responsibility: Marginalization of Elderly People in the Post-totalitarian Society." In *Développement local et développement social, Québec, Canada*, 89–94. Université Laval.

Szablowski, David. 2007. *Transnational Law and Local Struggles: Mining, Communities and the World Bank.* Oxford: Hart.

Takirambudde, Peter, and Joanna Weschler. 1999. "Letter to U.N. Secretary-General Kofi Annan on the Sierra Leone Conflict." Human Rights Watch, July 6. Accessed

December 11, 2014. http://www.hrw.org/news/1999/07/06/letter-un-secretary
-general-kofi-annan-sierra-leone-conflict.

Tap, Relinde. 2007. "High-Wire Dancers: Middle-Class Pakeha and Dutch Childhoods in New Zealand." PhD diss., University of Auckland.

Taussig, Michael. 1999. *Defacement: Public Secrecy and the Labor of the Negative.* Stanford, CA: Stanford University Press.

Tavuchis, Nicholas. 1991. *Mea Culpa: A Sociology of Apology and Reconciliation.* Stanford, CA: Stanford University Press.

Teitel, Ruti G. 2003. "Transitional Justice Genealogy." *Harvard Human Rights Journal* 16:69–94.

Thelen, Tatjana. 2003. "The New Power of Old Men: Privatisation and Family Relations in Mesterszallas (Hungary)." *Anthropology of East Europe Review* 21 (2): 15–21.

Thompson, Grahame. 2007. "Responsibility and Neoliberalism." *Open Democracy,* July 31. Accessed September 6, 2014. https://www.opendemocracy.net/article/responsibility_and_neo_liberalism.

Thompson, Grahame. 2011. "The Paradoxes of Liberalism: Can the International Financial Architecture Be Disciplined?" *Economy and Society* 40 (3): 477–87.

Tilley, Helen. 2011. *Africa as a Living Laboratory: Empire, Development, and the Problem of Scientific Knowledge.* Chicago: University of Chicago Press.

Towarzystwo Inicjatyw Twórczych "ę." 2012. "'Zoom Na UTW': Raport z Badania," 110. Warsaw.

Trnka, Susanna. 2013. "Forgotten Pasts and Fearful Futures in Czechs' Remembrances of Communism." *Focaal* 66:36–46.

Trnka, Susanna. 2017. *One Blue Child: Asthma, Personality Responsibility, and 21st Century Patienthood.* Palo Alto, CA: Stanford University Press.

Trnka, Susanna, and Laura Busheikin, eds. 1993. *Bodies of Bread and Butter: Reconfiguring Women's Lives in the Post-communist Czech Republic.* Prague: Gender Studies Centre.

Trnka, Susanna, Christine Dureau, and Julie Park. 2013a. "Senses and Citizenships: An Introduction." In *Senses and Citizenships: Embodying Political Life,* edited by Susanna Trnka, Christine Dureau, and Julie Park, 1–32. New York: Routledge.

Trnka, Susanna, Christine Dureau, and Julie Park, eds. 2013b. *Senses and Citizenships: Embodying Political Life.* London: Routledge.

Trnka, Susanna, and Catherine Trundle. 2014. "Competing Responsibilities: Moving beyond Neoliberal Responsibilisation." *Anthropological Forum* 24 (2): 136–53.

Trundle, Catherine. 2011. "Biopolitical Endpoints: Diagnosing a Deserving British Nuclear Test Veteran." *Social Science and Medicine* 73 (6): 882–88.

Trundle, Catherine. 2012. "Memorialising the Veteran Body: New Zealand Nuclear Test Veterans and the Search for Military Citizenship." In *War and the Body: Militarisation, Practice and Experience,* edited by Kevin McSorley, 194–209. London: Routledge.

Trundle, Catherine. 2014. *Americans in Tuscany: Charity, Compassion and Belonging.* Oxford: Berghahn.

Trundle, Catherine, and Brydie Scott. 2013. "Elusive Genes: Nuclear Test Veterans'

Experiences of Genetic Citizenship and Biomedical Refusal." *Medical Anthropology* 32 (6): 501–17.

Truth and Reconciliation Commission, Sierra Leone. 2000. "The Truth and Reconciliation Commission Act 2000." Accessed February 16, 2015. http://www.sierra-leone .org/Laws/2000-4.pdf.

Truth and Reconciliation Commission, Sierra Leone. 2004. *Witness to Truth: Final Report of the Sierra Leone Truth and Reconciliation Commission*. Accessed December 11, 2014. http://sierraleonetrc.org/index.php/view-the-final-report.

Truth and Reconciliation Commission, "Sierra Leone," final reports, table of contents. Accessed August 2, 2016. http://www.sierraleonetrc.org/index.php/view-the-final -report/download-table-of-contents.

TV Nova. 2013. "Ostrava žaluje stát a ministerstva kvůli znečištění ovzduší!" October 18.

Ungar, Michael. 2011. *The Social Ecology of Resilience: A Handbook of Theory and Practice*. Berlin: Springer.

United Nations. 2004. "Report of the Secretary-General on the Rule of Law and Transitional Justice in Conflict and Post-conflict Societies." http://daccess-dds-ny.un .org/doc/UNDOC/GEN/N04/395/29/PDF/N0439529.pdf?OpenElement.

University of Auckland (UoA). 2013a. "Continuing Capability Development Guide." Auckland: University of Auckland. Accessed September 9, 2014. https://cdn .auckland.ac.nz/assets/staff/HR/career-development/documents/Continuing %20Capability%20Development%20Guide%20booklet%20layout%20March%20 2014.pdf.

University of Auckland (UoA). 2013b. "Guide to the University of Auckland Leadership Framework." Auckland: University of Auckland. Accessed September 6, 2014. https://cdn.auckland.ac.nz/assets/staff/how-the-university-works/documents /Guide%20to%20the%20Leadership%20Framework%20-%20Capabilities%20 Defined.pdf.

Utas, Mats. 2005. "Building a Future? The Reintegration and Remarginalization of Youth in Liberia." In *No Peace, No War: An Anthropology of Contemporary Armed Conflicts*, edited by Paul Richards, 137–54. Oxford: James Currey.

Valverde, Mariana. 1996. "'Despotism' and Ethical Liberal Governance." *Economy and Society* 25 (3): 357–72.

Vance, Andrea, Tracy Watkins, and Danya Levy. 2012. "What Have I Done Wrong?" Stuff.co.nz, November 6. Accessed September 6, 2014. http://www.stuff.co.nz /national/politics/7909810/What-have-I-done-wrong.

Van Dijck, José. 1998. *Imagenation: Popular Images of Genetics*. New York: New York University Press.

Vaněk, Miroslav. 1996. *Nedalo se tady dýchat*. Prague: Maxdorf.

van Opstal, Debra. 2006. "Moving beyond Security: The Resilience Imperative." *Cutter IT Journal* 19 (5): 12.

Velinger, Jan. 2015. "Health Reports Says that Air Pollution Leads to More than 5,000 Deaths in Czech Republic Annually." *Český rozhlas*, October 3. http://www.radio.cz /en/section/czech-life/health-reports-says-that-air-pollution-leads-to-more-than -5000-deaths-in-czech-republic-annually/.

Verdery, Katherine. 1996. *What Was Socialism, and What Comes Next?* Princeton, NJ: Princeton University Press.

Villa, Dana R. 1996. *Arendt and Heidegger: The Fate of the Political.* Princeton, NJ: Princeton University Press.

Vossler, Teri, Libor Cernikovsky, Jiri Novak, Helena Placha, Blanka Krejci, Irina Nikolova, Eva Chalupnickova, and Ronald Williams. 2015. "An Investigation of Local and Regional Sources of Fine Particulate Matter in Ostrava, the Czech Republic." *Atmospheric Pollution Research* 6 (3): 454–63.

Všelichová, P., dir. 2010. *Intolerance: Když vzduch zabíjí* [film]. Accessed March 4, 2014. http://www.ceskatelevize.cz/porady/10275866938-intolerance/41023510014 1006-kdyz-vzduch-zabiji/.

Walker, Jeremy, and Melinda Cooper. 2011. "Genealogies of Resilience from Systems Ecology to the Political Economy of Crisis Adaptation." *Security Dialogue* 42 (2): 143–60.

Walklate, Sandra, Gabe Mythen, and Ross McGarry. 2012. "States of Resilience and the Resilient State." *Current Issues in Criminal Justice* 24:185.

Warmuz, Stanisława. 2004. "'Moje' Seminaria" ["My" seminars]. *Kurier UTW* 9:21–23.

Warner, Michael. 2002. "Publics and Counterpublics." *Quarterly Journal of Speech* 88 (4): 413–25.

Washick, Bonnie, and Elizabeth Wingrove. 2015. "Politics That Matter: Thinking about Power and Justice with the New Materialists." *Contemporary Political Theory* 14:63–89.

Watney, Simon. 1987. *Policing Desire.* London: Comedia.

Watson, Peggy. 2006a. "Stress and Social Change in Poland." *Health and Place* 12:372–82.

Watson, Peggy. 2006b. "Unequalizing Citizenship: The Politics of Poland's Health Care Change." *Sociology* 40 (6): 1079–96.

Watson, Peggy. 2010. "Poland's Painful Market Reforms." *British Medical Journal* 340 (c2837): 1336–37.

Webster, Andrew. 2009. "Innovative Genetic Technologies, Governance and Social Accountability." In *Handbook of Genetics and Society: Mapping the New Genomic Era*, edited by Paul Atkinson, Peter Glasner, and Margaret Lock, 486–501. London: Routledge.

Weeks, Jeffrey. 1995. *Invented Moralities.* New York: Columbia University Press.

Weismantel, Mary. 1995. "Making Kin: Kinship Theory and Zumbagua Adoptions." *American Ethnologist* 22 (4): 685–709.

Welker, Marina A. 2009. "Corporate Security Begins in the Community: Mining, the Corporate Social Responsibility Industry, and Environmental Advocacy in Indonesia." *Cultural Anthropology* 24:142–79.

Welker, Marina A. 2014. *Enacting the Corporation: An American Mining Firm in Postauthoritarian Indonesia.* Berkeley: University of California Press.

Werner, Emmy E. 1993. "Risk, Resilience, and Recovery: Perspectives from the Kauai Longitudinal Study." *Development and Psychopathology* 5 (4): 503–15.

Werner, Emmy E., Jessie M. Bierman, and Fern E. French. 1971. *The Children of Kauai: A Longitudinal Study from the Prenatal Period to Age Ten.* Honolulu: University of Hawai'i Press.

Werner, Emmy E., and Ruth S. Smith. 1982. *Vulnerable but Invincible: A Study of Resilient Children and Youth.* New York: McGraw-Hill.

Werner, Emmy E., and Ruth S. Smith. 2001. *Journeys from Childhood to Midlife: Risk, Resilience, and Recovery.* Ithaca, NY: Cornell University Press.

Whitehead, Gregory. 1990. "The Forensic Theatre: Memory Plays for the Post-mortem Condition." *Performing Arts Journal* 12 (2/3): 99–109.

Whittier, David, Janet St. Lawrence, and Salvatore Seeley. 2005. "Sexual Risk Behavior of Men Who Have Sex with Men." *Archives of Sexual Behavior* 34 (1): 95–102.

Widdows, Heather. 2009. "Between the Individual and the Community: The Impact of Genetics on Ethical Models." *New Genetics and Society* 28 (2): 173–88.

Wildavsky, Aaron B. 1988. *Searching for Safety*, vol. 10. New Brunswick, NJ: Transaction.

Williams, Raymond. 1975. *Keywords.* Glasgow: Fontana.

Wilson, Richard A. 2001. *The Politics of Truth and Reconciliation in South Africa: Legitimizing the Post-apartheid State.* Cambridge: Cambridge University Press.

Wnuk, Walentyna. 2004. "Różne Wymiary Opieki Nad Ludźmi Starszymi Na Przykładzie UTW We Wrocławiu" [Different dimensions of care for older people in the example of the UTW in Wrocław]. *Kurier UTW: Nieregularnik Uniwersytetu Trzeciego Wieku* 9:3–6.

Wnuk, Walentyna. 2005. "Postawa Wobec Własnego Życia" [Attitude toward one's own life]. *Kurier UTW* 10:15–16.

Wolff, Larry. 1994. *Inventing Eastern Europe: The Map of Civilization on the Mind of the Enlightenment.* Stanford, CA: Stanford University Press.

Woźnicka, Alina. 1997. *Regulamin UTW, 1979–1997* [UTW rules, 1979–1997]. Wrocław: Universytet Trzeciego Wieku.

Xstrata. 2011. "Creating Shared Value." Accessed September 12, 2014. http://public.thecorporatelibrary.net/Sustain/sr_2011_31280.pdf.

Yakinthou, Christalla. 2008. "The Quiet Deflation of Den Xehno? Changes in the Greek-Cypriot Communal Narrative on the Missing Persons in Cyprus." *Cyprus Review* 20 (1): 15–34.

Yakovleva, Natalia. 2005. *Corporate Social Responsibility in the Mining Industries.* Burlington, VT: Ashgate.

Young, Allan. 1995. *The Harmony of Illusions: Inventing Post-traumatic Stress Disorder.* Princeton, NJ: Princeton University Press.

Young, Iris Marion. 1989. "Polity and Group Difference: A Critique of the Ideal of Universal Citizenship." *Ethics* 99:250–74.

Zigon, Jarrett. 2011. *"HIV Is God's Blessing": Rehabilitating Morality in Neoliberal Russia.* Berkeley: University of California Press.

Zigon, Jarrett. 2014a. "Attunement and Fidelity: Two Ontological Conditions for Morally Being-in-the-World." *Ethos* 42 (1): 16–30.

Zigon, Jarrett. 2014b. "An Ethics of Dwelling and a Politics of World-Building: A Critical Response to Ordinary Ethics." *JRAI* 20: 746–64.

Zigon, Jarrett. 2015. "What Is a Situation? An Assemblic Ethnography of the Drug War." *Cultural Anthropology* 30 (3): 501–24.

Zigon, Jarrett. Forthcoming. *World-Building: Critical Hermeneutic Essays on Ethics, Politics, and Ontologies.* New York: Fordham University Press.

Zubrzycki, Genevieve. 2001. "We, the Polish Nation: Ethnic and Civic Visions of Nationhood in Post-communist Debates." *Theory and Society* 30:629–68.

Zubrzycki, Genevieve. 2002. "The Classical Opposition between Civic and Ethnic Models of Nationhood: Ideology, Empirical Reality and Social Scientific Analysis." *Polish Sociological Review* 3:275–95.

Zubrzycki, Genevieve. 2006. *The Crosses of Auschwitz: Nationalism and Religion in Post-communist Poland.* Chicago: University of Chicago Press.

Zwart, Hub. 2007. "Genomics and Self-Knowledge: Implications for Societal Research and Debate." *New Genetics and Society* 26 (2): 181–202.

Contributors

BARRY D. ADAM is distinguished university professor of sociology at the University of Windsor, and senior scientist and director of prevention research at the Ontario HIV Treatment Network. Adam came to HIV work with an extensive research record on the dynamics of domination and empowerment, LGBT studies, HIV prevention, and issues of living with HIV. Some of his recent articles have appeared in *AIDS Education and Prevention, Culture Health and Sexuality, Canadian Journal of Law and Society, Critical Public Health, Health Education Research,* and *Sociology of Health and Illness.* In 2007, he received the Simon-Gagnon Award for a distinguished career in the study of sexualities, presented by the Sociology of Sexualities Section of the American Sociological Association. In 2012, he received the Community Partners Award of the Ontario AIDS Network; in 2013, the Queen's Diamond Jubilee Medal; and, in 2015, the career award for outstanding contributions to the sociology of HIV/AIDS, presented by the Sociologists AIDS Network of the American Sociological Association.

ELIZABETH ANNE DAVIS is associate professor of anthropology at Princeton University, where she is affiliated with the Seeger Center for Hellenic Studies. Her research and writing, grounded in the European horizons and the Ottoman history of the Greek-speaking world, focus on the intersections of psyche, body, history, and power as areas for ethnographic and theoretical engagement. Her first book, *Bad Souls: Madness and Responsibility in Modern Greece,* is an ethnographic study of responsibility among psychiatric patients and their caregivers in the multicultural borderland between Greece and Turkey. She is currently working on her second book, *The Good of Knowing: War, Time, and Transparency in Cyprus,* a collaborative engagement with Cypriot knowledge production about the violence of the 1960s–70s in the domains of forensic science, documentary film, and conspiracy theory.

FILIPPA LENTZOS is a senior research fellow in the Department of Global Health and Social Medicine at King's College London. Her work focuses on social, political, and security aspects of the life sciences, and she is particularly interested in contemporary and historical understandings of the threat of biological weapons and bioterrorism. Her book *Biological Threats in the 21st Century* was published in 2016 and her book *Synthetic Biology and Bioweapons* will be published in 2017.

JESSICA ROBBINS-RUSZKOWSKI is assistant professor at the Institute of Gerontology and Department of Anthropology at Wayne State University. She is a sociocultural and medical anthropologist who studies how experiences of aging—especially of health and illness—are part of broader social, cultural, political, economic, and historical processes. She is currently writing a monograph on aging, memory, and personhood in Poland, based on almost two years of ethnographic fieldwork. She has an ongoing project on the (pre)/(post)socialist histories of the sciences of aging in Poland, and is developing new comparative ethnographic studies of urban gardens/*działki* (allotment gardens) in Detroit and Poland. Previous work has appeared in journals including *Anthropology and Aging Quarterly*, *Cargo*, and *Forum Oświatowe* [Educational forum], and in multiple edited volumes.

NIKOLAS ROSE is professor of sociology and head of the Department of Global Health and Social Medicine at King's College London. He was trained as a biologist before switching to psychology and then to sociology. He is founder and coeditor of *Bio-Societies: An Interdisciplinary Journal for Social Studies of the Life Sciences*. He has published widely on the social and political history of the human sciences, on the genealogy of subjectivity, on the history of empirical thought in sociology, on law and criminology, and on changing rationalities and techniques of political power. His most recent books include *Neuro: The New Brain Sciences and the Management of the Mind* (written with Joelle Abi-Rached), *Governing the Present* (written with Peter Miller), and *The Politics of Life Itself: Biomedicine, Power, and Subjectivity in the Twenty-First Century*.

ROSALIND SHAW is associate professor and chair of the Department of Anthropology at Tufts University. She has published extensively on memory, religion, transitional justice, and Sierra Leone. She is the author of *Memories of the Slave Trade: Ritual and the Historical Imagination in Sierra Leone* and coeditor of *Localizing Transitional Justice: Interventions and Priorities after Mass Violence*; *Syncretism/Anti-syncretism: The Politics of Religious Synthesis*; and *Dreaming, Religion and Society in Africa*. Her book in progress, *Anticipating Memory: The Production of Post-conflict Time in Sierra Leone*, explores postwar reconstruction in Sierra Leone through the lens of memory and futurity.

CRIS SHORE is professor of anthropology at the University of Auckland. He trained as a social anthropologist at Sussex University, where he carried out anthropological fieldwork in Italy, studying the Italian Communist Party and the lives of its activists. His second major fieldwork project explored EU cultural politics and the emerging organizational culture of the EU civil service in Brussels. His main research interest is political anthropology, particularly the ethnography of organizations and the anthropology of policy, a field that he has pioneered since the 1990s. He has also published extensively on other related themes including audit culture, elites, higher education reform, and the anthropology of corruption.

JESSICA M. SMITH is assistant professor in Liberal Arts and International Studies at the Colorado School of Mines. Her research engages two major areas: the sociocultural dynamics of extractive and energy industries, with a focus on corporate social responsibility, social justice, labor, and gender; and engineering education, with a focus on socioeconomic class and social responsibility. She is the author of *Mining Coal and Undermining Gender: Rhythms of Work and Family in the American West*, which was funded by a fellowship from the National Endowment for the Humanities. Her current research project, "The Ethics of Extraction: Integrating Corporate Social Responsibility into Engineering Education," investigates the sociotechnical dimensions of CSR for engineers in the mining, oil, and gas industries and is funded by the National Science Foundation.

SUSANNA TRNKA is associate professor of anthropology at the University of Auckland. Her research focuses on the intersections between the body, citizenship, and subjectivity. In addition to her long-standing research interests in the Czech Republic, she has conducted research in New Zealand, the United States, and Fiji. She has completed a book on responsibility and the politics of childhood asthma in the Czech Republic and New Zealand, *One Blue Child: Asthma, Responsibility, and the Politics of Global Health*, which is being published in 2017. Her other works include *Bodies of Bread and Butter: Reconfiguring Women's Lives in the Post-communist Czech Republic*; *Young Women of Prague* (coauthored with Alena Heitlinger); *State of Suffering: Political Violence and Community Survival in Fiji*; *Up Close and Personal: On Peripheral Perspectives and the Production of Anthropological Knowledge* (coedited with Cris Shore); and *Senses and Citizenships: Embodying Political Life* (coedited with Christine Dureau and Julie Park).

CATHERINE TRUNDLE is senior lecturer in cultural anthropology at Victoria University of Wellington. Her research centers on the politics of inclusion and exclusion, citizenship, medical anthropology, and intersubjective ethics. Her book, *Americans in Tuscany: Charity, Compassion and Belonging* (2014), examines the role of charity practices in migrant communities. Trundle's current research explores military veterans' claims for health care and the politics of recognition and responsibility. Her publications include *Detachment: Essays on the Limits of Relational Thinking* (coedited with Matei Candea, Joanna Cook, and Thomas Yarrow) and *Local Lives: Migration and the Politics of Place* (coedited with Brigitte Bonisch-Brednich). She is currently completing a monograph that examines the medical and legal claims made by veterans of British nuclear testing in the Pacific.

JARRETT ZIGON is associate professor in the Department of Anthropology at the University of Amsterdam. His research interests include morality and ethics, political ontology, and the relationship between anthropology and philosophy. These interests are taken up from the perspective of an anthropology strongly influenced by post-Heideggerian continental philosophy and critical theory. His forthcoming book is tentatively titled *World-building: Critical Hermeneutic Essays on Politics, Ethics, and Ontologies*.

choice: burdens of, 217; consumer choice, 101, 104, 212n8; and care, 11–12, 216; and freedom and autonomy, 4, 5, 10, 11, 102, 107, 215; and humanist thought, 59; lifestyle choices, 218, 226; limited choice, 43, 85, 161, 206

Christianity, 4, 9, 29, 30, 182, 183; Catholicism, 13, 182, 195, 207, 208, 209; God, 61, 71, 136, 165, 173, 174, 175; priests, 27, 80, 214

Churchill, Winston, 96

citizenship: active citizenship, 101; biological citizenship, 218, 223, 228; and the civilizing process, 28; and corporate power, 121; ethical citizenship, 33; and ethnicity, 74, 94; democratic citizenship, 30, 101; and environmental health, 74; flexible citizenship, 13, 201; historical transformations in, 5; military citizenship, 213; and neoliberalism, 181, 186, 194–95; technologies of, 28; university citizenship, 108

class, 13, 15, 29, 93, 106, 143, 182, 195, 208; class aspiration, 209–10; elites, 18, 29, 157, 176; working-class labor, 21, 74; working-class women, 101

clientism, 32

Clinton, Bill, 103

cognition, 15, 41; cognitive flexibility, 38

Cold War, 152, 156–58

Colombia, 42

colonialism, 157, 158; Atlantic slave trade, 159; British colonial rule, 159

commerce, 62, 73, 97, 105

community: as interface between citizen and state, 42; concept of, 10; community empowerment, 35, 121; community outreach, 17, 123; community organizers, 119, 183, 184–85; community protection, 82, 97; community self-governance, 33, 42, 102–3, 185; corporate community development, 121–31; ethnonational community, 144; politics of community life, 22

compassion, 185

Confucianism, 13

corporations creating shared value (CSV), 21, 118–19, 126–30; citizen-corporation relations, 19, 21; corporate social responsibility (CSR), 10, 17, 19–21, 23, 75, 85–86, 97–98, 118–32; and democracy, 74; infrastructure

projects, 120; legal personhood, 125; multinationals, 1, 17, 122

corruption, 29, 76, 105, 151–52, 198

crime, 31–32, 97–98, 138, 144, 152, 158, 161–62, 174, 177

culpability, 3, 16–17, 34, 82, 160, 213, 226, 227, 228, 229

Cyprus, 16, 135–54, 155n3, 155n4, 155n5

Czech Republic, 9, 16–17, 71–95

dependency, 3, 10, 12, 17, 22, 30, 32, 33, 40, 124, 152, 163, 185, 188, 195, 213, 216, 229

democracy, 4, 18, 42, 74, 105, 121–22, 141, 158, 186, 197–98; civil society, 120, 161, 194–95, 197–98, 202, 209, 211n4; elections, 84, 101, 152; market democracy, 194; property-owning democracy, 101

Derrida, Jacques, 97

Descartes, René, 51, 61

deviancy, 97–98

disability, 19, 36, 210, 218, 228, 230n1

drug treatment, 12; harm reduction treatment, 12, 49–68

duty, 5, 10, 12, 14, 21, 23, 32, 79, 86, 99, 100, 102, 126, 163, 226

Eastern Europe, 13, 158, 194, 197–98, 209

economics: economic crisis, 39, 80, 152, 169; economic restructuring, 72, 101, 104, 194, 198; economic prosperity, 82; financial institutions, 34; Homo economicus, 18; influence of Milton Friedman, 118; non-market economies and values, 122, 129, 130; sustainable economic growth, 128; tax, 34, 98, 101, 152

egalitarianism, 32

Elias, Norbert, 28

emotion, 14, 56, 57, 110, 148, 173, 187, 192, 202–3, 224, 227; lack of emotion, 12, 149. *See also* love

empowerment, 2, 4, 9, 11, 16, 35, 39, 44, 84, 102, 112, 121, 124, 214–16, 229

England, 29, 98, 101

environment, the: air pollution, 76; ecosystem, 39; ecologists, 80, 86; environmental challenges, 35; environmental activists, 21, 76, 82–87; environmentalism, 76, 85, 131; environmental health, 129; environmental regulation, 122, 128; environmental well-being, 34, 131; pollution, 34, 71–95, 116, 225; sustainable development, 125, 128, 131

equality, 12, 47n13

ethics: attunement ethics, 64; audit ethics, 106, 116; bioethics, 219; ethics of perseverance, 64; ordinary ethics, 24

ethopolitics, 28, 31

European Union (EU), 72, 137, 142, 152, 198, 199, 204, 209

experts, 32, 35, 36, 37, 45, 168, 176, 215; anthropologists, 93, 139, 145, 148, 149, 154, 224; archaeologists, 139, 146, 147, 148, 149, 154; international legal specialists, 156, 157, 158; lay knowledge, 222; public health specialists, 84, 87, 93; scientific experts, 72–79, 141–46, 221–27

family: childhood, 40; familial responsibility, 98, 213–30, 230n3, 231n10; female reproduction, 74; and gender, 13, 181, 204–6, 209, 216, 229; grandmothers, 155n2, 204; and patriarchy, 182; nuclear family, 182; parenthood, 13; pregnancy, 66, 130, 214; spousal obligations, 205; and the state, 90, 218

Fassin, Didier, 18, 74, 89, 90, 154

filial piety, 13

fitness, 38

food, 7, 39, 149, 199, 200, 223, 224

forensic scientists, 16, 139, 144–49, 153

forgiveness, 19, 136, 160, 173–75, 176

Foucault, Michel, 7–10, 52, 100, 105, 214

freedom, 2, 4, 7, 18, 31, 44, 45, 96, 101–2, 106, 198

French Revolution, the, 4

Freud, Sigmund, 96

friendship, 2, 23, 67, 188, 197, 202–3, 205–6, 209–10

future, the: and calculation, 8, 30, 35; futures relationship to the past, 158, 224; and prudence, 29, 30, 31, 32, 215; and risk, 34, 40, 44

gender: gender roles, 13, 90, 195, 205–7, 208, 213, 225; gender disparity, 204; masculinity, 21, 74, 89, 90, 225, 231n10; and national identity, 212; spousal obligations, 205; women's groups, 197

genetics, 16, 72, 147, 213–30, 230n3, 231n9

Germany, 75, 83, 208

Ghana, 122, 129–130

globalism, 22

Gluckman, Max, 23n2

government: governance, 2, 4, 5, 8, 13, 21, 22, 48n14; governmental rationalities, 36, 103, 115; governmentality, 2, 7, 24n4, 28, 103, 107, 110, 115, 186, 214; government policy, 7, 21, 39, 43, 97, 98, 102–3, 107–9, 111, 152, 158, 176, 184, 187, 190, 196, 197

gratitude, 19, 148

Greece, 10, 137–38

Guatemala, 139

guilt, 16, 19, 28, 81, 114, 116, 151, 181, 183, 217, 226, 227, 228

Hage, Ghassan, 4, 18, 20, 75

Hawaii, 37

health: debility, 89, 193, 194, 210, 213, 219, 228, 230n1; disease, 19, 29, 31, 55, 72, 129, 181, 184, 190, 210, 218, 228, 231n7; environmental health movement, 73, 84; and exercise, 38, 186, 199, 201, 202, 206, 218; genetics, 16, 72, 147, 213–30, 230n3, 231n9; genomic responses to radiation, 219; harm reduction practices, 49–50, 53–55; health care delivery, 191; health monitoring, 19; HIV, 13–14, 56, 57, 181–92; hospital, 12, 29, 54, 86, 101, 120; hygiene, 29, 199; illness, 2, 5, 16, 21, 41, 73, 79, 92, 193–94, 208, 210, 214–18, 222, 225–26, 228, 230n1; molecularization, 215, 217, 223; malaria, 129; medication, 187, 191, 199; nutrition, 127, 130, 200, 202; patient choice, 11, 19, 215; post-traumatic stress disorder, 38; preventative health behaviors, 199; radio-biology, 16, 213, 219, 230, 232n11; rehabilitation, 203, 210; respiratory illnesses, 16, 21, 71–79, 84, 92; talk therapy, 56; trauma, 36, 38, 177, 189. *See also* disability

Heidegger, Martin, 51, 62, 97

Hobbes, Thomas, 17–18

hope, 17, 18, 23, 33, 43, 44, 46, 54, 64, 67, 75, 82, 214, 228, 229; economies of hope, 228

humanitarianism, 89, 137, 145, 153, 166

identity, 10, 33, 100, 138, 139, 146, 160, 206, 216, 232n10; national identity, 208–9, 212n15

idleness, 31

Newton, Isaac, 48n14, 51
New Zealand, 5, 23n1, 79, 96, 98, 99, 102–3, 106–7, 108, 110, 111, 112, 113, 218, 219, 222
Nietzsche, Friedrich, 27, 46n1
North America, 29, 64, 187
nuclear tests, 16, 231–32

Obama, Barack, 5
obligation, 1–23, 23n2
Ong, Aihwa, 13, 201
optimism, 35, 38, 39–40, 43, 44, 228
Other, the, 3, 10–11, 12, 14–15, 17, 22, 61, 68, 93

Pacific, the, 16, 213, 218, 223
Papua New Guinea, 122, 224
paranoia, 18
paternalism, 11, 124
personhood, 4, 11, 45, 100, 111, 125, 164–66, 194–96, 206, 210, 213–15, 217
Peru, 122, 124, 125, 130, 176
pharmaceuticals, 7, 34, 155n7, 191
philanthropy, 123, 127, 130, 131; donors, 124
philosophy: advanced liberalism, 2–24, 32, 97; liberalism, 3–13, 21, 27, 32, 37, 50, 95n2, 97, 101, 126, 157, 158, 174, 175, 176, 186, 196, 229; metaphysical humanism, 49–68; ontological reductionism, 230n4; posthumanism, 59–61; shortcomings of humanism, 59
Plato, 17–18
Poland, 9, 71, 86, 193–211, 211n1, 212n14
politics: activism, 17, 23, 56, 68n1, 74–77, 82–86, 92, 95, 102, 125, 126, 138, 158, 176, 228; antiliberal, 45; austerity, 151–52, 158; biopolitics, 16, 50, 53, 58, 63, 67, 213, 226, 229; Bush administration, 182; Communist Party, 76, 89; civic engagement, 85, 228; civil society, 13, 84, 119, 120, 131, 132, 161, 194–95, 197–98, 202, 209, 211n4; dissidents, 77–78; geopolitics, 35, 152, 218; global governance, 157; grassroots activism, 126; imagining alternatives, 132; leftist politics, 63; policy failures, 43; political activism, 77, 83; political authorities, 36; political experimentation, 63; political programs, 36, 40; political rallies, 9, 65; political repression, 169; political struggle, 21, 74, 76, 78, 88, 137, 218; politics of resignation, 76; postpolitical projects, 63; progressives, 8, 29, 43, 46, 49;

public officials, 33; public protests, 72, 76, 78, 91, 94, 119, 144; Reagan administration, 101, 102, 182; Republican Party, 182–83; Third Way politics, 33, 103; vital politics, 61, 215
poor, the, 29, 34, 124, 152, 170
postconflict, 140, 148, 158–59; cease-fire, 137, 155n1, 160, 163; combatant reintegration, 163–67, 177; demobilization, 164; postconflict states, 158–59; reconciliation ceremony, 173–74; redemption, 158; truth telling, 159, 163, 166–68, 170, 173–75. See also reconciliation
postsocialism, 75, 77, 196, 202, 211n3; East-West imaginary, 194
prison, 29, 37, 77, 169, 171
protest: blockades, 144; instruments of assertion, 144; labor strikes, 144; mass demonstrations, 144; media campaigns, 144; petitions, 73, 82, 83, 184; public demonstrations, 76, 77, 82, 144; street protests, 144
prudentialism, 30, 32
public, the, 140
punishment, 136, 143, 157

race, 15; racialized rural irrationality, 171; racist hysteria, 184; racism, 43, 93, 189
Rancière, Jacques, 53, 58, 60
rationalism, 188
rationality, 4, 105, 112, 115, 130
Rawls, John, 18
Reagan, Ronald, 101, 102, 182
recognition, 3, 11, 14–15, 22, 36, 62, 75, 95, 153, 158, 175, 228, 229; failure of recognition, 149
reconciliation, 16, 159, 161, 164, 166, 177
reflexivity, 1, 109, 110
relationality, 11, 13, 68, 213, 219; dependency, 3, 17, 22, 30, 152, 163, 188, 213, 229; entanglement, 22, 61, 96, 106, 137, 157, 214, 216; isolation, 45, 53–55, 62, 68n2, 189, 203, 204, 205, 209, 220, 230n4; proximity, 61, 225; reciprocity, 3, 17–22, 33, 34, 74, 75, 88, 90–95, 163, 165; risky relations, 225. See also sociality
religion, 15, 23n2, 29, 30, 38–39, 80, 81–82, 123, 138, 144, 182, 184, 186, 192, 207, 208, 209, 212n15; religious leaders, 123
resilience, 8, 29, 34–48, 104

responsibility: and answerability, 4, 126, 130, 228; cellular responsibility, 225; definition of, 4; and dutiful response, 126; environmental responsibility, 127, 131; genetic irresponsibilization, 217–18; historical and institutional responsibility, 158–77; individual legal responsibility, 158, 162, 177; masculine responsibility, 225; postwar responsibility, 162; public responsibility, 166, 184; responsible sexual subject, 189, 192; therapeutic responsibility, 159. *See also* familial responsibility (under family)

rights: civil rights, 5, 17; and democracy, 101, 121, 186; rights-based language, 121; right to health, 23. *See also* human rights (under law)

risk: and anticipation, 36–37, 46, 75, 95n4, 149, 217; and liability, 129; preparedness, 31, 35–36, 46n4; risk society, 34, 100, 109; and uncertainty, 29, 34, 35, 40, 46n4, 47n10, 202, 219, 221, 222, 230; unacceptable risk, 113, 125; and well-being, 186

Roma, the, 92–94

Rose, Nikolas, 2–10, 23, 28–32, 38, 40–44, 46n3, 84, 102–7, 119, 130, 196, 215, 216, 223, 228

Rousseau, Jean-Jacques, 18

rumor, 154, 169–72, 176

Russia, 54, 211n7, 212n14

Rwanda, 148, 158

safety, 5, 97, 105, 113–14, 116–17, 128, 227

Sartre, Jean-Paul, 97

science: contested science, 222, 229; forensic science, 138, 140; mathematics, 52, 60, 62; and the public, 231n6; quantum physics, 60, 61; scientific colonialism, 157; scientific struggles, 21; scientization, 147. *See also* scientific experts (under experts)

Scotland, 5

Scott, James, 99

secrecy, 137–41, 143–44, 152–54, 227

security, 8, 17, 29, 30, 31–45, 46n4, 47n11, 78, 122, 127, 152, 162, 163

sexuality, 8, 29, 53, 185; heteronormativity, 182; HIV, 13–14, 56, 57, 181–92; homophobia, 184, 189; homosexuality, 183; safe sex, 182, 185,

186, 187; sexual abuse, 37, 41, 189; sex education, 183; sex work, 57

Sierra Leone, 15, 156–77

slavery, 18, 159, 170

social contract, 1–24

social theory: agential realism, 60–61; ontological turn, 52, 58, 60, 62; vital materialism, 59, 61

sociality, 13, 40, 193–212, 223; collective ties, 11, 13; social, the, 10. *See also* relationality

South Africa, 90, 124, 129, 130, 151, 157–59, 167, 191

space, 10, 18, 29, 31, 46, 54, 56–57, 62, 65–66, 89, 101, 107, 140, 142, 155n7, 197, 207, 225; neighborhoods, 10, 33, 41, 55, 62–66, 73, 149, 205, 208, 209; urban space, 202

Spain, 139, 140, 155n3

state, the, 3; asylum seekers, 100; corruption, 29, 71, 76, 105, 151–52, 198; coup, 80, 137, 152, 160; development, 7, 30, 38, 39, 40, 41, 46n5, 86, 89, 110, 119–25, 128–32, 158, 190, 195, 198, 203, 214; devolution of governmental authority, 121; modernist state, 198; and modernization, 75; nationalism, 13, 18, 74, 86, 144, 152, 208; post-welfare state, 104; public authorities, 8, 35, 104; reunification, 137–38, 141, 151; socialist state, the, 74–81, 89–90, 95n2, 194–206, 211n4, 212n8; state-citizen relations, 4, 20, 75, 94, 122; state regulation, 122, 127–28

statistics, 79, 91, 92, 93, 190, 204

stigma, 19, 57, 163, 167, 186, 188, 217

stress, 38, 41, 47n5, 105, 226, 231n5

subjectivity: and governmentality, 7; rational, self-interested subjects, 186; self-care, 7–10, 13, 194, 199, 201, 202, 214–15; self-control, 28, 166; self-improvement, 102, 106, 112; self-judgment, 28; self-managing subjects, 2, 4, 10, 54–55, 57, 58, 63, 67, 102, 106, 110, 121, 201; self-responsibility, 3, 8, 9, 13, 14, 28, 30, 84, 97, 103; self-sufficiency, 3; subjectivization, 52

suffering: alleviation of suffering, 17; bodily suffering, 19, 208, 228; figures of suffering, 74, 88, 91; and the state, 74, 89, 90; and sacrifice, 89

surveillance, 2, 7, 104, 106, 231n5

technology, 4, 21, 27, 28, 29, 30, 32, 40, 45, 46n4, 53, 62, 65, 80, 98, 105–7, 110, 111, 116–17, 118, 213, 216, 223

Thatcherism, 98

Timor-Leste, 176

truth, 53, 140, 141, 151, 155, 156, 157, 158–59, 161, 166–68, 172, 174; contested truth and the past, 141; Truth and Reconciliation Commission (TRC), 15, 23, 156–77

Turkey, 138, 142, 152

United Nations (UN), 140, 142, 161, 176

United State of America, 2, 29, 64, 129, 138, 187, 198, 224, 225

urban spaces, 54–55

victimhood, 16, 149, 216

violence: combatant leaders, 164; domestic violence, 15, 182, 189; mass arrests, 169, 176; mass violence, 157; police oppression, 54; political violence, 16, 149, 159, 171; public execution, 162; sexual violence, 2, 189; structural violence, 16, 159; urban violence, 42; victims and perpetrators, 16, 151, 176; war, 15, 38, 41, 136, 142, 160, 164, 165, 166, 167, 168, 169, 174, 228

vulnerability, 21, 34, 39, 40, 45, 47n5, 74, 90, 183, 188, 190, 192, 225, 229

war, 15, 38, 41, 136, 142, 160, 164, 165, 166, 167, 168, 169, 174, 228; civil war, 143, 156, 159, 164, 168; depoliticized armed conflict, 176; and grief, 139, 143; and human remains, 139–45; mass crimes, 158; Spanish Civil War, 139; terrorism, 34, 39; war crimes, 142, 161–62, 174

welfare, 11, 12, 30, 31, 32, 43, 98, 100, 102, 124, 125, 193, 196–97, 215

Western Europe, 4, 17, 29, 72, 80, 95n2, 138, 155, 182, 211

Williams, Raymond, 98, 99

Wittgenstein, Ludwig, 99

work: coworkers, 205; entrepreneurialism, 101, 109, 111, 119, 123, 124, 125, 128, 130; good labor vs. bad labor, 57; productive work, 165–66; regulations, 86, 87, 120, 121, 122, 127; unemployment, 73, 80, 94, 215; workplace, 1, 3, 5, 10, 31, 33, 105, 111, 205, 113. *See also* labor

World War I, 38

World War II, 39, 196, 207, 218